Mother
Country

Mother Country

A STORY OF LOVE AND LIES

Monique Charlesworth

MOTH
BOOKS

First published in the UK in 2023 by Moth Books,
in partnership with whitefox publishing

www.wearewhitefox.com

ISBN 9781915036698
Also available as an ebook
ISBN 9781915036704

Edited by Martin Fletcher and Sam Boyce
Copyedited by Jenni Davis
Designed and typeset by Seagull
Cover design by Simon Levy
Project management by whitefox
Printed and bound by TJ Books, Padstow, UK

To my big sister Lorie with love

PRAISE FOR
MONIQUE CHARLESWORTH

For *The Children's War*

'It is one of the strengths of this novel that children are seen not only as victims of warring states, but of the emotional entanglements of their parents ... [in] the intensely moving story of Ilse's emotional awakening.'

Gerard Woodward, *The Telegraph*

'Richly satisfying and utterly absorbing ... Charlesworth tells the story so artfully that she brings an utterly fresh perspective to bear on familiar psychological territory.'

Robert MacNeil, *The Washington Post*

'[Charlesworth] has a keen eye for detail and wide sympathies. She tells it as it really was ... Sometimes you get the feeling that a certain novel is one that its author has been preparing for years to write. This is such a one, and it is really very good indeed.'

Allan Massie, *The Scotsman*

'Rich in local color and character detail ... powerful and poignant. With her cinematic eye for description and her story's propulsive narrative rhythm, Charlesworth thrusts us into the very heart of chaos.'

The Boston Globe

'Breathlessly suspenseful … Charlesworth uses two apparent opposites – a timid, sensitive Nazi boy, a bold, red-headed Jewish girl – as a way of exploring what good people have in common and how innocents learn to be decent in a world swarming with evil. She moves her story through fast, terrifying intricacies of plot: journeys, battles, smuggled papers, love affairs, carefully calculated loyalties, heroic sacrifices and endless duplicity … Charlesworth's greatest success is to show how these children grow into morally mature adults, learning about treachery not just by seeing it around them, but by making difficult and some-times terrible choices themselves … Engrossing.'

Polly Shulman, *New York Times Book Review*

'*The Children's War* breathes a well-earned authenticity, even as it recounts circumstances that test human character to belief-defy-ing limits.'

Eva Hoffman, author of *Lost in Translation*

'Ilse grows from a passive child, observing events, into an active participant, driven by the same mixed motives as everyone else. With Ilse as unblinking guide, Charlesworth travels the morally ambiguous alleyways of war to create a deeply satisfying read full of richly complicated characters.'

Kirkus Reviews (starred)

For *The Glass House*

'There are, as the publishers suggest, hints of Heinrich Böll in the working-out of the novel's themes, although the skilful blending of realism and allegory, the deft plotting, the characters that come dangerously close to caricature and yet live, and the sharp intelligence of the writing equally recall Muriel Spark. Ultimately, however, the author's style is her own and so is her engagement with Germany, which she views as an informed outsider.'

TLS

'An impressive debut. Monique Charlesworth combines a sharp wit with a rich sense of time and place in a very distinctive blend.'

Graham Swift

'*The Glass House* introduces a writer of significant accomplishments, among them a gift for describing her characters as if they themselves had taught her how to place them perfectly in context.'

Jonathan Keates, *The Observer*

For *Life Class*

'Somebody – God, perhaps – is grooming Monique Charlesworth as the next Muriel Spark. Improving on her strong debut in *The Glass House*, she shows herself unnervingly assured at the deft interweaving of comic and philosophical observations: the hallmark of Spark's writing at its best … Miss Charlesworth succeeds in reaching the heart while being brutally funny; no mean gift.'

Patrick Gale, *Daily Telegraph*

'... here clearly is a writer to follow wherever she may go next, gifted with the urge and talent to explore, a high sense of style and spurts of grim humour. This is a book to read again and savour.'

Christopher Wordsworth, *The Guardian*

'*Life Class* makes it clear that she is a novelist of very considerable talent. It has that rare quality: authority. Her mastery of structure is proof of her talent. The story ranges widely in space, time and mood, but it never loses coherence. It is a very good novel.'

The Scotsman

For *Foreign Exchange*

'Monique Charlesworth's sharply observed novel ... hovers tantalisingly between farce and tragedy.'

Daily Express

'A charmingly droll drama of sex, food and ethics ... beneath a soufflé-light storyline, Monique Charlesworth tucks away great wisdom on the subject of marital boredom and fantasy.'

She

CONTENTS

Seizing the day: Inge in her eighties in the Jardin des Tuileries in Paris

CHAPTER I

· · · · ·

Madame
la Marquise

In provincial France, a person can live well and hide their secrets. My mother has chosen to spend the last decades of her tumultuous life combining these activities in Tours, in the centre of the Loire Valley. This rich merchants' town with a medieval heart is beautifully situated on the Loire and Cher rivers. Romans planted vines and made wine here. Skilled metalworkers forged Jeanne d'Arc's armour, yards from the Rue Bernard Palissy where my mother lives. The kings of France built fabulous chateaux where they could disport with their mistresses in this lush countryside. For thirty years, my German-born mother has been known as a charming English eccentric. She pushes her empty wheelchair along the boulevards, using it as a Zimmer frame and shopping trolley. Everybody recognises her. Her secret life brought her here and her great gift for misdirection sustains her. How scathingly she dismisses people who make things up: 'so-and-so is just a fabulator'. But it turns out that she is a fabulator too, possibly the best. I studied her carefully for sixty-seven years. I thought I was her confidante, but I was fooled. This woman means everything to me, yet I don't know her at all.

When I visit, I mustn't be late. I hurry past the Chien Jaune bistro, the Charcuterie Hardouin, prize-winning maker of succulent pork rillons and rillettes, the father-to-son photography studio and the ubiquitous boulangerie. An inner monologue strikes with each footstep: be generous, be kind. But I am not sure that I can be relied on. Let's not forget my mistakes and errors of omission. How many times have I been told to greet everyone politely? Bonjour Madame! Bonjour Messieurs, Mesdames! But let's not start with the ways daughters and mothers find to frustrate and irritate each other. Let's start as each visit surely does, in a spirit of daughterly and motherly love. And wild excitement – that's always in the mix. For days before I arrive, she is in some kind of altered state. I'm not calm either. I love my mother deeply and unquestionably, but I often don't like her.

I ring the bell. She buzzes me in and up I go in the lift. She's breathless, waiting in trembling, overwhelmed anticipation. Her face is ancient, lined yet still attractive; she is forever and unchangingly herself. She is ninety-two and looks it. Me in twenty-five years' time – a weird thought. But my life has been so happy! As if a happy life didn't produce wrinkles. People often say that I look like her – now, what daughter appreciates that? This strong face, quivering with emotion, inspires a mixture of affection and repulsion, strangeness transmuting into familiarity.

'Hello, Mummy! You look great!' I say, because at this early stage of the visit I can still be free with compliments. I can see how she is and it's not good: an old frail person in great pain, held up by willpower. The word 'Mummy' is irritating, but I am not permitted to call her by any other name. I once referred to her as Inge in her presence – that was a disaster. 'I am the mother, and you are the children' – how often have I heard that? Inge is short for Ingeburg. For years I spelt it wrongly, Ingeborg with an o, as she herself did in some kind of Freudian memory slip. But perhaps it was deliberate, and she was hoping that people might assume that she was Swedish. I lean forward. A tentative embrace – she is too fragile to be touched. I fear the oohs and aahs, the evident pain, the false bright I'm-OK smile. The physical turmoil echoes the emotional; she yearns for my embrace, but if I touch her without warning, she will jump like a startled deer. It's not altogether clear whether my inability to put my arms around her is psychological, or physical, or both. Put it this way: I have already failed.

'You look marvellous, darling!' she says. 'I love the lipstick.'

She is a skinny, tiny and bent figure smartly dressed in sweater and black trousers, wearing one of the Hermès scarves I've given her, pinned with her gold brooch. She always smells of Chanel No. 5. Her chignon is immaculate. She's carefully made up. I tell her she is very chic (she is wearing the striped favourite sweater I particularly dislike) and she sways from side to side and clicks her fingers, doing a look-at-me this-is-the-life mini twirl. Why do I hate it when she's in her happy mode? I want to tell her that she is unchanged, which is true, but I can't quite bring myself to utter a second compliment this soon. *Be kind, be generous.* She wheels her chair away and I follow.

She's given to excesses of emotion – excesses of all kinds really – always justified by the cry of 'It's my day!' That means that she must be indulged because she's feeling marvellous. She has no truck with Mother's Day because children should be marvellous to their mothers every single day, not once a year under duress. Depending on her mood, most days of the year can be claimed as 'hers'.

Today is one of her special days. I can read the curve of her back, the way it expresses enthusiasm and delight and recognition, alongside some kind of pre-disappointment. But maybe these are emotions I am projecting. This once upright, energetic woman has scoliosis. 'You see?' she said in her eighties, indicating the hip that had begun visibly to jut out. 'I never could get the hem of my skirts to sit straight and now I know why.' She was an excellent seamstress and still has a wooden box full of bobbins and cotton reels, thimbles and a darning egg. It turns out that you can spend a life looking at yourself and not see what's there. Just as a daughter can spend a lifetime looking at her mother and still know nothing.

The white ring around the iris of her blue eyes is cholesterol; I have it too. Her good strong nails are different from my soft useless ones. Her skin is thin, literally and metaphorically, as is mine. We have everything and nothing in common. Here is the angry red patch on one hand that has been there for years, a burn mark that never faded. Her inner self is the same: injustice has been burning through her for decades. Writing this at home in London, I wonder whether the emotion she terms wild excitement, the sort that makes her want to throw up, is another name for anxiety and dread. What are we so afraid of? Each other. *'Man erzieht seine eigenen Feinde'*: you bring up your own worst enemies, as my grandmother Tilly used to say. She had an aphorism to suit every occasion. Not all Germans recognise the sayings knitted into me that date back to the 1930s. Some, like 'fish and guests stink after three days', are well known. For years now, my mother and I have agreed that three days are just perfect: code for the fact that neither of us can stand a minute longer.

But this is the mother I worshipped, the centre of my universe. Though heading for my seventh decade, inside I feel perhaps thirteen – the age at which consciousness of self arrived. I remember rocking on a swing, watching the sky, thinking this: *I am me, separate from the others, and this is the world, and these things will never change.* At what age did her internal clock stop? Inside this old lady is the nineteen-year-old who adored babies and small children and flaunted her youth in halter-neck tops on the beach. We're trapped behind the façades and the decades; we've lost each other.

Inge sits in her special chair with her back to the window and the balcony, the view of the gardens below always ignored, and I take my usual place on the far sofa under the Tree of Life rug that hangs on the wall. Every inch of floor is covered with Persian carpets. A cup of tea – a glass of wine? Coffee. She is beaming, enjoying these early moments of joy and excitement. She's also looking tired. 'I'm not the woman I was a year ago,' she says. She sips her coffee; it doesn't taste the same without a cigarette. She gave up smoking two years ago after seventy-six years and still misses it. Now and then she tells me she's going to have a cigarette, enjoying the look of horror on my face. She loves catching me out being pious.

'You've changed your hair,' she says. 'I liked it better how you had it before.'

My mother – pale-blue eyes alert behind her huge South Park spectacles – sees very well, better than me. She is familiar with every wrinkle and furrow on my face, just as I know hers, but I subscribe to the fallacy that she can't know me as I know her. I am occluded, hidden, so much cleverer. She can't guess at these cruel thoughts, which circle and recur to land, unforgivably, on this page. I can't imagine that sons inspect their fathers with quite the same visceral dislike and fascination – just as they don't talk about their emotions. What dark currents swirl through mothers and daughters in their mutual criticism, their intense lifelong study of each other, entwined with deep and helpless love. How to be. And, especially, how not to be.

We've always been in touch, and we've never spent time with each other. She adores my children but wasn't there to babysit or advise on childcare. I'm not here to look after her in her old age, were she to allow it. Inge gleefully refuses every offer of help. 'I shall be "autonome" to the end,' she says. 'I am Madame la Générale.' The pecking order is clear: Inge believes that she dominates, and I know that she doesn't. Protestations of love are always made; the relationship has always needed a bit of buttressing. Each highly anticipated meeting generates stories both absurd and sad. My telling of these has created the Inge myths our family knows well. Our relationship has been a succession of encounters – high drama all the way. Other mothers and daughters seem to get on without such peaks and troughs.

When I sit to eat (she's not hungry – she's never hungry), Inge pushes her wheelchair over and stands nearby in what purports to be a spirit of companionable interest, urging me to try each of the cheeses while assessing how many calories I ingest with each bite. Eventually, she releases the observation that's burning through her.

'You know, darling, if you lost five kilos, you would be just perfect.'

How do I respond? Not always well. After all, there's no monopoly on pettiness. Telling my friends that she's 'the world's oldest anorexic', for instance. Although I agree with her about my weight, I am not going to admit it.

Food is just one of the many contradictions that link and separate us. She adores me but she can't really stand having me around. We have much in common, not least the fact that we never openly admit to these complex and negative emotions. There must be a very particular tension between her relief at being herself at last – with a daughter who knows all about her troubled, sad past – and her simultaneous need to be somebody completely different. How many days can a person put up with this kind of stress? Three, until the fish stink.

Because she's very old now, I fear for her. In bleak moments she sits, head hanging, in a miasma of pain, before she recovers herself. What if Inge cannot uphold the effort of being this person she has invented – might there be a total collapse one day from sheer exhaustion? God forbid that she should develop dementia: what if a German word were to slip out? To be found out is her deepest fear. She used to count in German; that was a bit of a giveaway. She's long since trained herself out of that.

The next morning, a couple of the loyal friends she's made through her English conversation classes come to visit. Her friends love her joie de vivre, her ageless good spirits and the sound advice she dispenses. At 11 a.m., a large 'petit kir' or the lethal 'red cardinal' (crème de cassis plus red wine) is produced, always accompanied by little Vache qui Rit cheese squares and cocktail biscuits. A second drink soon follows. Talk is carefully orchestrated. Inge holds forth in a way I find false and tooth-gratingly strange, yet it is a performance to marvel at. The sprightliness of this charming lady of a certain age! The elegant scarf and outfit, which must be admired! The vivacious gestures – the eruptions into song! For years she has suffered from a terrible condition called *polynévrite*, which attacks the entire body in unexpected and excruciating ways anywhere from the sole of the foot to the roof of the mouth. It's agonising to see and hear, and there are times when her entire body hurts. If a friend ventures to say 'Are you all right, Inge?', she bursts into a version of 'Tout va très bien, Madame la Marquise!' in a voice rising from deep baritone to shrill, complete with flamboyant arm gestures. This comic song – iconic in France – features the Marquise telephoning home to be told by her various servants that her grey mare has died – but not to worry, all is well. Verse by verse it transpires that her husband discovered he was ruined and committed suicide, the candles he overturned set fire to the chateau and the flames spread to the stables – each incident the result of a far graver one. Insouciance in the face of total disaster: that's my mother. Insane, and yet admirable. She cannot bear any sympathy whatsoever. '*Ooh – ah – je fais la comédie!*' and once again she bursts into song. The act never varies. Everyone else finds this absolutely marvellous.

Everything is about her. No matter where we start – politics, the weather, the gilets jaunes, books – any topic whatsoever – she forcibly inserts herself, demanding attention and admiration. Presenting herself as the sympathetic, wonderful host, Inge is consciously setting herself up as the reverse of her mother, Tilly, whom she found callous and flawed. Tilly's oft-repeated sayings drove her mad. One of her favourites was *Selbstlob ist das schönste*: 'self-praise is the best of all'. In Tours, I'm vividly reminded of this.

Inge demands recognition for her elegance, her wit, her popularity and kindness. '*Et modeste avec ça ha ha!*' – and modest too! – is her running joke. An impossible tiresome gaiety and sustained self-praise under a thin veneer of self-deprecation – these are the hallmarks of marvellous English Inge, so idiosyncratic and ageless. Nobody else seems to notice or mind. No matter how much admiration is showered on her, she always needs mine. But I can only squeeze out the most miserly amounts. Why? I love her. Why can't I be a better person? Why can't I rise above it, be charming and compliment her, like my kind husband? I am as stubborn as she is. When I play my part in this masquerade, I resent it, and her. To need – to crave – so much praise, a person has to be terribly damaged inside. But it's hard to have sympathy, because this charade drives me bonkers.

When the audience departs, she rolls her wheelchair into the kitchen, ingests her many medicines and visibly flags. By one o'clock, the two-kir euphoria has abated and she's irritable. She is also hungry because she normally eats at noon; she hasn't eaten a thing since three o'clock the previous day. She has had a tiring morning being wonderful. She's thrown her considerable intelligence and energy into these efforts. And now she is exhausted and needs lunch and a sleep.

In the afternoon she wakes, sadder and smaller. As the day wanes, the mood darkens. Because the present is so awkward, the past is where we connect best. We drift into talk of her sad childhood and the never-to-be-forgotten awfulness of her mother. The rehashing of events decades old is as far as I ever venture in the blame game. The past feels like the honest place where we meet as equals – yet there is always something more I need to know, something she holds back. By contrast, everything in the present feels false, and not just because of the deception we collude in. We are always out of joint; I can never quite articulate why. Soon, she's had enough. I've exhausted her, and vice versa. When it's time for me to leave for the B&B she chose for me, she can't bear to see me go, yet can't wait for me to be gone. She needs to be back inside the safe bubble she has made for herself. She is a veteran of self-invention; this French idyll must be her fifth or sixth life.

I'm simultaneously fascinated and exhausted, longing to get away yet racked with guilt. When, after three days, I board the TGV for Lille and home with my iPad charged up, I burn to record the latest incident. My voluminous notes go back years. Like her, they return again and again to the past she cannot forget but has never dealt with. I worry away at the mystery: who is she really, and what exactly is she hiding?

CHAPTER 2

* * * * *

Expelled from the Heimat

Ingeburg Cocard (née Rosenbaum) was born in Germany of a Jewish father and Lutheran Protestant mother, exiled at the age of thirteen in 1939 and forced into misery and hardship in Belgium with her parents. Her difficult, supremely political communist father was picked up in Brussels and deported when the Nazis invaded. He probably died the day he arrived in Auschwitz. Inge and her mother survived. They were refugees, stateless, penniless and homeless, expelled from the Heimat. That word for home holds deep connotations of safety and belonging that don't really have an English equivalent. The loss has left its mark. When Inge was a small child, she believed that some people were children forever and some were adults – and she was terribly unhappy, knowing that she would always be the former and ordered around. Somewhere in her, alongside the adult who knows best and must be obeyed, that powerless child lives on.

Inge supported her mother as they lived in exile underground; her enterprise and courage got both of them through the war. Events that anybody else would be proud of are for her sources of the deepest shame. She is the Holocaust victim who wanted to be a member of the Bund Deutscher Mädel, the girls' equivalent of the Hitler Youth. She is the little girl who yearned to be normal and safe and said to her mother: 'Why did you marry the Jew?' Her father had no truck with religion and so she had no positive connection to it. Being a Jew meant being tainted, having bad blood – being vermin. The bullying and taunts of school friends struck home. Cruel words poisoned her mind and cruel acts permanently damaged her sense of self. Inge's catastrophic childhood taught her that she was a second-class human being, and that the world was a dangerous place. She didn't want to be a Jew or to have any of her loved ones bear the taint. She refuses to be defined by this tragic past.

The stateless refugee married my father, Tom Charlesworth, a soldier she met at the liberation of Brussels, moved to Birkenhead and became English. After their divorce, forced to start again, she moved to South London with her two little girls. Years of hard work followed as Inge moved through a succession of jobs, always striving to improve her situation. As we grew up, relationships became difficult. The problems of teenagerhood were exacerbated by Inge's poor relationship with her mother, who had come to live with us. In her early forties, Inge fell in love with René Cocard, a married friend of our grandparents, and they had a passionate affair. After they broke up, she took residential jobs, eventually leaving London to start again in Kent. The final act was that move to France at the age of sixty to marry René after the death of his wife. He was the great love of her life, but died far too soon, after only seven years together.

The Rosenbaum family circa 1928 with Inge on the right

Though devastated, our mother never considered leaving this street where René was born and where her heart had found peace. Tours is a well-planned town packed with interesting shops; the doctor, dentist and pharmacy are accessible on foot. On utility bills and bank statements, Inge chooses to style herself as Madame Ingeburg veuve [widow] Cocard. In this way, René defined her. He was the rose-coloured lens through which she viewed the world. It was but a short step from this to becoming an Englishwoman in France.

Slowly recovering from grief, Inge reinvented herself one final time. For the last three decades of her life, she has been the cultured English lady who gives conversation classes to a select group. She's the charming bookish woman who reads for hours each day, who has taught the children of many of her friends and acquaintances to speak English well and would never dream of charging. Inge has a mild but definite German accent, which I have never been able to hear. The French can't hear it either, which is just as well. To me, she sounds like herself. As children, we assumed that she was English like us.

Inge created my sister Lorie and me with her enormous strength, her willpower, despite the pain of her wrecked childhood and the sadness of a divorce she never wanted. We created ourselves around her and because of her, albeit in our very different ways. She was absolutely everything to me. She defined the parameters of my life and I loved and worried about her in equal measure. From my earliest days, I always felt some cause for anxiety: something unexpressed but almost palpable. I wanted to make her happy and didn't know how. I always took her side, never questioning if it was right or wrong. How could I question the ground on which I stood?

How does it feel to be something you can't stand being? What if you also happen to be subject to extremes of emotion? '*Himmelhoch jauchzend – zu Tode betrübt.*' That's the expression Goethe coined, which Inge uses to describe herself – from heavenly exaltation to deathly depression. She is subject to a range of emotions so overwhelming that they literally make her ill. Is she a manic depressive? And yet Inge is always cheerful and upbeat, always presenting a brave face to the world. She is known all around her district for her good humour and smiling demeanour. She literally never complains. Her emotions aren't arbitrary, though. She cares enormously about justice and fairness. Passionately outraged at the cruelties of the world, she will give fifty or even a hundred euros to a beggar one day and chastise her the next for being so impudent as to ask for more. She's furious with Marine Le Pen and deeply upset at the rise of the right. She shudders at the sight of French police in riot shields – they're just like the SS. She's a monster sacré, super strong yet weak, vulnerable in her deception yet ruthlessly determined. She is, in my sister's marvellous phrase, the diva who thinks she's a mouse.

Not even her immense willpower can hold the weaknesses of the flesh at bay. She has started giving away books, the good Limoges china, the crystal glasses and, disconcertingly, once or twice has said that 'the rainy day has come'. For years she has had 'a decent sum of money in the bank for the rainy day'. I ask her what she means but she won't say. Is there something wrong that she's not telling me about? Secrecy is one of her specialities. She'll ring up out of the blue and announce triumphantly that the operation has been a great success – what operation? 'Well, I didn't want to worry you, darling.'

Another entry for my notebook. For some time now I have been wanting to write down her extraordinary life story. I've already published a novel that took her flight into exile aged thirteen as its starting point, but thereafter was pure invention. My fourth, it proved to be my most successful. She read *The Children's War* with the utmost care; she corrected the French translation; she loved being my editor. Obviously, facts had to be concealed. I wrote a personal piece for the publishers that made my mother Belgian and definitely not Jewish. In this way, I came to fictionalise her story both as fiction and fictitious non-fiction. A double whammy. Nobody else would have given a hoot, but Inge cared deeply. This pre-emptive act of bad faith arose from my anxiety about betraying her, which runs as deep as her anxiety about herself. I have no idea why. Inge has always been part of everything I write, from the first draft I send ('this is the most boring book I have ever read, darling') to the eventual dedicated signed copy.

The worst thing I could ever do is to expose this tender, vulnerable woman to her friends. I need her to approve of me: I can't bear her to be angry or unhappy with me, guilt would undo me. As I type, I am worrying that reading this will destroy her. How cruel to demean and embarrass her! And yet I write on. I'm already calling her Inge in these pages; she won't like that. But I can't bring myself to type 'Mummy'.

CHAPTER 3

. . . . .

Too old to feel like this

It's five months since I've seen Inge. Two weeks before Christmas 2018, I am in Tours for the weekend with my husband, Alex, whom Inge adores (having long since come to terms with the catastrophe of his – and indeed my – being Jewish). Because he's there, we are having the most relaxed time ever. We joke and laugh together. Alex and I are even permitted to go out for dinner; Inge no longer goes to restaurants – she can't cope with seeds, or herbs, or strong sauces. 'I am such a pain,' she says. She doesn't go out at all because the weather is so chilly. I can see how weary she is. Because she hides her aches and pains, I don't always appreciate how much effort it takes for her to hold herself together each day.

The two of us venture out for a walk round the old town and buy chocolate and good wine in the market. In a design shop nearby, we choose a fancy corkscrew to replace Inge's old one and have it gift-wrapped. Inge rips open the paper, tries it and announces that it is useless. Alex opens the good wine; Inge tries the corkscrew again and pronounces it wonderful. She wants to please him, not to be 'a pain'. We drink the red wine cheerfully and she tells us about the neighbour who dropped dead of a heart attack in the lobby of her building. '*Quelle belle mort!*' she says, lowering her voice a full octave. 'What a beautiful death!' After we leave, she feels wobbly and tells her good friend Martine that she fears she will never see us again. Less than a month later, on Sunday 13 January 2019, she dies. Her death is sudden, and unexpected, and every bit as dramatic as her life.

I always ring Inge on a Sunday. The timing is precise. I am to ring after Toscan, her favourite pupil, has left but before her afternoon sleep, because mornings are her best time. Toscan — always described by Inge as 'Toscan with the dancing eyes' — is preparing for his baccalaureate and Inge is helping him with his English. Seventy-five years apart, these two are true and loving friends, Inge a substitute for the grandmother he never knew. Heaven forbid that I interrupt this special session. But on Sunday 13 January, when I phone at the appointed time, it is Toscan who answers.

'How are you, Toscan?'

'Very well, thank you,' he says. 'Did Hélène call you?'

His mother, Hélène, a close friend of Inge's, is not in the habit of telephoning.

'No, I don't think so. Is she well?'

Along the non sequiturs, my mother's life is unravelling. That morning, Toscan rang Inge's bell scores of times and she didn't answer. He ran to Franck's bike hire place opposite to use the phone and call the police. The emergency services came — the police — the *pompiers*. The firemen set a ladder on the balcony of the flat below, climbed up and saw her lying on the floor of the study. Unable to force the front door, they smashed the window and broke in. She is conscious, Toscan says; she is being taken to hospital.

The first rush of emotion is relief that Toscan went for his usual lesson that Sunday. For years I have been afraid that she would fall and injure herself, that she would lie far from the telephone and no help would come. Some time back, I forced the Présence Verte on her – the old-age call button. She refuses to wear the call 'watch' on her wrist. It lives neatly wrapped around the wheelchair in the living room, potentially near but usually unreachable. Another small act of rebellion against her interfering daughter.

Toscan calls the paramedic to the phone. In French too rapid for me to take in, this man explains that they are taking her to the Hôpital Trousseau, the big one with the A and E department. I ask how it is spelt. I give him my telephone number; we both struggle with the numbers. No, I can't speak to her, everything is in train: they will close the shutters covering the window they have smashed and the keys to the flat will go with her to the hospital. Meanwhile, an email arrives from Hélène, asking me to call her and explaining that Inge has fallen but is 'conscious' – this I realise later is code for 'alive'.

At noon, Inge's close friend Martine calls me in tears to say that she is leaving the South of France to return to Tours. She will be at the hospital at 9 p.m. and will call me from there. A highly experienced former nurse, she knows it well. I spend some time wondering how she found out about Inge, concluding that the paramedics called her. This is complete nonsense. I must have called her myself after speaking to Toscan and the paramedic. I remember nothing of that call; I am falling into that rabbit hole of shock where some details etch themselves on your soul while others vanish forever.

I text Martine to remind her that Inge is allergic to morphine. I email our adult children, Sophie and Jonathan. I call my sister,

Lorie, leave a voicemail, text then email. She is in New Zealand visiting her elder daughter and family. No reply. When Martine calls back towards midnight, Alex and I are in bed, unable to sleep; everything is topsy-turvy.

'I am so very sorry,' says Martine in a gentle tone. '*Je suis desolée.*' This word, often used politely, swells to encompass its full meaning. She was, and remained, desolate. Typing this page many months later, those words still induce tears. Martine puts me on to a woman doctor, who talks super fast in technical language. There is no pen on the bedside table, no paper to hand, no time. Time has abandoned us. '*Madame le docteur, parlez plus lentement,*' I say twice, but she can't slow down. 'Blood in her stomach – haemorrhage of the stomach – she was cold – had been on the floor – some other complications – all the vital signs were extremely low – arrived in a coma. Many interventions. Awake about 5 p.m. At her age and in these circumstances, it seemed impossible that she would survive and yet she rallied.'

We're talking about my indomitable mother. She is always going to rally.

Around 10 p.m. Inge had a heart attack so massive that she could not survive. The gabbling doctor regrets that Madame did not have a chance to say goodbye. This I get. Tenacious Martine, waiting in acute anxiety for two and a half hours, was not permitted to see her, to hold her hand. The doctor understands that the lady '*avait sa tête*', meaning that my mother was completely with it: worth saving. What a dressing-down Martine must have given the doctor, forcing the mobile into her hands. *You talk. You explain this.*

I am incredulous. I cannot believe that this time, unlike previous times, my mother has not been saved. I need the doctor's name, but she rings off too soon; I need to make notes. If I can write down the doctor's exact words, then my mother will still be alive in France, albeit with these difficult symptoms. What is this bizarre mania I have, about recording events? Everything to do with my mother and her life seems so important.

Alex and I lie awake for hours, talking. I cry quietly, so he can get some sleep. Though it doesn't bear thinking about, I think about it all night. She was not alone in the end. There were people with her. Doctors and nurses working on her. Bright lights. She didn't die alone on the big Persian carpet in the study, which Martine will scrub before I arrive, I don't have to see the blood stains. (Her favourite striped jumper – the one I dislike – is so badly stained that it has to be thrown away.) Later, Martine will tell me that she rang Inge from holiday the previous day – 'we laughed, we were joking' – and this is a comfort. While booking train tickets, I imagine my mother lying on the floor of the study alone all night and freezing cold. They found her surrounded by cotton reels from the sewing box. Did she go in there to mend something? Please God, let this have happened on Sunday morning, just before Toscan arrived, and not on Saturday during the day.

I think that I should probably thank the doctor, but how will I get her name? I also hate her for not having let Martine sit with Inge. That same night, I will later learn, a father died in A and E while his son waited outside in vain. At some point, it comes to me that René also died in the Hôpital Trousseau; Inge was by his side. Nobody held Inge's hand. Nobody told her what was happening. Do we die as we live? I don't know. Every death in our small family so far has been painful and sudden.

The next day, Alex has an operation on a ruptured Achilles tendon. I collect him from the hospital. Two to three weeks in a cast, total bed rest, then twelve weeks in a boot: no funeral for him. Our children rally round. Late that afternoon, I rush to the hairdresser. I am going to see my mother and a very cold critical eye will be upon me ('I see you've changed your colour, darling, I like the old one better').

The journey to Tours is out of joint from the get-go. There is a major delay at St Pancras, where I idiotically get out my phone to call my mother and warn her. The most trivial things upset me. I write down the emotional flux and drama of the last twenty-four hours and make a list of what to do. I've been making lists since I first learned to write. Aged five, I planned my Saturdays: Get up early. Make bed. Arrange shell collection. Read book. I understand that my mother has died but I am also in a state of disbelief. On the final shuttle train, I fall apart. Though it is wholly unreasonable to expect a woman of ninety-two to live forever, it turns out that there is no good age to lose a mother, especially ours, mother and father to her two girls. She is the constant in my life, the starting point: how can she no longer be in the world? Only drunks and babies may exhibit uncontrollable emotion in a public place. People look away as I sob and gulp, dabbing at my face with a wet ball of tissue. I hurry across the platform and out of the station, still crying. Fortunately, women my age are invisible.

I'm scared to go to the flat alone, in the dark, with that broken window. Lying awake in the B&B, I am too sad and worried to sleep. At some point during the long night, it comes to me that there must have been something horribly wrong with Inge, an inoperable stomach thing she kept to herself. How typical of the mistress of deception. I remember the tale of her favourite Doctor Lepagney, who wrote her a note sending '*bisous*' – kisses – and told her how elegant she was. He was probably in on it. She told us everything about that check-up, except the truth. That was why she announced that the rainy day had come. Why didn't I force her to tell me? But I never could make her do anything. She was constructed of iron.

Thinking bad thoughts, I keep bursting into new outbreaks of tears, like a desperate small child. I am too old to feel like this! This can't be real! At some deeper level below the irritation and rage, I still love her with the total adoration I had for her as a little girl. My mind goes racing back through the last phone call – the last visit – the last time we had a proper conversation. I told her that I loved her every time I called. That was hard to say in her presence, but easy in my kitchen in London with a cup of coffee to hand and a newspaper spread to amuse me in case she repeated herself too annoyingly. She hated the idea of the duty call – any kind of duty really. 'You really don't have to call me,' she used to say, meaning it. Often her answerphone wasn't working – the last year of her life was a long litany of phone disasters and rage that she couldn't make these stupid machines work.

It belatedly occurs to me that my deaf mother, without her hearing aid yet attuned to the slightest of slights, could hear my impatience and indifference. I am staggered at the conversations I neglected to have, the opportunities thrown away. I need to know everything about her, and I don't. Inge and I had sixty-seven years to talk, but it wasn't enough.

I let myself into the flat early the next morning. Everything is tidy, the plants in their usual place, the bed made, all clean and orderly. Dear Martine has made everything right. I can feel my mother's presence strongly. It occurs to me that she might not know that she has died. It happened inexplicably and fast, so I tell Inge about the collapse and that she was on the floor, but hopefully not for very long, and also that the hospital did its utmost to save her. (No need to be negative at this stage of events.) I feel something of her all through these days when I am on my own. Not scary, just sad. I know that I will never again see her push her wheelchair into the kitchen, pour a kir or sit to cut green beans at the correct angle. I will see her face in the morgue, and that is it. I keep the connection going for as long as I can. 'I'm going to have coffee now,' I tell her, taking my usual place on the sofa, explaining that my big sister, Lorie, is coming, and our children, Sophie and Jonny, and also informing her about Alex's operation – because otherwise, obviously, he'd be here with me. I talk like a mad woman all day, telling her everything I feel she needs to know, stopping when the family arrives. By then, her presence has gone.

Her big funky glasses sit on the Michelle Obama autobiography I gave her in December, with the bookmark on page 14; this is the woman who used to read for six hours a day. (She bought these particular glasses because the optician insultingly remarked that 'these are too expensive for you, Madame', thus fixing her choice.) I begin to hear some of the things I blocked: 'I'm not the woman I used to be.' Her young German friend Lili will later tell me that Inge always said '*Ich bin zwar alt – habe noch solche Lust zu leben*' – I'm old but I still have such an appetite for life. The last time they spoke, Inge took a different tone: '*Es wird alles beschwerlich.*' Everything is laborious. She never said as much to me. Madame la Générale would never tell the subordinate troops how awful she felt. There are always things parents keep from their children. In my mother's case, these would turn out to be fundamental.

Martine, some thirty years younger than Inge, is her last great friend. The two of them found each other when Martine came to replace Inge's long-standing cleaning lady, who was on holiday: it was a mutual *coup de foudre*. Love at first sight. 'Next time you come, may I embrace you?' asked Inge as Martine left. The two of them laughed and sang, they danced the tango and waltzed together. They shared countless interests, from Buddhism to South America to the many charities Martine supports. She is a rare soul with endless energy, a powerful desire to help other people and full of fun. Inge had a go on Martine's scooter – Martine tried out the wheelchair. She rang frequently and her visits and calls were a source of great pleasure. With her beloved Martine, Inge reverted to being a joyful eighteen-year-old.

Though devastated by the loss of her friend, Martine insists on accompanying me everywhere in Tours and is kindness itself. She drives me to the hospital morgue; pressure is on to arrange the funeral because space is limited. We walk down the long ramp and ring the bell; a man in white scrubs opens up to a bleak basement with harsh lighting, a few chairs and a pot of orchids. Empathy is beside the point. 'Chère Monique,' says Martine, hovering outside the room where the body lies. 'I can't do it.' But I have to. I need to be certain that my mother really has died, though the idea makes my stomach cramp with dread.

The large formal room is lined with wooden panels. The body lies on a white bed with wheels. My tiny mother is very straight, very collected, neatly covered with a white sheet. Her chignon is immaculate, her face calm, just caved in a little. Every day by eight in the morning, Inge was ready to meet the world: bathed, coiffed, made up, carefully dressed, though this effort might take her as much as two hours. Her dignity is intact. The lines of her face are clear and clean. I study her hairline and her nose and the special shape of her ear and the smallness of her and there is no doubt that she is both completely herself and completely gone. There is bruising and a red mark on her forehead, from the fall. Poor little Mummy.

Inge often made me swear that in the unlikely eventuality of her ever dying, I was to prick her with a pin, just to make sure. The thing she feared most was being buried alive; that was an extra reason to be cremated. So I touch her very gently with the end of my pen (a pin would hurt), telling her what I am doing, and I kiss her. She is very, very cold. I reassure her that she is definitely dead. Not to worry then! I have my phone and sort of want a close-up, but this isn't her true self and she would hate it; never photogenic, she loathed having her picture taken and always made dreadful gurning faces. After some minutes, I take one illicit picture from a distance, pretending it doesn't count. Her death does not remove my compulsion to please her. If anything, the reverse is true. I get out my notebook; there are other ways to record everything about and around her.

From the morgue, we drive to the town hall in Saint-Avertin to register the death. The sun shines, the receptionist is kind and friendly, the large airy space is nearly empty. Yes, they have the notification from the hospital. The exact time of death is 22.50. Forms are filled in by the doctor declaring the death. I copy the name of that woman carefully into my notebook. There! Got you! As the trainee registrar begins to fill out the death certificate, up comes Inge's maiden name: ROSENBAUM. Every Frenchwoman is forever known by her maiden name legally and on her ID: why should a woman be the property of a man? The nice young woman studies the unfamiliar name, writes it down – turns her computer and shows it to us. Is that right? I nod. Where was she born? It is on her identity card. The careful checking goes on: Mülheim with an umlaut. Or Mülheim/Ruhr? There can be no discrepancy or anomaly. French bureaucracy is very exact. The German word is carefully copied and spelt out. All this would have been fine if I were alone, but I am not.

And so I nod and smile and avoid looking at Martine and pretend Rosenbaum is an English name. Inge's dear friend says nothing. Does she notice? Of course she does. Heaven alone knows what she is thinking about her English friend. I cannot reveal this deepest secret and dare not ask Martine if she knows anything. They shared many confidences – but surely not this one. When some days later Martine says something about Germany, I hear myself launch into a rambling diatribe about our family – what silly old English eccentrics we are! – being born in odd countries. Alex was born in Bombay, India – Sophie in Hong Kong – this, I imply, is how we like to arrange things. Maybe Inge chose to be born in Germany, for fun. For some reason, Martine humours me in this.

The constant surfacing of ROSENBAUM, INGEBURG COCARD always brought Inge grief. A decade or so back she wanted to join her wine-buff pals on a gourmet trip round Bordeaux but could not risk them seeing her maiden name at the hotel check-in. A fierce supporter of *Liberté, Egalité et Fraternité*, she insisted on exercising her democratic rights – but what if she chanced to be queuing at the town hall polling station next to somebody she knew? What if they happened to see or hear the name on the card? Being ill and forced to give your ID to your neighbour or friend to collect your parcel or recorded delivery letter – that was a nightmare. And fate knows how to laugh at those who try to frustrate it. The town of Tours is twinned with Mülheim an der Ruhr. German coaches park near the town hall and disgorge people her age. One of those Nazi pupils who terror-ised her might one day step out of the coach in front of the Mairie or in the Rue Nationale. Whenever she saw a German coach, she and her wheelchair would speed past.

Death cannot remove the problem of my mother's maiden name. Nothing can. And thus her problem becomes mine.

CHAPTER 4

. . . . .

Flowers are for the living

I request twenty copies of the death certificate – I know there will be lots of paperwork. Each is signed by hand and stamped; each has the recurring German Jewish name. The name comes up at the undertakers in full force. If she wasn't already dead, Inge would be beside herself. Perhaps she is. ('Don't make that face!') Rosenbaum is ubiquitous except for one document, which offers the exciting variant of ROSENBRAUM.

I have to make Inge the English lady she purported to be. Even in death, I have to do exactly what she wanted. Especially in death. I understand her. I too have spent a lot of my life pretending to be something I'm not. Am I the girl from the Birkenhead council estate? Yes and no. I don't sound northern, or feel it. I come across as posh. The committed convert to Judaism? Yes and no. More of a Buddhist, these days, though I have raised my children as Jews and given them that positive identity. From North to

South, at school, at university, living in France or Germany, changing religion, I too have remade myself several times. I am indeed my mother's daughter. It just happens to be the case that my various selves are sequential and don't conflict, or so I choose to think.

Madame la Générale decided long ago what shape her funeral should take; in 2011 and again in 2016 she telephoned to remind me 'no religion, darling, no prayers', with the names of the three songs she wanted played. I wrote it all down each time, though her choice didn't vary. I was to remember that 'flowers are for the living, not the dead'. A cardboard coffin would suit her just fine. She described the sweater she wanted to be dressed in (decent quality, a polo neck, white or black, but not the good cashmere). In May 2014 she announced that she had paid for her coffin and cremation at the crematorium in Esvres, where René's ashes had been scattered, calling me triumphantly to say that it was the cheapest available deal. She sent a photocopy of her choices: basic oak coffin, white taffeta lining and so on. The cost was €3,586.19.

Martine and I search through her papers for the contract. When we cannot find it, we ring every firm in town. It eventually transpires that she had never followed up on that initial quote. She visited a second firm, signed a contract and then cancelled it within the 14-day grace period. I expect she decided to save her money for the rainy day.

Looking through her papers, I find a yellow Post-it sticker placed on top of the little green state folder *Démarches et Formalités/ Dossier Familial*, which is the French state's 'how to organise procedures and formalities' booklet. This reads as follows, in pencil:

From me with love – underlined once. *I am asking you very sincerely to make sure to take the cheapest option in regards to the 'funerailles'* [funeral arrangements] – underlined twice.

(Don't be influenced by your emotions). Xxx 2013. On the other side she has written in ink *DO NOT PUT AN ANNOUNCEMENT in the papers.* I know that's because of the maiden name, also because she thought herself to be unimportant 'and anyway, nobody will come'.

The kind woman at the funeral parlour, familiar with heartbroken, frantic and emotional relatives, goes through the choices while I insist that my mother wanted the very cheapest funeral. She explains gently that they cannot supply cardboard or for that matter wicker coffins, and that pine is the least costly option. Two walls of the funeral parlour display various woods, coffin handles, fabrics and gaudy artificial flowers. I choose the cheapest thing in every category with breakneck speed. The pine coffin will have padding in white satin, a frilled volant, with matching pillow (white). Inge will be made up and wear the black polo-neck sweater; she will be lavishly perfumed with her favourite Chanel No. 5. I toy with the notion that she should leave this world in a cashmere sweater and Hermès scarf because frugal Inge so adored luxuries. Now I see the error of my ways. 'The waste, darling!' There is a saving of €206.88 on the original quote, which would have delighted her. The most generous of women, she loathed wasting money, especially on herself.

We go through the details of the ceremony: thirty-five minutes to fill, with no religious content. The funeral director explains that a plaque with maiden name and date of birth engraved on it will be fixed on her coffin. This is obligatory in France: that way, there can be no mix-ups. The body will be verified, and the coffin officially sealed by the police. I find more questions. Yes, the pleasant lady agrees, the lid of the coffin will be standing against the wall and visible in the morgue when people come to see her and say farewell before the ceremony, as is customary. During the ceremony, everybody will be asked if they wish to make the '*geste d'hommage*'. I enquire further. The usual homage is to approach and people can touch the coffin with petals or flowers. There will be a one-minute silence while they stand around it. Shit. That is more than enough time to study the plaque with the maiden name.

Galvanised, I explain to the slightly confused funeral director that my mother (that charming English eccentric) simply hated bureaucracy. This independent-minded lady fought all her life against domination by the state. So the plaque of the freedom-fighting Che Guevara of Tours has to be as small as possible.

'But they are all the same size, Madame.'

'How big exactly is the plaque?'

'It is official.'

She gestures mild bewilderment with her hands, giving me no idea how big the bloody thing is going to be in relation to the coffin. It is ridiculous and funny and sad. My efforts to cover up the Rosenbaum name now move from the figurative to the literal.

Inge was insistent: flowers are for the living. Covering that plaque is going to involve the sort of floral abundance that would be wasted on the dead. I tell myself that it is OK if the flowers are nice. Inge loathed white lilies, calling them '*Totenblumen*' – flowers for the dead. She rarely used a German word, and when she did it was to express a particular loathing. She didn't much care for cut flowers but quite liked freesias – well, there are no freesias at this time of year. She quite liked yellow tulips because I love them – tricky in January, but not impossible.

I go to Beauchesne, the florist in the old town. The sales assistant says they can get red, white and pink – but Madame la Générale, loud in my head, is insisting on yellow. Yes, a special order can come from Holland. I order 250 euros' worth of yellow tulips and ask for a carpet to be laid covering the entire coffin. Just in case. The florists are busy making funeral wreaths – sadly, their proprietor has recently died, and a book of memories lies open for customers to write in. They don't do 'carpets'. The young woman assistant says that the arrangement has to have some sort of structure. Don't we all. They need foam and wire and also green leaves and other smaller flowers – what about mimosa? I say no, they explain practicalities, we discuss small yellow flowers at length. Customers look askance as the eccentric Englishwoman rants on about the things her dead mother liked. Intransigent and unreasonable though I am, I accept the structure and agree to mimosa mixing with her tulips because I remember Inge being greeted by her favourite uncle, Willy, with an armful of mimosa when we visited the South of France as teenagers.

I have turned into my mother, or some version of her. I am her and she is inside me and we are complicit. The arrangement I have ordered will undoubtedly be huge but, just in case it isn't, the person delivering it to the morgue is instructed to place it at the end with the plaque to cover it. I make the florist write this down on the order. The wishes of the eccentric madwoman will be done.

For two weeks I wander around the neighbourhood, weirdly compelled to tell the world she is no more. Now I'm inside my mother's life.

'I am the daughter of Madame Cocard,' I say, going into a shop – and sometimes, if that doesn't ring a bell, 'the old English lady who pushes the wheelchair round the quartier.' Everybody tells me how marvellous she was – always witty, good humoured, always pausing for a chat. Nearly all of them know of her dramatic death; Monsieur Franck, the proprietor of the bike hire shop, has told lots of people. His wife is terribly upset. I do the rounds of the local chocolatiers. I discover that her 'wows' – her word for the extravagant gifts she loved to give us – come from a shop in the Rue de la Scellerie, the best chocolatier in town. 'Too good for the poor – but we'll have it anyway!' is another of Inge's expressions. Monsieur Hardouin, who sold her favourite cheese tart ('it's not quiche, darling, quiche has ham in it'), tells me how every time she came into the shop, he would attempt to help her with the wheelchair up the steps and every time she flatly refused.

Notes start arriving from her neighbours in the Allée du Manoir, expressing sorrow. I begin to understand how deeply embedded she was in this place with its routines and rituals and that all those polite and tiresome Bonjour Mesdames et Messieurs had meaning. She created a world in which she was safe and respected, and I cannot let her down. Years ago, I asked Inge what should happen after the service. 'Nothing,' she said and then, when I pushed, grudgingly added, 'Maybe the Restaurant de la Gare.' A good restaurant in René's day, it stands a hundred metres from the flat and was convenient when she didn't want to peel and deseed tomatoes for his preferred hors d'oeuvre. Renovated and expanded, it is now a standard station bistro, big and bluff and noisy. Martine and I have lunch there to check it out. Melted cheese sits greasily on a bowl of undercooked gelatinous fish. The steak is passable, but I don't eat meat. Yet I have no other option. Though I ask everyone what they think is appropriate and would be better, I am incapable of taking them to a restaurant my mother has not pre-approved.

Lorie arrives from New Zealand via Liverpool, totally jet-lagged. My two children, Sophie and Jonathan, arrive and the four of us put up a good front. On the day of the cremation,

22 January, snow turns to hail with lashing wind. At breakfast in the B&B I read out the French version of the eulogy I have spent many days writing, giving Sophie and Jonny named copies. The children will take turns to read out the English version. (The copy I give Lorie is marked 'spare'. 'Well, that's just typical,' she says. Miscommunication always has been our forte.) We time it. The whole reading comes to seventeen minutes, which is perfect. With the three songs, the 'homage', the silence and the waiting while the coffin goes into the flames, our slot is filled, to the minute.

Martine drives us to the morgue. In freezing rain, we scurry down the steep ramp; it's part of the tradition for friends and family to see the departed. Inge's dear friends Philippe and Maryvonne Fort are there and have already seen her. Our mother is made up, her face normal, ready. She seems calm. I kiss her. The lid of the coffin stands against the far wall; the plaque is quite small. Nevertheless, as we watch the sealing of the coffin by the police, I remind the two men from the undertakers that the flowers have to cover it fully. The seal is red wax, the screwing down of the coffin inexplicably horrible. Outside, relief erupts noisily and we are told to shush by the guy in the white tunic and trousers because another grim and silent family is waiting. The sense of trepidation grows but also some kind of weird exultation, because now the day is unstoppable and everything I planned is coming to pass.

At the cemetery, people are gathering; not just Inge's other dear friends Hélène and Hortense, but people we don't know from the neighbourhood. Maybe eighteen or twenty in all; given the lack of a newspaper announcement, this is a terrific turnout. Simon and Garfunkel sing 'Bridge Over Troubled Water' and their message of friendship when darkness comes is moving. The absence of religion and prayers is unusual, but the audience listen intently to the eulogy as I tell the story none of them have ever heard about the great mad amour Inge had for René Cocard, the man she came to Tours to marry.

When Inge was in her forties, she fell in love with René, a family friend who was already married, and they embarked upon a passionate affair. When she decided to end it, each suffered a breakdown, but Inge – made of sterner stuff – eventually recovered. René did not. From then on, he was a semi-invalid and they were parted. Nearly twenty years later, his wife died. She too was called Renée – everybody used to call them '*les deux Renés*', the two Renés. He summoned Inge to Tours, meeting her at the station with a huge bouquet of sixty red roses and the urgent question: 'Will you marry me or would you prefer to be my mistress?' Indifference was never an option. Her life was transformed. She was no longer the reject, second-class citizen, but the deserving object of a grand amour. She moved to Tours, married him and settled into the routine of being a French housewife and mistress of innumerable plates. Sadly, they would only enjoy seven years together.

In English and French, we explain that these last three decades in France were the happiest of her life. Nana Mouskouri sings 'La dernière rose de l'été', a beautiful song about love and seizing the moment. With tears in my eyes I realise, belatedly, that the songs she always insisted upon are not arbitrary at all. This is the soundtrack of her life. Everything she chose and did was more deliberate than I ever understood. I knew the depth of her feelings, and now I feel them. I'm very proud of her. She has achieved her oft-stated intention to be autonomous to the end.

The tulip with mimosas arrangement is glorious and immense and hides the plaque. Can the flowers go to the hospital? No; they can only be laid in the 'garden of memories', a freezing area of mud and grass where the ashes are to be scattered. Sophie pulls out a tulip to give to one lady – and suddenly we are inspired. Flowers are for the living, not the dead – haven't we just said that? And now we start pulling apart the structure, giving people armfuls of flowers – careful, meanwhile, to leave the base of the arrangement lying on the coffin, covering the plaque. Euphoria breaks out. People cradle their bouquets and tell us about Inge's charm – her joie de vivre – her appetite for life. We go out to the upbeat rhythm of 'The Girl From Ipanema' by Joao Gilberto and Stan Getz, and it is the perfect song, full of sunshine and hope. People mill about in the bitter cold; they don't want to leave. Snow falls in thick flakes at weird and intrepid angles, but everybody makes it to the station restaurant. The lunch passes in an outpouring of affection and talk; we drink a lot and (being French and taking lunch seriously) they eat all the food.

By the time we get back to the crematorium late that afternoon for the scattering of the ashes, the sun has come out. We sit in the car waiting for the ashes. Lorie, the children and I sing 'Waterloo Sunset', one of Inge's favourite songs, to an incredulous Martine. It is snowing in Paris – a blizzard is turning all France white – but here the sun sets gold and my lovely children scatter their grandmother's ashes where those of the great love of her life were scattered twenty-six years earlier. As Inge has written: *Je m'envolerai dans l'air de Tours*. I shall fly away in the air of Tours.

Sophie and Jonny leave for London. Lorie and I are choosing a few things to take home when I notice a blue folder at the back of the sideboard where Inge keeps her good china and glass. There, neat in bulldog clips, are handwritten notes and texts labelled *childhood, Meknes, Morocco, Brussels, Tours*. The date on the papers is 1993, the year René died. Mad with grief, Inge did not know what to do with herself. As a distraction, she started writing about her life, as I had often begged her to. She sent me the section about her childhood. I had no idea that she had written more.

Do I start with French troops being stationed in the Ruhrgebiet when I was born? Do I start with early reminiscences of babyhood, girlhood, marriage (the first one) or being the mother of two delightful little girls?

Do I start with my German, stateless, English or French nationality?

Do I start at the age of 43, when after living 17 years on my own I fell madly in love with a gorgeous, elegant, exciting Frenchman who already had a wife?

CHAPTER 5

. . . . .

Why did you marry the Jew?

I sit on the sitting-room carpet beside the cupboard, furtively tearing through the first dozen pages as if they were love letters from some illicit tryst. How well I know this voice and this characteristically rolling and upright writing that never changes. I flick through crossings-outs and corrections, revisions more to do with expression than content. She would no more change the content of these stories than rearrange her furniture.

I would so love to begin my life's story with an unforgettable first sentence; in my first line, my literary ambitions are revealed. Like mother, like daughter. I see a copy of the covering letter she sent me back in 1993 and read it again: *This by the way is not written for any outsider*, it says, *you and Lorie fine, but at present I don't think it should go beyond that.* This note will return to worry me, just as it should. She was writing at a time of wretchedness and her childhood as a half-Jew (*Mischling*) in Nazi Germany – appalling to experience – was painful to read. Her story isn't mine to share. Does my compulsion to write about her outweigh her wish for privacy? Her friends loved her, no matter who she was – my worry is not for them, it's for me, it's for her.

In the next sentence, Inge gives a partial permission: *If at any time bits are useful to you the 'Author' you are free to use whatever – but it is so humdrum I doubt it.* Humdrum? I don't think so. At the bottom of the letter, she added: *Whatever your comment I'll carry on writing because I have become completely involved with the past and have no time to think + weep.* Then caution returns: *I'll tell you however, I don't want it to make the rounds. Anyway, not that it could possibly interest anybody else.* She see-saws between anxiety and self-deprecation. Her letter ends: *I love you darling, love to you all – Mummy.* That's a bit more love than she usually sent. There always was love between us, even if it went underground at times.

Here is the compliment I often denied her: she was a truly remarkable woman and her story should be told. She lives on in these pages, collaborating with me from beyond the grave. I think she would enjoy that idea. I've italicised her written words without inverted commas so it's clear where I am quoting directly from her written account; I've paraphrased where there's too much detail. And I have speculated a good deal about her – it should be obvious where – because I can't resist. I'm the storyteller in our family. Fiercely critical of my work when she thought it second-rate, my book-loving mother was also my greatest admirer. We both knew how fiction and fact entwine. Wasn't her life in France a carefully crafted mixture of both? Inge loved editing my work. I can see her sitting in her white winged armchair with her back to the window, carefully annotating these pages in pencil with a secret smile. Ha ha ha! Monique thinks she knows it all, but she doesn't.

I was born on the 26th March, 1926 in Mülheim Ruhr.
Up to the age of 6 or 7 I have no consciousness of existing.
I only have flashes of events and I remember them clearly to
this day. My first awareness of being is at 18 months to 2
years, lying in my cot and the doctor wanting to look at the
spots on my tummy, lifting my nightie to see the extent of the
chickenpox or whatever. I remember very clearly the feeling
of outrage. Then, as a three-year-old playing in a sandpit
with my sister Hanne Lore I noticed that I had lost my brace-
let and was overcome by such a feeling of loss that I screamed
so fiercely that I lost my breath and was very frightened. Years
later, when I mentioned this to my mother, she was amazed
that I remembered that episode. I had turned blue and she
had feared that I might choke.

Mülheim an der Ruhr lies on the meandering River Ruhr between
Duisburg and Essen, twenty minutes' drive north of Düsseldorf
in the Rhineland. Germany's industrial heart boasts steelworks
and factories and plenty of work, but this part is also green and
pleasant. The town, founded in 1093, has an ancient castle and
medieval heart and at the time of Inge's birth was prosperous. Her
family on both sides had lived around here for hundreds of years.
Everyone in Hitler's Germany was told to make a family tree to
demonstrate their pure blood; I wish I had the one my grandmother Tilly drew up, which went back to the fifteenth century.

For centuries, the Lindemanns, on my maternal grandmother's
side, were small-town people, with a sprinkling of musicians and
choir masters. The paternal Rosenbaum side of the family, dealers
in coal and empty bottles, were better off. Great-grandfather
Salomon Rosenbaum lived in a big house with a courtyard housing

the numerous horse-drawn carts he owned. He and his very religious wife, Luise, had eight children, three boys and five girls. One of the boys died in infancy. The disaster of Inge's life was that her Lutheran Protestant mother, Mathilde Johanna Lindemann, chose to marry their elder boy, Arthur, a committed communist. The three crucial relationships of Inge's young years were with her mother, from whom she could not be parted even for one night, with the father she barely knew and with her elder sister, Hanne Lore, after whom my sister Lorie would be named. Each relationship was flawed, albeit in a different way.

I have been as truthful as my memorie [sic] *allows me to be,* writes Inge. *In lots of parts it is not a very flattering picture at all. To be so sensitive and on dramatic occasions to appear totally devoid of any feelings whatsoever. I am not justifying myself. I was although at the end of my tale 12 years old, a very very young 12-year-old. So darling your advice is very welcome. Please be brutally frank.* And I was. I welcomed and admired her honesty; that's my kind of writing. When I wrote back in 1993, I told her how much I liked what I'd read about her childhood and begged for more. The writings I find in the cupboard vary and don't have the consistency of her description of childhood. The pages on Meknes and her war years in Brussels are gnomic, practically bullet points; later I will decipher these, looking for all the events she chose not to mention. Even in these rough notes, Inge was economical with the truth.

What was Inge's model for motherhood? Total loyalty was the duty of a wife. Inge's mother, Tilly, regularly urged by the Gestapo to divorce the Jew, supported her husband through persecution and the years in prison and concentration camps; she ran the business and refused to divorce him even when all was lost. Kicked out of Germany, she walked with him over the border into Belgium at night. When in 1940 the Nazis invaded Belgium, the local authorities in Brussels rounded up their German and foreign Jews with great enthusiasm. Arthur was deported. My grandmother Tilly sent food and clothes to his camp in the South of France, but refused to join him there. Had she done so, she and my mother would also have ended in Auschwitz, where he met his fate.

The text in Inge's blue folder describes the start of this marriage promisingly enough. Arthur Rosenbaum was a keen cyclist. Bicycling through the forests near Lintorf in Düsseldorf, he somehow met Tilly's mother. When she showed him a photograph of her daughter, he fell in love at first sight: beautiful blue-eyed Tilly had red hair in long plaits to her waist and a terrific figure. For a time, the family had lived in Hamburg. Aged fourteen, Tilly was confirmed in the St Michaeliskirche there and told by her father that, if anyone asked, she was always to say that she was a 'Lutheran Protestant'. Tilly was one of five children, her lifelong favourite being her handsome older brother Willy, who attended the Fine Art Academy in Hamburg. Inge inherited her soft spot for this notorious romantic, an uncle as generous as he was unreliable. Always sporty and keen on the outdoors, the country girl wanted to be a gym teacher, but straitened circumstances meant that Tilly became a kindergarten teacher instead, working in Düsseldorf and returning home at weekends.

Tilly's mother promoted the courtship, arranging an 'accidental' meeting with Arthur the smitten. To the chagrin of the Rosenbaum parents, their last unmarried son would follow his brother and marry out. All but one daughter did the same. In the 1920s, the Jews of Germany were the most integrated in Europe. In 1922, the year of their marriage, Arthur was thirty and Tilly twenty-three; his profession on the wedding certificate reads coal merchant. He wooed and won, but he was a communist and atheist and family was not his priority. *His motto was first the party, and then the party, and then the family.*

Inge reports that Tilly had been wooed by another young man she liked, but who was already engaged. He wanted to abandon his fiancée, but she discouraged him. *One is as good as another*, our grandmother apparently said. Also: *Your father was very attentive, kind, very generous and was well off.* The defensive tone makes me wonder how often Tilly came under attack on this score. Did Inge regularly criticise her mother, dwelling on that nice Aryan boy Tilly refused, the fantasy father she should have had?

Tilly may well have settled for security with Arthur and what (until the advent of Hitler) promised to be the good life. Looking back at her sensible and unromantic choice, it's worth remembering that these were the tumultuous post First World War years of unrest and German hyperinflation, when ordinary folk wheeled around bundles of cash to buy a loaf of bread or a cabbage.

Despite family opposition, the young married couple were offered a flat in the big Rosenbaum house. Hanne Lore was born on 2 November 1923 and Inge nearly two and a half years later. From 1928, Arthur ran a successful bakery business. They moved several times and in 1931 settled in a handsome and spacious flat in the Schreinerstraße. Early childhood featured frequent expeditions to the countryside and family life. Nice (and less nice) aunts, uncles and cousins on both sides of the family lived nearby. Inge describes it thus:

There were river trips on the Ruhr, long walks, Indian file through the woods dressed in our Sunday best. An unwritten law in Germany at that time was that on Sundays

A Sunday walk in the countryside with one of the aunts. Hanne Lore, in front, was adored by the family. Inge, behind, is playing with a small cousin

*one dressed up. So we wore the most unsuitable dresses for
excursions through ferns and brambles, along narrow little
pathways and through the woods.*

The whole family met frequently and organised big Easter egg
hunts for all the children. Everyone visited Tante Nelly's summer
house, and everyone celebrated Christmas.

Arthur's mother, Luise Rosenbaum, came round to her favourite son's unfortunate marriage after the children were born. She
got on so well with Tilly that she even ate her food; this was a great
accolade. Inge wondered why grandmother Luise had a special
set of china in its own cupboard in their flat; nobody explained
that a kosher household served meat and milk on separate dishes.
Nobody told her anything about Judaism. The first time she set
foot in a synagogue would be when I married Alex.

Unlike her elder sister, Hanne Lore, who was adored by
everybody, little Inge got into scrapes and misunderstandings of
all kinds. She went in for crazy self-inflicted haircuts not once
but several times. She sat so long in the cinema watching Shirley
Temple on repeat that – o shame! – a notice was put up on the
screen saying *Inge Rosenbaum must go home straight away.* She
offended her least favourite aunt, the dreaded Tante Mally, when
she spat out the artificial children's coffee she was given at her
place because at home she drank real coffee. Dramas ensued if she
was offered margarine instead of butter; eventually she refused to
eat in anyone's house.

Her childhood was not a happy one. This came about partly
through circumstances and partly because of her temperament.
Inge wrote that all her life she was an *all or nothing* sort of person,
no matter what the cost: *Once I have started with A no matter*

what, I continue right through to Z. Hunting for Easter eggs in the meadows with the other children, she would panic and rush and fail to find even one; the adults had to fill her little basket. One year she discovered the Christmas tree abandoned in the cellar of the house and was heartbroken to realise that it wasn't magical after all. *Indeed I was a difficult child and would weep, not because I didn't get the presents I wished for, but because I had.* Highly possessive of every object she owned, Inge would cry helplessly if anyone dared to touch the collection of handbags in which she kept cherished scraps of paper inscribed with *rubbish I thought was French.* Desperate for a pram to wheel her dolls in, she refused the one Hanne Lore offered to lend because the dolls could only go out in a pram that she herself owned. (Fifty years later, for this very reason, she insisted on buying my two-year-old Sophie the most lavish dolls' pram to be had.) Since they could not go out, her dolls lived on her bed, covered up to be safe from germs. She would cry if anybody touched one. And *I learnt little or nothing from my past mistakes. They were never the same mistakes.* Her sister, by contrast, was beautifully behaved.

Super sensitive on the one hand, on the other Inge was a tomboy who lived for roller-skating with the gang. The sisters had *the most modern, double axel* [sic] *ball-bearing skates money could buy.* She and Hanne Lore practised on the wonderfully smooth surface of the market square outside the town hall. *We had twirling dark blue skirts and cream polo neck jumpers for artistic skating and dark blue track suits for all other rough and tumble activities.* Inge and her gang ran races, rang people's doorbells and fled before they were caught. Her knees were richly cross-latticed with scars from these escapades. She also had wooden-wheel skates on glamorous white boots for skating indoors. The only threat to

The roller-skating sisters. Inge shades her eyes

have any effect whatsoever on Inge was that her skates would be taken away.

Her mother was the star of the show, often-absent Arthur a bit player. Inge begged her father to let her go up in a plane from Mülheim Airport and *he gave his 'word of honour' which was never to be broken*; they went together. She remembered that the plane window wound down and that she had stuck her arm out through it, but almost nothing of him. Once he played marbles with her in the street. Sometimes she was allowed to help soak stamps for his collection. Apart from that, they never spent time together:

> *I say we – for my mother is vividly present on all occasions – but my father and my sister are shadowy figures. Writing down my memories I realise that my sister Hanne Lore, lovely, slim and 'douce' [sweet] with beautiful auburn hair just like my mother's, with the neatest most beautiful hand-writing, always a good and obliging girl, dearly beloved by all the family, didn't play any part in my life.*

Hanne Lore, three years older, was clued-up. She knew what was happening in Germany. But Inge yearned to be like everyone else, to wear the neat little 'Berchtesgaden' Hitler top under a brown jacket, belong to the Bund Deutscher Mädel (League of German Girls) and sit round the campfire singing patriotic songs.

She was soon made to realise that she was not good enough. Even before Hitler came to power in 1933 and banned the party, communists were hounded. The First World War had radicalised my grandfather. Deeply involved with politics from the time he was demobilised in 1918, Arthur became a member of many anti-fascist organisations. During the Weimar Republic, he was imprisoned several times: in 1919 for eighteen months for resistance to the state and six weeks for disturbing the peace (singing communist songs). He was a ringleader and a major figure in the town. When the Nazis took power in 1933, he was arrested; from this time onwards, he shuttled between prison and concentration camps.

All through the 1930s, people started to disappear. First to go was Gerta, *the youngest, smartest and prettiest* of the Rosenbaum sisters and the only one who had married a Jew. Inge missed her favourite aunt and uncle:

Tante Gerta and Onkel Wolf, her husband, suddenly disappeared from my life. They emigrated to America. Lucky for them, they left Germany early and were able to take all their possessions and money with them. It must have been 1934 or 36. They settled in the Bronx. 1934/36 was the time when most Jewish families left Germany or arranged to obtain a quota number to enable them to emigrate to America. My father felt 'German'. He had fought in the First World War, had lost a finger at Verdun and got some sort of war decoration. All his ancestors as far back as one could trace them had lived in Germany, Mülheim an der Ruhr to be precise. He was not a religious man and wasn't involved with the Jewish community. Our friends were the family, all mixed marriages, and of course he was a committed Communist. Some combination, to be Jewish, a communist and to live in a small town.

Arthur was active, the treasurer of the local party. He paid the rent for the local meeting place, signed as guarantor for the black shirts purchased – after all communists should be as smart as the Brownshirts – later of course most of these communists joined the SS and were able to wear the same black shirts. My father had to pay the bill, not just for a dozen or so, but for all the communist members in Mülheim. I remember the bailiffs coming and sticking 'Kuckucks' – 'cuckoos' – on our dining room and sitting room furniture and various other items and later on removing all items with the cuckoo sticker to cover some of the cost of the black shirts.

Adolf Hitler visited Mülheim an der Ruhr. Inge saw him standing up in a large limousine: *to this day I cannot forget the extraordinary look. I felt sure, he had only looked at me. It was a strange experience.* School, with its Hitler fanatics, soon became a living hell for the only (half) Jew in the class. Inge's teacher, a terrifying one-armed man, continually persecuted her. Unable to learn, paralysed by fear, she used to throw up daily before leaving the house. Persecution by her peers was even worse. She describes their name-calling, ostracising and physical attacks as former friends ganged up on her. When they shouted 'Jew' at her, she would sometimes shout back *Half-Jew! See? You're completely wrong!* She was constantly reminded that she was not as good as the others. Told to take toys to school for needy children, she took a dear little doll's armchair, which she greatly loved, and was told to take it home again by a nice teacher *because I can see you like it so much.* Her journey home with the all too visible toy was accompanied by catcalls all the way. Only later did she realise that *one could not expect a pure-bred German child to play with a contaminated toy.* It was around this time that she asked her mother why she had married a Jew.

As well as roller-skating, Inge was good at sewing: she had the novel experience of being praised and held up as an example to others. She describes how one day, for no very good reason, she sewed her mother's good stockings together at the top with beautiful tiny stitches; fortunately, Tilly was amused. Inge learned to knit, sew, crochet and embroider beautifully. These skills proved useful in later life, but she mourned her lack of education and never stopped trying to make up for it.

The family were on a downwards trajectory. The secret police searched the flat on a regular basis, looking for incriminating pamphlets and political material:

> *My father was accused of listening to Radio Moscow. It was of course well known in Mülheim that at one time my father had been chosen to attend some conference in Moscow, but it never came to pass. The early visits, always around 6am or 7am, were repeated with regular frequency and each time the newly purchased radio vanished.*

They never found incriminating material. Tilly would hide political pamphlets under her apron because nobody dared search her. Both parents would watch closely to see that nothing was planted and Inge reports that the flat was not trashed but left in good order.

Hanne Lore developed diabetes, Inge thought most probably from the shock and stress of the Gestapo visits. She grew steadily more ill, and no treatment was available. Events took a yet more tragic turn when the Gestapo started taking Arthur away with them for questioning and would not say where. Tilly was *totally fearless* and always found out: others didn't.

> *I think by then my mother had realised what an attractive woman she was. She had a marvellous figure, dressed*

in simple but very well-cut suits and to top it her beautiful auburn hair . . . one could not have missed her in a crowd. One of the men actually apologised to my mother for taking her husband away.

The periods of imprisonment grew ever longer. The Gestapo wouldn't leave him alone.

Once my mother took us with her to visit my father in prison, at that time he was in Oberhausen. I remember the police being very courteous. It was very strange to leave the cell, the door closing and your father being locked in.

Inge resented being forced into public displays of courage:

I remember with horror having to march at the head of a demonstration organised by the Communist Party to the prison in Mülheim where on another occasion my father was locked up.

What a desperate life. Tilly's struggle to support a family with a dying child, a business to run and a husband in prison does not bear thinking about. The bakery business in the Sandstraße had been put in her name. Large letters on the window announced 'owner Mathilde Johanna Lindemann'. On Kristallnacht in November 1938, when all Jewish shop windows were smashed, these would be left intact. She and her girls were by now living above the shop in a flat with three rooms and a large kitchen/living room; Inge was stunned to hear that they would have to go into the hallway with a key to use the bathroom and loo that came with the flat. Her parents were doing everything they could to get out of Germany, to no avail. No help came from the Aryan side of the family, some of whom had decided it wasn't a good idea to know the Rosenbaums. With Arthur constantly under arrest and no family support, how desolate and alone Tilly must have felt.

Tante Gerta in the Bronx offered to be a guarantor for the family in order to secure a permit for them to leave for the USA, but there was a quota numbering system and too many people ahead of them in the queue. The usual Jewish channels were overloaded and not interested in people who had married out of the faith. The Quakers in Britain did not respond. By now, the writing was literally on the wall: 'Jews not allowed in parks'; 'Jews not wanted'; 'Proudly announcing the reopening of a former Jewish business, now owned by a German'.

As Hanne Lore's health deteriorated, Inge describes helping her carry her satchel to school. They had been ordered to leave Germany, but couldn't:

> *It wasn't enough to be persecuted, one also had to have sound health, and my sister was diagnosed as a diabetic. No one, not one country, was willing to take a family with a sick child.*

She writes that her sister was protective and kind, and always told her parents to let the little one play:

> *I don't remember ever playing or talking to her – I feel I must have done. She was somehow grown up, indeed a grown-up person. Even now I can hear her say Mutti, let Inge go and play marbles, I'll wipe the dishes – let her do this, let her do that. She is only a little girl, Inge doesn't understand. At*

times I wanted to know what she and her friend Hildegard were talking about. She would look at her friend and say 'lass, sie weiss doch nicht wo die Glocken hängen' [leave her, she doesn't know where the bells hang: meaning she hasn't got a clue] *and I would rush out to play. There were never any bad feelings between us, and I didn't know what the word jealousy meant. I shared a bedroom with her until she died. I feel sad now, that I did not know her.*

Hanne Lore was christened and confirmed – Inge says that looking forward to her confirmation kept her going – before her death, aged fourteen, on 12 April 1938.

It was very important to my mother that I should say goodbye to Hanne Lore. We went into the room and I remember thinking, she is dead, and being frightened. Here was my mother kissing her and stroking her head and weeping. She told me to kiss my sister goodbye. Finally I approached her and I did it very quickly. All I wanted was to leave the room.

I didn't find it easy approaching my mother in the morgue in Tours; I can well understand how terrible this forced kiss was for a child of twelve.

The beloved child was buried in her black velvet confirmation dress and the real silk stockings she had so longed to wear, wearing the little diamond ring that had been her confirmation present. To her lasting bitterness, Inge was neither baptised nor christened, which served to confirm her underlying belief that nobody cared about her. During their years living underground in Brussels under German occupation, Inge enterprisingly had herself baptised by a Belgian pastor, Raoul Bordarier, in L'Église Evangelique de l'Observatoire. I found the handwritten document dated Sunday 13 December 1942 among her papers. She had kept this safe for seventy-seven years.

The funeral was devastating, Inge's memory of it dreamlike and unreal. She could not process the trauma.

I had never been to a funeral before and nothing had been explained to me. I was 'dépassée' [overtaken] by the events and all I remember was feeling very foolish. The service was held in a chapel, so we entered and there lay my sister in her open coffin dressed just like she had been for the confirmation. My mother and father went and stood each side of her then I saw them throwing themselves over the coffin with such weeping and agitation. I stood and looked; the pastor who had confirmed her was present. Next I remember standing with my parents at the open grave and a never-ending stream of people filing past us shaking hands. When we eventually returned home, I remember asking if I could go roller-skating – this caused consternation to all those present but my mother said yes.

Remembering that day now as an adult is dramatic, as I write tears are streaming down my face. I can feel this minute in Tours the heartbreak of my parents at losing their beloved Hanne Lore.

Perhaps Inge imagined that she would now be special, that she would be cherished as her sister was – this didn't happen. Sadly, she adds, any ideas she might have formed about being an only child *proved erroneous.*

The studio portrait of Inge, with older sister Hanne Lore on the right

At the very back of the cupboard with these handwritten notes is a framed sepia studio portrait of Inge and her older sister that must have been taken around 1930, before Hitler came to power. They are around four and seven. Inge's guileless blue eyes gaze sideways; Hanne Lore, so much more knowing, seems to be looking at the photographer. This is the first image I have ever seen of the child Lorie was named for.

All her life, Inge kept this and her sister's '*Poesie Buch*', the book of poems and inscriptions fashionable in the 1920s. Among Inge's effects is a small green plastic folder of photographs that belonged to Tilly, sized to fit in a handbag. Inside are pictures of her children and of Heinz, her second husband, in swimsuits on the beach. There is no image of Arthur. Right at the back, behind a picture of Inge and Hanne Lore on roller-skates, lies a bright lock of Hanne Lore's auburn hair. How Tilly adored this child of whom she never spoke. Perhaps she couldn't bring herself to, in the presence of Inge.

Inge and her sister lived together but apart. Inge was unable to understand what was going on. She knew her sister was ill but could not anticipate or process her actual death. Herself ill at ease, she endlessly kept putting her foot in things. Nobody told her how to behave; nobody shared information with her. Nobody showed her how to read a situation. Nobody read to her. The first book she was ever given was *Die Heimlichen Fünf – The Secret Five*. School friends presented her with this when she left Germany in March 1939, aged twelve. Yet one of her Lindemann aunts, Tante Lenchen (Lena), ran a big bookshop in the town. In later years, the bookworm was incredulous that there had been no books in her life. She was neglected by parents whose attention, inevitably, was channelled towards her sister. Inge never uses the word neglect. The way she put it was that adults acted and judged things by different rules and she couldn't work out what the rules were. But the lack of love is visible between the lines.

Yet how this child bloomed when an adult showed her the slightest bit of attention. When she was very small, her mother played a hide-and-seek game with the towel at bath times; she never forgot the joy of it. When her lovely Aunt Röschen called her Ingemaus (Inge mouse), she was in raptures. She remembered all her life how Willy Zimbehl – a family friend – once brought her chocolates packed into a special cup because he had heard that she was sick. When he told her that she was his friend, she was in seventh heaven. To hear endearments or receive presents out of the blue – such things were unheard of. How desperately she wanted and needed praise and how little she seems to have received. When she describes these moments, you feel the

Tilly in 1939, after Hanne Lore's death. This
photograph was probably taken for her passport

immense gulf of her parents' seeming indifference. That terrible things were happening does not take away the pain. Other people in extremis managed to be loving to each other. And yet I find it hard to judge my grandmother, who suffered so much and who was so kind to me. The only thing I am sure of is that in circumstances of true terror such as these, I would have failed. This is the knowledge that forever hangs over us, the fortunate children of the survivors.

After Hanne Lore's death, Inge and her mother were alone together and their circumstances, already dire, worsened yet further. Tilly was in a state of deep grief. Arthur Rosenbaum was living underground as a 'submarine'. The bakery in the Sandstraße was gone. Tilly had been driven out of business; I don't know how. In November 1938, Inge and her mother moved to their last address in Mülheim, a miserable room in the Eppinghofer Straße, a poor run-down district. They had nothing; even the furniture wasn't theirs. *By then I accepted everything, I don't know why.* That Christmas it was just the two of them, no tree and no festivities.

In January 1939, Inge was told that she was being sent out of Germany on her own to Morocco, to stay with her mother's favourite brother: handsome, romantic Uncle Willy, whom she had never met. Her mother explained that she and her father were going to Shanghai and would join her later in Meknes. This was not true: they had only managed to obtain one ticket to Shanghai and they used its existence as a lever to get Arthur out of Dachau.

Inge and Tilly traipsed round innumerable offices in search of a passport and *my mother was not intimidated by anyone.* Willy had helped them obtain a visa by guaranteeing to the authorities in French Morocco that he could support the child. An official letter was then sent to Germany, stating that Inge had a three-

The last photograph of twelve-year-old Inge taken in Germany

month visitor visa and required a passport. This unlocked the door that was so firmly shut. Nearly three months later, the passport arrived. On the morning of her departure, it was still dark when Tilly and Inge came out of the building into the taxi. One street away the car stopped, and her father stepped out of the shadows to kiss her goodbye. *I don't remember any emotions.* It drove on, taking her to Karlsruhe and the German border, where she embraced her mother and crossed, alone, to meet a Red Cross woman at the French checkpoint.

> *From there someone would take me to Strasbourg to a Catholic convent. From there someone would make the journey with me to Marseille and then by boat to Oran (Algeria) where Onkel Willy would meet me.*

Her tone is flat, her acceptance total. All the stuffing had gone out of her. Inge, who remembers the doctor lifting her nightie when she was two, can barely summon a detail of this memorable journey. She had never been on a train before, as the family always travelled by car. She had never seen the sea or been on a boat. She wonders at her surprising lack of recall; she was in deep shock but did not realise this then, or later:

> *I went, I didn't cry, I who had never spent a night away from home without my mother. I don't remember what I felt – is it possible I felt nothing at all?*

CHAPTER 6

. . . . .

Parallel lives

Lorie and I study the studio portrait of Inge with Hanne Lore that Inge kept all her life and never showed us. Two little German girls born two years and five months apart wear smart dresses with white collars, shiny hair brushed. Their heads touch; the photographer has aligned them in sisterhood. Hanne Lore has a sensitive, clever face. The aunt we never knew about is starting to become a person. Because we had no aunts or uncles or cousins, Inge's sister never felt real. She existed as the source of Lorie's odd name.

Inge's old black-and-white photographs tell two stories: her childhood and ours. The two girls in matching roller-skating outfits on the smooth tarmac of the town hall square could be twins. They're us, just sportier. We too grew up with an absent father and hard-working mother in an all-female triangle. There's a further parallel. Lorie and I were strongly connected until I was rising thirteen. Then everything went wrong. We lost each other emotionally – and things remained that way for decades. Now we're falling back into our childhood.

Inge, who so wanted a big family, had two daughters and three miscarriages. Both births were grim: Lorie was a breech birth and Inge spent three days in labour. The pain, she said, was indescribable. Lorie Rosamund Charlesworth – named for Hanne Lore – was born on 25 June 1949 weighing 4 pounds 12 ounces. The first photo shows her upright, contemplating the universe from her pram in the unruly garden of our rented house in Egerton Park, a nice part of Birkenhead. Lorie, always said to be the image of our father, was nicknamed 'the professor' for her high brow and her calm air of knowing things. *Nomen est omen.* When I was on the way, Inge was told bed rest was needed if she wasn't to lose me. She lay in bed in hospital reading *War and Peace* and crying. Every time the nurses tried to cheer her up, she said she was fine – it was just that it was such a wonderful book. She must have acquired English very fast, alongside excellent literary taste.

In March 1951 I arrived early at twenty-eight weeks after another difficult labour and days of torment. I weighed 2 pounds and 2 ounces, one kilo precisely, and was put into an incubator and given oxygen. I was not expected to survive. Each day my indomitable mother bicycled to the hospital with her expressed breast milk. She fed me with a pipette before bicycling home to make lunch for our father (obviously) and look after her twenty-one-month-old little daughter. I was *a tiny wizened thing with a monkey's head the size of an orange.* The tiny monkey grew chubby and round-faced; unlike the 'professor', I wasn't held to be the image of anyone. Inge spoke French to us until our father put a stop to that. My first word was '*pomme*'. Thirty years later, my daughter Sophie's first word was 'apple'; genes do operate in wonderful ways.

Tom and Lorie bond

Grim, grimy Birkenhead was changing. The NHS had been created three years earlier and in a time of rationing and austerity I was one of those fortunate British babies fed orange juice each week (it was rather sour) plus a big spoonful of cod liver oil, which I hated. The old slums were being demolished, and the long promised New Jerusalem was rising, brick by brick, on fields around towns. Around 1953 our parents moved into number 15 Boswell Road, a newly built three-bedroom council house in Prenton on the outskirts of Birkenhead. A primary school was rising up a short distance away to accommodate the baby boom. When I went back after forty years, I was surprised to see how neat and nice it was – green spaces everywhere and no cars on the road. For a decade, until the council started churning concrete to build the rest of the Prenton Dell Estate on the fields beside our house, it was a quiet and pleasant place. Adjoining streets were named Johnson, Garrick, Dickens and Byron; the planners had aspirations.

A generous triangle of regularly mown grass sat in front of our neat red-brick house, the last in a row of four. We had a decent bathroom and kitchen and a big coal shed that was jet black inside; everyone had coal fires then. There was space for the rockery Inge would later build to one side and a long back garden giving on to an old meadow that was untilled, full of wildflowers and wilder rabbits. A long lane took us to Prenton Primary. Ancient, deep and rutted, once used by carts and stagecoaches, it had a strip of velvety grass running down the centre. This beautiful pathway was lined by tall hedgerows brimming with blackberries and elderberries, the habitat of innumerable birds and creatures. Skipping our way to school unsupervised, we stained our mouths black with berries. Prenton was a village then, all fields beyond.

Lorie on the left

My first memory is sitting on the top stair in Boswell Road listening to screaming and shouting from downstairs: our mother's voice hysterical, our father's angry. Lorie is beside me. Rising five, she knows everything. I'm young and clueless – maybe three? If so, this happened in 1954, when Inge was twenty-eight. Our father had left Inge for an older woman – a double insult.

One of the few conversations I remember with my father came one Saturday when I was four or five and he took us to the grand Central Library in Borough Road for our usual quota of books. We spent hours in that airy sunlit space: we children got three compared to his six and I had always read mine by Wednesday, so choosing the right book was an important matter. That day, as we returned home, he told us that they were divorcing. This didn't go well. We howled and sobbed at the bus stop and clung to him, and then, somehow, he had to get us on to the bus and deliver us back home – he'd already been gone for a couple of years. This staggering ineptitude probably came about because Inge insisted that he deliver the bad news in person. Their divorce was always going to be his fault, not hers.

After the split we three lived inside a bubble of otherness, a triangle of female solidarity in a man-less world, wholly different from other Prenton children. We had no family in Birkenhead. We had a grandmother who lived in Morocco whom we called Omi: Omi/Tilly travelled to England to meet us and there are photographs of her in the garden of Egerton Park carrying us. Later, she visited our Boswell Road council house with Heinz Steinberg, her second husband. Heinz was charming and friendly and wore a black-and-white-striped dressing gown. This exotic zebra smelled of Eau de Cologne and fragrant tobacco; his pipes came from Dunhill. In every picture, this beautifully dressed man is smoking a pipe. These fabulous creatures then moved to Peru, a place further away than the moon.

Omi/Tilly was known to be German, but it didn't occur to me that my mother was – nobody mentioned it, and I have never been able to hear her accent. She was our Mummy, who loved us and played with us. I was happy at home with my mother until I was four and a half and Lorie came home from school with a letter saying I was to start at the local primary full time. And so, skipping the kindergarten or nursery stage, I went to school and Inge out to work. Bored because I could already read, and was unable to see the blackboard, I spent my time staring out of the window counting the motes of dust, which I decided were fairies flashing on the windowpanes. Eventually, somebody realised that I couldn't see. With spectacles, my life came into focus. Inge had found a secretarial job at Belmont Slumberwear, a factory making pyjamas, and with her usual energy and drive soon rose to become the boss's secretary.

I didn't want us to be latchkey children. I wanted to be like my friends Jacqui Durban and Susan Parsons with a mother who stayed home. Lorie and I always sensed that we didn't fit in, that we were out of place, without knowing why. As a little girl, I wasn't ashamed of the council house – that came later – but I badly wanted us to be a proper family. I longed to live in one of the nice houses on the other side of Prenton Primary School with a father and a car parked in front of a neat garage.

Lorie and I lived entwined. There was always an hour or two after school to kill before Inge came home at six o'clock; the house didn't have central heating and we were not allowed to light the fire. A blanket thrown over the dining table became a warmish cave where we created an alternative world. Lorie needed to be entertained so I told her stories. The Mouse Kingdom saga evolved, a kind of junior *Gormenghast*. Most unfairly, she insisted on being the beautiful adventurous Princess Jemima, while I – titular King of the Mice – was known for being fat and greedy. This was undeniably true, because my father had nicknamed me 'fattun pattun', which did little to enhance my self-esteem. King Montmorency (later shortened to Monty) did all the narration, making it up as I went along. Lorie wasn't an easy audience because she got bored quickly and then grew sardonic like our father, forcing me to up my game. I told her stories at night too, when we couldn't get to sleep.

We understood very well that everything had gone wrong because Daddy had left us, and I long entertained the fantasy of reuniting them. But how? We plotted to make them meet between Woodside and Hamilton Square stations – and they did – but nothing happened. Aged ten, I pestered my mother to take us to see *The Parent Trap* featuring Hayley Mills playing twins, divided at birth. Using all sorts of cunning tricks, they defeat the pushy prospective stepmother and bring their divorced parents back together. We couldn't afford the cinema; this was the first film I had ever seen. I must have been very insistent. Off we went to that giddy fleshpot, the Savoy Cinema on Grange Road, Birkenhead. Did my naked and futile ambition sadden Inge? I don't think so. She would have loved the Technicolor glamour: the Californian cars, the fabulous frocks and hairdos of 1961. By then, she was plotting her getaway from Birkenhead.

According to Inge, Tom's departure so broke her heart that for decades she could not look at another man. We saw for ourselves that she wouldn't look at him. On Saturdays, when he came to collect us, she refused to budge. We would hear the sound of his car – a relative rarity in Boswell Road – and run to the door. She remained at her Singer sewing machine pedalling away, roaring down seams. On those days out, our father drove us to the funfair at New Brighton for the day and gave us five bob each. We wasted this huge sum rolling pennies down shelves and steering grab-the-toy claw machines. Lorie and I queasily enjoyed the extravagance of these outings, but it also felt strange under the neon, with the stench of greasy food. The day went slowly and stickily. Once we clamoured for a go on the Ferris wheel and then screamed so hysterically after a proper rotation at full speed that Tom had to get the man to stop it. It occurs to me now that he might have wanted to take us to his house, which would have been a lot nicer and cheaper, but couldn't because his new wife, Flo, so disliked us. In the late afternoon Tom would drop us home in his car, nauseous on toffee apples and encrusted with candy floss, with no envelope for our mother. I remember the vague guilt I felt, and the look on her face when we arrived empty-handed.

In 1958, the year of the divorce, Inge was thirty-two. I was seven, Lorie nine. That summer we travelled to Brussels for the World Expo and stayed with Inge's friend Nina at her tall, narrow house in Wenduine near Blankenberge on the coast. This was a very big event in our lives and Inge spent every free moment knitting cardigans and making us all new summer skirts and dresses. A boulevard photographer captured her striding into the future white-gloved, hand in hand with her girls. She'd made every stitch we are wearing. In Brussels we met the widow of 'Uncle George', whose sweet factory Inge had worked at during the war. Lorie remembers a creepy stuffed Pekingese on a pillar, which she was on no account to touch. I remember going up the Atomium, the shiny structure with nine spheres that is still there. Lorie and I were filmed in the Russian pavilion and appeared live on a television screen, just like Laika, the first dog sent into space, in 1957, on Sputnik 2. We were very keen on Laika the stray mongrel and on the pavilion showing footage of our canine heroine. It would be years before it was revealed that poor little Laika, the first animal to orbit the Earth, had died within hours.

By 1960 the concrete mixers had started up and Inge was looking to move from Boswell Road. Change was afoot. Heinz and Tilly had received reparation money from the German government. As her share, Inge received £2,500 from Tilly and Heinz, which in Berkenhead would have bought a nice house. In South London it supplied the 50 per cent deposit on a small two-bedroom garden flat. Inge took out a mortgage for the rest, which was a struggle for a divorcée in those days.

She wanted to stay in the North of England where she had friends and to open a boarding house in Chester. But Heinz was pulling the strings and holding the purse strings too. Metropolitan and suave, with a cousin who'd settled in London, he talked Inge round. She found digs and a job in London at the international phone exchange. And so in 1961 we were foisted on to Tom and Flo, the lovebirds, for a memorably gruesome six months, commuting to school where I was due to take the eleven-plus.

It was because her lodgings were in Lordship Lane, East Dulwich, that Inge concentrated on south of the river. Her landlady and new friend was a recently widowed mother of three, known to us as 'Auntie Myra'. Myra took Inge under her wing and drove her about, later introducing her to catering and thus gaining herself an able assistant at Midland Bank in the City. The flat Inge found was newly built and a short walk from Sydenham High School, part of the Girls' Public Day School Trust. Lorie was at Park High School for Girls grammar school; I won a free place at Birkenhead High School, also GPDST, through the eleven-plus. Sydenham High was the school for us. But we arrived in London in the summer of 1962, too late to sit school entrance exams. Inge, who so passionately believed in education, would have to pay fees. She would eventually work as a bursar at GPDST schools, thus obtaining a 50 per cent discount. Good linguists, Lorie and I shed the much-mocked northern accent within a couple of weeks as we all set about remaking ourselves.

A first small rift occurred when we found out about our Jewish heritage. In the summer of 1963, Inge's favourite uncle, Willy Lindemann, invited us to stay in the hotel he managed in Nice. We'd heard a lot about how kind and artistic he was. We knew that when Inge was our age, she'd travelled on her own all the way to Morocco to stay with Uncle Willy, and that she'd had a marvellous time. The fabulousness of the South of France was discussed in depth. There was a lot of talk about miniskirts and bikinis and the usual whirlwind of sewing.

Lorie and Inge were chatting in the bathroom, sitting on the edge of the bath. Lorie was doing her make-up, staring into the big mirror opposite. Smoothing on her panstick, which doubled as pale lipstick and was all the rage, she had a question.

'So what was Omi called?'

Omi was what we called our grandmother Tilly. It was our version of the German word Oma, meaning Granny, not that we knew that.

'Mathilde Johanna Lindemann.'

'So she wasn't married then.'

Lorie was fourteen and sharp as a whip.

'Of course she was.'

'Well, she didn't marry her brother. Did she marry some-body else called Lindemann? I mean, that would be very unusual, wouldn't it?'

'No.'

'What was her name then?'

I can see Lorie drawing her cat's eyes with a black brush before applying the endless layers of mascara. I can hear the pause before our guileless, trapped mother replied.

'Rosenbaum.'

'That's Jewish. Are we Jewish?'

How on earth did Lorie know such things?

'Great! That means I don't have to go to assembly.'

That was all being Jewish meant to her. But this moment was huge for all three of us. I was weedy and bookish and nothing this exciting had ever happened to me. Later that year I read Leon Uris's *Exodus*, which made me cry and fixed the idea of Jews as romantic, special, and overwhelmingly attractive in my mind.

Lorie had pinned Inge down; our mother would later say how remarkable it was that my sister had worked it out, how clever she was. But being forced to share her deepest and darkest secret in this way also changed the trust between them. I am sure that Inge would have suppressed this information forever if she could have. Yet it was bound to come out; like Hanne Lore, my sister always was ahead of the game.

The following year – to Inge's utter dismay – Tilly and our step-grandfather Heinz turned up to live with us. This was unex-pected. For twenty years they had lived in Morocco, then they had spent a happy six years in Peru. Heinz, who had befriended Willy in the French Foreign Legion, was an entrepreneur who famously exported Panama hats to Panama. In Peru he dealt in guano, exporting it to Germany. Holding both German and French passports, our grandparents decided to retire to France. Heinz bought a house near Toulouse, then discovered that an aircraft factory was being built nearby. They sold it and announced they were coming to London instead.

The Heimat abruptly landed on our doorstep. For Inge to have the hated past return was catastrophic. She would have to suffer the awfulness of her German-speaking mother blowing her cover. When asked what her accent was, Inge ('It's Ingeborg with an o') tended to shrug, implying vague Swedishness, adulterated by her years in the North of England. Heinz was not just utterly German but another powerful man telling her what to do. It must have felt like a rerun of her childhood. She could not tell them she didn't want them there. Who can tell their mother that they don't love her? So the disaster unfurled.

Tilly, so kind and unassuming, could be tough if crossed – I never experienced that side of her, but Lorie did. Terrible Sturm and Drang ensued as the grandparents settled in to our small flat and started building an extension in which they would supposedly spend all their time but never did. Tilly called the builders (Bridge Walker) Bricks and Mortar and endlessly wondered why site meetings always had to be at our place. They paid for the extension but Inge, who made the mortgage payments, was considered to be still beholden to them for the deposit – it was not a happy state of affairs.

Though Lorie couldn't stand Tilly and Heinz, I loved the Continental atmosphere, Heinz's Jewish jokes, the careful way he cleaned his prized Dunhill pipes and the fragrance of his tobacco. A charming man (albeit with a fierce temper), he was always beautifully dressed in elegant suits and Sea Island cotton shirts, his shoes highly polished. No fighter, he always said his area of expertise in the French Foreign Legion had been making donkey salami. A bachelor for decades, he had smoothly progressed from one married lover to the next until Tilly came along. He looked after his clothes and possessions himself and he did it well.

A routine evolved; he cut out chess problems from *The Times* and solved a week's set on Saturday mornings, looking at each one for perhaps a minute and then laying it down with a nod. Tilly played croquet and they made friends in the neighbourhood. Inge's friends loved them and they were included in every invitation, to her great annoyance. Now and then Heinz's temper would surge up and he'd throw a blue fit about something, generally of no importance. By the next day it was always forgotten. Tilly used to say that in the night she would hear a very small voice saying '*Liebst du mich noch?*' – 'Do you still love me?' Of course she did.

Through these years, Inge worked hard with little incentive to get home early. Tilly cooked each day. When we came home from school, there was always a hot, fresh currant loaf to be slathered with butter. Gigantic grilled pork chops lounged on mounds of mashed potatoes with warm apple sauce. Tilly was, of course, an accomplished confectioner. We had Continental manners: the table was properly set for every meal and food served from dishes, not directly on a plate. Good Melitta coffee and home-made cakes were a daily institution.

I loved Tilly, who was sweet and even-tempered and often said '*Je suis la balance*' [I am the weighing scales] to illustrate this. Her scanty stock of English was very funny. She and Inge only spoke English at home. Heinz spoke English well, but he and Tilly veered from French to German and back to English. A bit of kitchen Spanish was regularly thrown in by my grandmother, searching in vain for the right word. Mistakes and idiosyncrasies that set Inge's teeth on edge charmed others. Tilly's complex mishmash expressed her thoughts perfectly without troubling the grammar books. Despite terrible losses in her earlier life, our grandmother found joy in the everyday. She gardened, she cooked; always sporty, she played croquet avidly and competitively for Sydenham Ladies. She undertook bold expeditions on three buses to the Swiss Centre in Leicester Square to buy black bread and Swiss cheeses obtainable nowhere else, returning triumphantly swinging her bulging string bag.

I benefited from being in their orbit. Naturally good at languages, I soon got better. Inge never helped with French or German homework, or indeed any homework. She might turn up at the school's annual prize-giving in a big hat, to our absolute horror, but was less keen on meeting teachers at parents' evenings and hated having to write letters. Her lack of education troubled her terribly. But like all the other extreme emotions fermenting away in that small flat, this was never mentioned.

Lorie was fourteen when Tilly and Heinz arrived, and she couldn't stand them any more than Inge could. She had been perfectly happy when there were just the three of us and now everything exploded. Lorie was a stroppy teenager, but the rows she and Inge had went way beyond normal. Their arguments were fierce, with shouting and door-slamming. Lorie was very clever and, like Tom, had a quick riposte to everything, which infuriated Inge. Our mother – already in a mental state of siege – could not stand to be criticised or contradicted. She worked late and at weekends collapsed with migraines. These never flared up when she went abroad and mysteriously abated on Monday mornings as she fled back to the office. Tiptoeing around the bedroom in which she suffered, I never once thought that these might be psychosomatic. I always took my mother's side. Not to do so was unthinkable. And in short order, Lorie became a pariah. Aged eighteen, she went off to live with our father and her relationship with us went further downhill.

Lorie and I have often met over the years, of course – but we never really talked about any of this. And now, alone in Inge's flat, the two of us can't stop.

CHAPTER 7

· · · · ·

Sisterhood

We haven't spent this much time together since we were teenagers. We regress and transgress. We leave dirty coffee cups in the kitchen sink and use non-approved linen when setting the table. We ferret about. For Inge's generation, who went hungry in the war, love was food, supply or deny. I feel the love in the Nespresso machine she acquired after noticing how much I liked mine and the decaffeinated coffee pods bought specially for me. Love was in the contents of the fridge, in overfeeding swiftly followed by fat-shaming.

We discuss provisions, their surfeit and lack. Our mother always announced that 'the fridge is full, darling, just help yourself!' Opening it, I would find an elderly jar of mayonnaise, a yellow plastic squeezie lemon that had been there for years, a scraped-out jar of Poupon mustard, two potatoes, a pack of butter and five full-fat cheeses. Supper would be a baguette, butter and cheese, each fattening mouthful carefully assessed for its calorific value as it went down, Inge herself eating nothing. Cheese, as we all knew, made her bilious. Soon enough though, she would ask

Lorie, left, wears the beads

for a piece 'just to try' – then another and another, 'because you're here', and happiness meant overdosing on cheese and feeling sick.

I tell Lorie about our fish wars. Lunch was Inge's main meal (usually her only meal). We always had fish because I am the expert who supposedly knows how to cook it. I would buy the fish plus a lemon, fearing the furry fridge one. Then I would make the mistake of squeezing lemon over the grilled fish. At once, Inge would push her plate away in disgust.

'Water everywhere. It's probably not cooked through. Nobody could eat that.' She was hungry, but it gave her more pleasure to leave the fish than to eat it. That way she won. So I'd mop up the juice with kitchen paper.

'It's cold. I can't eat cold food.'

I'd put the plate in the oven. When it reappeared, it was worse. 'It's dry. Overcooked.'

The piece of foil I'd used was wrong – it was never clear how. Too large? Too small? The wrong way up? By now, her hands would be trembling with rage. She had a very particular way of pushing the plate away, hard, with a crooked 'I'm bravely putting up with this' smile. Then she went off for her afternoon sleep.

Inge's rage at her own mother, Tilly, came out in the same way, channelled into remarks about boiling the coffee or using the wrong cup. Lorie tells me how Inge used to inform her grand-daughter Oriel – Lorie's second daughter – exactly how to hoover when she came to stay with her granny and slaved in the August heat. Inge would correct her slave if she took too much butter, just as she'd criticise the quantity of green beans I prepared ('nobody needs more than 100 grams') or how they were boiled.

'Have you set the timer? Four minutes? Well, they'll be hard. Too bad.'

'Is that your usual gunge [salad dressing]? It's not as nice as it used to be. In fact, it's inedible.'

Her rage was never about the dust or the fish. Inge had a self she didn't know she possessed: a frustrated woman with no idea what was driving her. We were set in ancient and familiar patterns that irked us both. We might snipe and be petty, but we never argued. Fury was vented on fish and innocent vegetables.

While sharing all this, Lorie and I drink Inge's wine. The good Vouvray was bought for us and guests. For herself, our mother bought the roughest €3 plonk in the local Atac supermarket: white to slosh into her petit kir and red for the red cardinal. We drink that too. We find bottles of crème de cassis and crème de pêche (15 per cent alcohol) for her favourite drink. 'Pure fruit, darling.' I can see her raising her glass with a big smile – it's my day! Any day could be 'hers'. Now everything is 'ours'. We fall back into being 'us' with a familiarity and ease long gone. We laugh a lot, with howls of recognition about how impossible Inge was. We can't believe how much there is to say. Because we have only a couple of appointments with the bank and the notaire, we are able to spend most of our days in Tours talking non-stop.

Something odd is going on; the invisible wall of distance and mistrust that lay between us for five decades has vanished. I hear what Lorie is saying and she makes sense. Before, she was muffled to the point of being inaudible. I couldn't, or wouldn't, listen to her. It will take a long time for me to grasp that it was my loyalty to Inge that created these psychological earplugs. To hear and understand Lorie was to fraternise with the enemy. Over the coming months, the desperate sadness of this will sink in.

As we swap and compare anecdotes, startling truths emerge. First, we unpick our long and bizarre failure to communicate about our mother. The way it worked was that one or other of us would say we were going to Tours – and did – then the other one would ask 'How's Mummy?' and we'd talk about the latest round of illness and never say that it was a complete nightmare or that she drove us round the bend. Why? Because we couldn't. Not while she was alive to divide and conquer. Invisible barriers held us in our allotted places. We never discussed her character. We never compared and contrasted the stories she told. The pieces of the jigsaw remained sealed in their box. Most mothers want their children to support and care for each other; Inge kept us apart. Did the experience of growing up alongside Hanne Lore teach Inge that sisters could be treated differently, that favouring one over the other was normal? Because that's what happened.

There's so much I don't know about my sister. I learn that as a troubled teenager, Lorie was referred to the Maudsley Hospital. The bad girl needed sorting out. She went there on Friday afternoons and talked to the psychiatrist, mostly about science fiction; she didn't see the point of this 'therapy'. Then the psychiatrist asked Inge to come in for a one-to-one chat, leaving the miscreant waiting outside. It must have been obvious that there was a lot going on at home. After half an hour, Inge emerged.

'Do you want to come back here?' she asked.

'Do I have to?'

'Not if you don't want to.'

Of course Lorie didn't want to; she was bored and miserable and wanted to go home. So off they went.

Years later, waiting to see a different doctor, Lorie was handed her dossier and read the psychiatrist's notes observing that she was very unhappy and would have benefited from inpatient care during the summer holidays. It was pointed out that her mother clearly needed help. But Inge could not bear any examination of herself: Lorie was always the villain of the piece. Any chance of help was missed that afternoon, when she manipulated Lorie into rejecting the opportunity offered to both.

As children, we couldn't know that Inge's pain and grief was not our fault. It wasn't her fault either. But she never acquired the tools that would have helped her to manage them; instead, she turned on Lorie. We didn't have understanding, let alone words, for this behaviour in those years: now we call it gaslighting. For my sister, being constantly gaslighted by Inge must have been exhausting. Lorie couldn't reconcile what she was being told with what she instinctively knew, and the outcome was profound self-questioning, sadness and depression.

I'm stunned by how little I saw or understood of what was going on in those years.

Lorie tells me she always sensed that our background was full of secrets and lies and she couldn't stand it. At some level, children know things. That's probably why we both have tended throughout our lives to extremes of honesty, however unwise. Inge made us complicit in her untruth, with its moments of tragedy and farce. Far more naive than my sister, I was very protective of my mother and never questioned a word she uttered.

We rapidly work out that Inge told us conflicting stories. I have always known that Lorie left us and went off to the North of England aged eighteen because she was desperate to live with our father and his wife, Flo. Fifty years on, I discover this isn't true. After A levels, the careers advisor talked to Lorie about the possibility of a job at the library in nearby Catford while she thought about what to do next. She applied and got it: 'I would have been so happy there, with 300 science fiction books,' Lorie says. She arranged to share a flat with a friend and was desperate to move out and be independent. But in January 1968, Inge despatched her off to the Wirral where our father lived, because she couldn't cope with her stroppy behaviour. I remember her saying that it was 'high time Tom dealt with the problem'. While living with Tom and Flo, Lorie started a foundation year at Liverpool Art School. Though she would later become a lawyer, she was and is a very talented artist. Later, when Lorie got into marital trouble, Inge refused to support her or to let her come and live at home where she could have made a new start. These were sad, bad years; Inge's snap judgements could be very harsh.

We probe further. Inge told me that Lorie deliberately chose her husband from 'the wrong crowd' after Tom ordered her to avoid them. And now I discover that this double typecasting of bolshie daughter and tyrannical father is also pure invention. Lorie tells me that our father didn't care what she did, providing she didn't annoy our stepmother, Flo. He was amiable and relaxed. Another Inge trope was that Lorie looked like Daddy and took after him. In other words, she was tricky and unreliable: another absconder. Every story fed this myth. I was cast as the good girl while my sister's bad girl status was continually embellished.

'But I'm good! I'm prefect material!' says Lorie as we sit in Inge's flat – amused but also sorrowful to hear herself saying this, fifty years on.

I am starting to assemble the pieces of the jigsaw in my mind. Lorie was the classic art school student type – creative, unconventional, clever, wacky. She remained mentally connected to the North of England, to our father, to the friends she had left behind. The small Sydenham flat where we shared a tiny bedroom felt like punishment to her. Sometimes it was. My Billy Graham evangelist phase must have been hard going. I would turn the other cheek piously and sometimes noisily when Lorie was particularly scathing about my purity and godliness. My Bible reading in bed really annoyed her, particularly when I chose passages to read out loud. I was always looking for some way to belong, without verbalising it or understanding what I was doing: my equivalent of the Bund Deutscher Mädel, the League of German Girls.

We agree, though, that the three of us were basically fine until our grandparents turned up. After that there was no privacy. Heinz sometimes had the sense to withdraw when something was brewing – but Tilly never did. Neither of them had any experience of contemporary teenagers. Lorie was hurt by constant criticism, which only made her more truculent.

What were Lorie's actual crimes? At school she underperformed with panache. She went in late and sloped off early, flouting uniform rules in her beatnik sloppy joe. The teachers liked her, so normal rules weren't applied. To demonstrate to Inge that work wasn't the problem, she once applied herself for a term, got top marks, and having proved her point, never did it again. This drove our mother crazy. Lorie didn't do anything useful in the house but read for hours, deeply immersed in novels and science fiction. There was the odd fag, occasional staying out late, answering back and liking boys. She monopolised the bathroom and spent an age doing her make-up and gluing on false eyelashes; boys liked her, and she liked snogging them. I was innocent, prudish, and massively jealous.

Once on holiday in Brixham Harbour, Devon, Lorie and a friend forced me to drink a murky black brew they called 'coffee' laced with mustard and her pal's anti-epilepsy medicine. Though I was ready to believe my big bad sister capable of anything, this experiment on the pious guinea pig was probably the nearest she got to drugs. The stuff she gave me tasted disgusting but under duress I got most of it down. Super wired, I was then up all night, hallucinating. Inge was horrified; I was baffled but also milked this incident for all it was worth. Lorie always made me laugh. But I was in my holier-than-thou phase, also looking for escape, albeit in less confrontational ways. I would never challenge Inge.

Lorie did. Her real crime was her inability to toe the party line when our mother demanded absolute obedience. 'I am the chief, and you are the Indians' was a favourite saying. Lorie's intelligence told her that the whole construct of our supposedly happy family was fake. She saw that our mother was lying and that the huge tension in our flat arose through her terrible relationship with our grandparents. Our mother couldn't face the truth and ran off to work. Lorie was so unhappy. She was clinically depressed, and Inge was telling her that she was the problem. I'm starting to feel terrible about this. My outrage is all the greater for my blindness at the time. I supported my mother in all things. Not to do so was literally unthinkable. There was no question of sisterly solidarity; that would have consigned me to her darkness.

We talk through those long-ago years when we barely communicated. Lorie doesn't know that Inge sent me away too. In the summer of 1969, after A levels, Inge packed me off on the ferry from Harwich to Hamburg for my gap year so fast that I missed the end-of-school parties and exam results. My mother told me I was naive and unworldly and needed to do some growing up, which was true enough. She arranged for me to spend a year as an au pair for German friends of our grandparents, which would also leave me time to study at the university there. I was set to do Oxbridge entrance, which in those days people took in the term after A levels. I'd done the exams as a dry run at sixteen and been encouraged to apply at eighteen. Dispatching me to Hamburg that summer scuppered that. I was fine about this; I already had a place at Bristol to study French and German and worried about how elitist Oxford might be for a South London girl of modest means. Looking back, it does seem strange that my mother, supposedly so set on her girls' education, took no interest in this.

Yet odder was the fact that the children of the family where I was going were away on holiday in Switzerland. I spent six weeks alone in the house with the maid; the father of the house was there but in the absence of his wife wisely avoided getting to know this rather innocent eighteen-year-old. I tell Lorie about the endless letters I wrote begging Inge to write to me and how she sent the most cursory of replies. Writing wasn't her thing. Because I never queried anything she did, it was twenty years before I wondered why my mother sent me away so fast and in a way that inconvenienced everyone. Yet for years Inge would tell me how desperate and lonely she was after I left, and how she 'had walked the streets'. That connotation was a little unfortunate.

I questioned nothing. Lorie questioned everything.

I have spent years thinking about how people behave and inventing characters, imagining myself to be some sort of expert. But I haven't realised some basic things about myself. After years of simmering tension, Lorie was always angry with Inge and now that our mother has died, her anger has vanished. She feels blank, unable to cry.

'I cried more about her in Mülheim in the archive,' she says. Years earlier, Lorie had looked up the Rosenbaums – the documentation on our family is harrowing.

I am bewildered by this new slant on our mother and confused, but I believe Lorie absolutely because everything she says rings true. I miss Inge terribly and I am sad; that great throb of misery keeps me awake at night. But inside my grief I am starting to worry away at what went wrong, and why. I have no idea why Inge needed to divide and conquer. She was all action and reaction – not a strategist. I don't think she set out to hurt us, but she did, and the upshot was that we sisters didn't speak for ten years. For a further forty years, any communication was weird and constrained. Now we're in full flow.

We do everything together, starting with the probate. The elegant maître receives us in her large sunny office in the centre of town. Teetering on her desk is the mountain of papers she has collected from the flat appertaining to Inge and the rental flats she owned. As well as being a solicitor responsible for official contracts, conveyancing and so on, the notaire manages probate and represents the French state, collecting death duties and official taxes. With strict deadlines to meet on tax, this goes at whistle-stop speed, documents processed and registered online. She zaps through the logic of the first stage document, the Acte de Notoriété, intended to establish the heirs. Us. Up on the screen comes the 'holographic' will of just two paragraphs that our mother made in this office, leaving all that she possesses to her two daughters as 'universal legatees'. The maître starts filling in the form: name, place of birth, residence, nationality, making the usual assumptions from the German name and birthplace. We correct her.

'Your mother isn't Franco-German?'

'No, she was Anglo-French.'

Inge, made stateless by Germany, spurned the post-war offer of German nationality, though Tilly and Heinz took it.

'Did your mother have any other children?'

Her question sounds amusing but is serious. Under the Napoleonic code, all children must inherit. In the bad old days, égalité and fraternité notwithstanding, illegitimate children received half the share of legitimate ones. In the twenty-first century, this anomaly has been smoothed out and now all the children receive equal shares. How aptly this translates into the Act of Notoriety. With perfect assurance, I inform our notaire that there is nothing whatsoever like that in our family. Given how little we know about our shared past, my confidence is ludicrous.

The big concept is *le partage*: sharing of assets and also of tax liability. We all know what happens when children are ordered to share. Siblings find ways to attack and counter-attack over such sentimental objects as a cherished dinner service. Back at Inge's flat, we institute our own partage. In the days when Lorie and I shared a small bedroom in Sydenham, it was divided by an invisible line down the centre. The teenage wars are over; we will share equally henceforward. As well, then, that my sister doesn't care about the documents or those handwritten notes in the blue folders that I am already putting in my suitcase. I own my mother; I needed to possess everything about her past. The counter truth that she owns me has yet to dawn. Our sharing of objects is helped by the fact that we have different tastes – Lorie is into vases and, apart from the papers, I want small sentimental things – plus the odd Hermès scarf.

Where is Inge now? Surely, at any moment she might roll her wheelchair in from the kitchen curious to discover what we are up to. 'Why are you laughing like that?' She isn't having her afternoon nap. She isn't on that muddy stretch of lawn where her ashes lie. She is everywhere and nowhere. For a long time after her death, I cannot bear for anything in this flat to change. I need her medicines to wait forever in the kitchen; her glasses and newspapers and paper knife never to leave their little tray beside her chair. Nothing is to be thrown away. I am going to have to keep the flat just as it is forever. To say that I cannot let go is an understatement. Inge holds me fast and I've only just begun unravelling the mysteries of her life. I will spend the next two years researching obsessively, revising facts that had seemed incontrovertible, assembling witnesses I didn't know existed. I start to question everything and everyone, not least myself.

Willy in the French Foreign Legion, circa 1928

CHAPTER 8

· · · · ·

A moi la Légion!

That night after we go back to the B&B, I arrange the blue folders chronologically and delve in. In the *Meknes* folder, Inge describes her journey as a numb and bewildered twelve-year-old in the spring of 1939 from Germany to safety in Meknes, Morocco. Her account differs from the trip I'd fictionalised. Wanting to start my novel, *The Children's War*, with that desperate flight from Germany, I researched everything: the detail of boats and trains, the station in Marseilles, the weather, the layout of the ports. The sadness of my fictional twelve-year-old turns to joy when the boat docks in Oran and marvellous Uncle Willy enters her life. In the novel I cunningly changed Inge to Ilse, since two different consonants obviously made her totally unrecognisable. I changed Rosenbaum (rose tree) to Blumenthal (valley of flowers) in another super-clever ruse. And I gave my heroine a wonderful welcome from her adoring uncle, who, like his sister Tilly, did indeed have film-star looks. I also threw in a big American convertible for the long but romantic drive to

Meknes, minarets rising from the pink dawn sky like a fairy tale in a child's Arabian Nights.

All of this was based on the romantic vision of Morocco that Inge always transmitted. The truth was more prosaic. The real Inge suffered from terrible seasickness all the way from Marseilles to Oran, though the sea was calm; the doctor on the boat kept making her drink water *so I drank and was sick, drank and was sick. Can't remember how long, it seemed forever.* That was in my book, but not the aftermath. Even on land she felt dreadful and the ground swayed under her feet. *Sick again – Eau de Cologne – sick again.* Willy, his wife Toni and Inge stayed an extra night in a hotel until she felt better, and the subsequent journey had nothing of Hollywood. *Here was North Africa – minarets – veiled women – beggars – and I worried about the hole-in-the-ground loo.* The three of them arrived in the Lindemanns' house, no. 25 Rue de la Voute, in Meknes on 25 March, the day before Inge's thirteenth birthday.

With some trepidation, she announced this important fact. When Toni said a birthday was a day like any other, Inge instantly understood that she hadn't wanted her to come. She was beginning to cotton on to things. But Willy winked! Nobody had ever winked at Inge before. When she read my novel, my mother was thrilled that her beloved uncle lived on in it. All her life, she adored this charming man who was so kind at that time.

The first note in the file is jubilant: *I had never had so much attention in my whole life.* Not all the attention would be welcome. Toni was tiny, slim, with a gamine crop and elegant in her high heels; Inge told me that she had been a philosophy professor in Warsaw and was Jewish. In 1937, desperate to get out of Europe, she distributed her photograph widely, seeking a white knight.

Romantic Willy fell in love and sent for her to make her his wife. Inge and Willy got on brilliantly and always would; perhaps Toni resented that. She was never going to play the kind aunt. She enjoyed criticising Tilly for not providing for the child; buying new clothes for Inge enabled her to play lady bountiful with her friends at the club.

Inge said that her trunk was coming, and eventually it arrived, packed with new clothes and shoes. The visit was supposed to last for three months, but here was enough clothing for far longer. That must have given Toni pause. She went through the trunk examining the dresses and swimsuits, commenting how extravagant Tilly was. (One can only imagine how hard Tilly had worked to clothe her child with some style.) This was the first criticism Inge had ever heard of her mother and for once she said nothing. Something seems to have clicked; she was no longer a little child who answered back without thinking. As she entered her teens, she was beginning to mature, physically and emotionally.

Having Willy's niece around cramped Toni's style. She wanted to go out to clubs and dance, not stay home baby-sitting. When Toni asked to read all the letters Inge sent to her mother, Inge replied that she preferred not to show them, because of possible spelling mistakes. Undeterred, Toni steamed them open. Inge's next note reads: *after one month told to write to Tante Gerta*. This can only mean that young Inge was told to write to her aunt in New York and ask her if she could find a way to sponsor and take her: this had of course already been tried to no avail. Toni was running out of patience. Evil stepmothers are a bit of a trope in our family; aged seven, I too was presented with one of my own.

Toni was always cast as the calculating villain in the tales Inge told – Willy remained the perfect uncle. He had been living in Morocco for fifteen years and was well connected. He had a lifelong attachment to the French Foreign Legion, a branch of the French army open to foreigners that swears allegiance not to France, but to the Legion itself. Born in 1897, he was twenty-three or twenty-four when he left Germany to join the Legion after the tragic death of his young wife and their baby in childbirth. He had fought in the Guerre du Rif and served in Sidi Bel Abbès, the Legion's base in Algeria.

Any man of any nationality who spills blood for the Legion is automatically entitled to French citizenship. When Willy left the Legion, he chose to become French and remain in North Africa. A talented artist, he set up a professional sign-painting business and soon branched out into property. He showed Inge round his building site. He employed artists using paint guns to create cinema signs, which impressed her. He knew everyone in the French community in Meknes, Fez and Casablanca. He was a bon viveur. Romantic and impetuous, he was clearly a soft touch where women were concerned. But he was no businessman, and his means did not always fit his ends. He had paid Inge's fare from Strasbourg and the Red Cross had agreed to take charge of her. A month after Inge arrived, an enormous bill was sent for the cost of accompanying her on this journey; this, she noted, caused consternation.

Inge was sent to a girls' school in Meknes and, despite the humiliation of being put in a class much younger than her, soon learned French. At the end of her first term, she won a prize for reciting a poem by heart ('Les Profondeurs de la Mer' – 'The Depths of the Sea') without understanding what it meant; no matter. At break time, the children ate delicious French bread stuffed with chocolate; she adored this. Morocco was heaven, with its ice cream parlours and good food, its clubs and cinemas

Artist of the nursery world: Willy was in fact an accomplished painter

and swimming pools. Willy's gentle Alsatian dog cured her of her terror of this Gestapo hound. She was taken to restaurants – impossible for Jews in Germany. She ate well and filled out and *after three months I blossomed with well-endowed boobs.* She was allowed to curl her hair. Like the adults, she enjoyed a siesta. She was given books. Willy and Toni took her to a wedding, and she enjoyed the dancing. She was a little woman now.

After six months, news came that her parents had gone over the border into Belgium and were in Brussels. She was to be expelled from Paradise. Inge always told us that she was sent back to Europe because when war came her uncle decided to rejoin the French Foreign Legion and fight for freedom. How happily she would have made her life in Morocco. She also said with some bitterness that though Toni was herself Jewish and should have been sympathetic, she flatly refused to look after her husband's niece.

Inge never said what in hindsight is obvious: she didn't want to live with her mother in mourning and her difficult father. She'd been given a vision of a different life, one of peace, freedom and luxury, with her uncle to protect her. Behind him stood that polyglot army of freedom fighters. Willy told Inge that a man in trouble could stand on any street corner in France and shout – 'A moi la Légion! To me the Legion!' And they would come to his rescue. This was a fantasy, as were many of his tales. Poor Inge's hope was fantasy too, given that her passport was German and her visa of short duration.

On that return journey in September 1939, thirteen-year-old Inge travelled alone. She didn't need an escort because she was now fluent in French. She was warned not to tell anyone where she was going as she didn't have a visa for Belgium and her French Moroccan one had expired. *If anybody asked, I was to say that I was returning to Germany.* She writes that she has no recall of this mournful return to Europe on the brink of war – it was too sad. She was now in France for the first time. In Paris, a journalist – I don't know who – was sent to meet her and put her on a train to Jeumont on the French/Belgian border. *By a lucky chance, my parents had taken a furnished room in a house in Brussels whose landlord had relatives living there.* They cooked up a plan to smuggle her into the country with the help of these relatives. Every day, Inge went back and forth over the border with the milk cart until the border guard got used to waving to her. One day she simply stayed on the Belgian side. She took the train to Brussels, where both parents met her. They didn't recognise this blossoming teenager: 'Is that really our Inge?' She had changed in more ways than any of them understood.

The three of them shared a room with another dreaded communal loo in a house in the Rue Traversière. The day after her arrival, the police searched it looking for 'fifth columnists' (pro-German spies); rumours of a Nazi invasion were rife. Terrified, Inge hid in a wardrobe, the base of which collapsed; the police found her but were apparently *charming*. Arthur and Tilly spoke Mülheim Platt, a strong Rhineland dialect, and made no effort to learn French. She was to interpret for them. The shops were filled with delicious food, but they had no money. Her father drove a car illegally for the landlord to earn something; he told Tilly that he regretted the years wasted on communism. *Too late*, writes Inge bleakly. She had grown so much and her figure had changed; she needed new clothes, but they could not afford them. Her coat now functioned as a shrunken jacket. She had no shoes and couldn't go to school until they managed, somehow, to find a pair two sizes bigger.

Tilly walked for kilometres to save bus fares. She worked intermittently as a maid making cakes and serving coffee at bridge parties for families they had become acquainted with: the Lucases, the Leffmans and the Katzensteins. Inge later told Lorie that Tilly, the experienced confectioner, had also made cakes for the wives of German officers. Such work was much sought after because a cook or waitress got to eat. But mostly work wasn't found. Inge said that they were always hungry.

When on 10 May 1940 war erupted, Inge thought it the most *marvellous fireworks show* until shrapnel hit the window and broken glass landed on her. In April 1940, Germany invaded Denmark and Norway. On 8 May the Belgian ambassador in Berlin signalled that the Reich was preparing an ultimatum and that attack was imminent. That same evening, German troops massed on the Belgian and Dutch borders. At 5 a.m. on Friday 10 May, the first bombings began, and the German army crossed the border. Holland and Luxembourg were invaded simultaneously. As German parachutists started dropping from the skies, Belgian civilians panicked and fled. Within hours, German troops were deep into Belgian territory.

The Belgian government rapidly rounded up all alien Jewish males, Arthur Rosenbaum among them, and organised trains and personnel to expel convoys of such refugees to France. The Belgian army surrendered on 28 May and the government fled into exile in France and Britain. Four thousand four hundred Jewish refugees, including Arthur Rosenbaum, were sent across the whole of France by train, landing at Saint-Cyprien. This was a makeshift camp set up on a beach in southern France, not far from the border with Spain. *Father St Cyprien, unoccupied Vichy government territory*, read Inge's notes. *Most men came back – father*

Tilly in wartime Brussels

wouldn't. Asked us to join – mother refused and sent all his clothes. I asked why – too late now, I am not giving up relative comfort to start again. Germans were trying to make her go back to Germany. There is a universe of suffering behind these gnomic words, which I tried to unpick in my novel.

Tilly had done everything she could to support her husband. She'd led where others followed. And now she was profoundly sad, mourning her adored Hanne Lore, cast into a world of strangers, a language she couldn't speak and bleak poverty. This hard-working, deeply decent and reasonable woman had reached the end of her tether. Did she have some kind of breakdown? It seems likely. At any rate, she could do no more and would run no further. And, as it turned out, this was a wise decision.

Standing in the Rue Royale near the Botanical Gardens, Inge and her mother watched the Germans march in. Because their landlord was among those who had fled, they were able to remain for a year in their attic room, paying no rent. The attic in the Rue Tiberghien had a bed, a skylight and a stove they could not light; it was bitterly cold and Inge had chilblains. She was hungry all the time. She had no winter coat and at fifteen stopped going to school because she had to earn money. Tilly and Arthur had left Germany with nothing. Mother and daughter had nobody to support them. Without the meagre support supplied by a Jewish welfare organisation in Brussels, they would have starved. Declared stateless, they had no right to ration cards, no coupons for clothes. Inge spoke French: that was their main resource.

She went to work in a sweet factory owned by a man she called 'Uncle George', whom she befriended. Standing for hours wrapping and packing sweets, Inge observed the women working in the office and saw how much easier their lives were.

She resolved to go to night classes to learn proper French and typing and (probably) shorthand. Food money was sacrificed to this end and once again they went hungry. Inge was determined to improve herself and by the end of the war was working in the office and answering the telephone. 'Uncle George' was a philatelist and she used to help him with his collection of stamps; this became her lifelong hobby. But her wages were very low. Inge and Tilly scraped together money for a sewing machine and spent hours putting hooks in ribbons for corsets, earning a pittance. *The hook and eye business was slave labour.* It took up all their time and *anyone who came for a chat was immediately put to slipping either hooks or eyes in never ending strips of material.*

I wonder, who came in for chats? Inge – always gregarious – had made a friend, called Nina. *There were bombers overhead. I knew the sound of the Flying Fortress from the brum brum. The cellar was made secure.* Aged fourteen, she had her first cigarette in that cellar with Nina, whose uncle and aunt owned a bistro. She would carry on smoking for seventy-six years. There was another friend called Menousch. Inge always made loyal friends; it's nice to think that the teenager had girl friends to gossip and smoke with. Possessing barely any French, Tilly was dependent on her daughter for every communication. What was their relationship like? It seems likely that it was here that Inge learned to blame her mother for the many troubles they were enduring.

Inge's notes about their war refer to some illegal banking transaction her mother got involved in, which improved their circumstances and enabled them to move to a second-floor flatlet. This episode is described by Inge in incomplete notes: *Then mother was approached by the Leffmans. The couple* [who had been their first contact] *'prêter son nom* [borrow her name]*' for the Banque*

Inge, left, aged around fourteen or fifteen, with either Nina
or Menousch, in the attic in the Rue Tiberghien

[bank] *(neither she nor I realised the complete foolishness of this) – really it was wicked of the Leffmans, think of all it implied. One per cent on all amounts of cheque. Flat furnished – cat fur coat – we had butter – black market – ration books.* All I can imagine is that this was some form of money laundering and that the Leffmans used Tilly's Aryan name, Lindemann, on the cheques they cashed. Perhaps Tilly was sent to the bank to get the money. She must have been desperate even to contemplate this. I hope the cat fur coat was warm. Poor cats.

In 1944, Brussels was liberated. On 3 September, the British Second Army swept into town to be greeted by a frenzied crowd. The German occupiers had left earlier that day – the change in mood must have been extraordinary. Hitler would subsequently attack the Ardennes, but nobody anticipated that then. It was five years to the day since war had been declared; the people of Brussels lined the boulevards, climbing on to tanks to embrace the conquering heroes, singing, weeping and generally slowing them down. Their joy is said to have far exceeded that shown at the liberation of Paris.

On the night of the liberation, Inge met our father, Tom Charlesworth, in a local bistro. I reckon it must have been the one Nina's uncle and aunt owned because eighteen-year-old Inge was not usually allowed to go out in the evening. I imagine her sitting in the corner, wide-eyed, while uniformed soldiers crowded the zinc bar. No doubt her mother – the eternal chaperone – was at her side. People were singing and dancing. Inge would have worn her best outfit; she must have polished her ancient shoes, which were falling apart. She and her mother must have been euphoric after years of misery and hunger. Everyone was tipsy; bottles hoarded for years were brought out. The air would have been pungent with tobacco, alcohol, testosterone, and the ripe possibilities of amour. This young thing with her blue eyes and clear skin must have had tons of sex appeal, yet – as she always told us – was utterly naive. She wore her soft brown hair combed up in the front and falling in waves to her shoulders. Inge loved a party. All her life she was ready to have a good time. She was undoubtedly flirting like mad, though she always claimed not to know how.

The Tommies were generous and attractive. In photos of our father with his army pals, they often personalise their looks – one wears an airman's hat and holds a dog under one arm. They look amusing and amused, light years away from the regimented, terrifying Germans. Because Inge spoke such good French, they couldn't know at first that she was German and a stateless refugee. Our father's repertoire may not have extended beyond Bonjour Mademoiselle and filthy parlez-voo songs, but he was an older man and I assume he was charming. Somehow, these misfits connected. He'd lost a beloved wife and was looking to remake his life. Any fool can see what he wanted from her – but it's not clear what she saw in him. A girl of eighteen wouldn't usually fancy a man of thirty-three – a widower to boot.

Inge and I never discussed that angle. Our childhood was dominated by the myth that our father was a truly wonderful and infinitely superior human being, daily mourned and missed despite the fact that he had left us so cruelly. The other dominant myth was Inge's total innocence – that she was a mere child. Yet she had already shown remarkable strength and enterprise.

Years back, I asked Inge about Tom's war. She wrote this artless account in a letter she sent in 2005: *Daddy was with the eighth Army – and I am sure he landed somewhere in Italy and according to him he had a lovely time drinking his way through Italy. He was one*

The 18-year-old girl Tom Charlesworth fell for. Inge's ID of 1944 was
obtained after the liberation of Brussels. It was updated to change her status
from 'Non enemy' German (the latter word heavily crossed out) to British.
The reality was that she had been stateless for years

Conquering heroes in Brussels: Tom is on the left

of the few men who never fired a single shot at the enemy. He lived in his 'camion' [lorry] *with his Morse equipment.* Reading Inge's notes, I get more of the story. The misfits connected in the simplest way. Knowing that they were heading back to the front, lots of soldiers asked girls if they would write. *I said yes to all of them but Charlie wrote and I wrote back.* She called him 'Charlie'; everyone did. His friend was called Gerry, which might explain why he didn't want to be Tom. He was a signals despatch rider; our father always did love cars. Transport to Brussels wasn't a problem. He came, *had tea, slept, showed me his signals van* – let nobody say that romance was dead. This does not mean that they slept together; there was no question of sex. Alongside naivety, Inge always stressed her virginity. She notes that he *asked her, if possible, not to wear ankle socks, because that made him look like a baby snatcher.*

Tom had a long face, dark hair and hazel eyes; he wore round spectacles and looked and was intelligent in a very English way. He was tall, slim, nicely made and resembled Aldous Huxley (which was generally felt to be a good thing). A clever bookish man, he should have gone to university but hadn't; it was beyond his reach financially but not intellectually. But this is probably a reflection of my ambition, not his. He was very witty, with a quick reply to everything, an easy-going convivial type. And he must have been subject to strong impulses.

Tom's war had been deliberately inglorious: a trained radio operator, he aimed never to be on the front line. Called up in 1940, he concealed his good education; coming from Birkenhead, he wasn't posh or privileged. He'd been a scholarship boy at an excellent grammar school but didn't want to be commissioned. When promotion upped him to non-commissioned officer, he went AWOL with purloined cartons of fags and a 'borrowed' lorry. Demotion came suitably swiftly. Or so he told Inge; I never heard him speak of the war.

The courtship progressed. More letters came and Tom took more leave, with or without permission. One day *he came without his stripes*, reports Inge. He was *stopped on the boulevard near the Jardin Botanique by the MP* [Military Police] *and told to button up his tunic*. When he was sent away to Germany, he wrote asking Inge to marry him. She wanted to say yes, but Tilly refused her permission; terrible tales were filtering back about girls who had gone off to America and been badly treated. Eventually, Tom returned and asked again. This time Inge defied her mother and said yes. *I said he is OK mother.* As good as that! She always told her credulous small girls that she had loved him madly, but I found no evidence of passion in these notes. Even here, though decades had passed, Inge was evasive about the truth. It would be a good half year after her death before I had the first inklings of what was really going on.

How quickly in this incongruous pair the hope arose of remaking their lives. Inge may have described herself as having been very naive, but that's not incompatible with ambition and grit. She was desperate to get away from the mother she'd been forced to support during their years of exile. Together, they had gone through great hardships; both women needed a new start and had few options. A return to vanquished, starving Germany was out of the question. Tom would make her English, and safe. It may be that the moral lightness I always associate with him was part of his attractiveness. Tom didn't appear romantic to me – whose father does? – but he seems to have been a fool for love three times in his life that I know of. He'd already married one young woman (Joan Bell), knowing she was dying from leukaemia.

During his absence, Tilly and Inge were getting into deep trouble. Throughout these years, they'd had intermittent contact with Germany. Tante Röschen, Arthur's sister (who fled into the countryside and survived), had given their address to German soldiers stationed in Brussels. These young men were the sons of friends. She'd asked them to check up on her sister-in-law and niece to see if they were OK. From time to time the soldiers had done this, bringing their much-welcomed rations with them.

After the war, Tilly and Inge were denounced as collaborators by their Belgian neighbours and sentenced to six months in prison – something our mother never mentioned. It's not in her notes either. She'd suppressed the shame and awfulness for seven decades and never told me about it. The subject surfaced just once in Tours, when Lorie was staying. During a discussion about awful people at work, Inge, then aged ninety, remarked that she had fought hard for a job in the prison office, typing and doing paperwork, because all the other women were forced to clean. In so doing, she had made an enemy of the (non-typing) woman she'd ousted from that position. Here is a glimpse of the real nineteen-year-old: intelligent, tough, enterprising, absolutely determined to make something of herself in the most awful circumstances.

What a hammer blow prison must have been, after all they had already gone through. Tilly and Inge had been rejected and expelled by the Germans for being Jewish and political, though they were neither. Arthur had vanished from their lives and they had nobody to protect or help them. And now, at a time of liberation and hope, they were again on the wrong side of history, demonised by the Belgians for being German. How ironic, how futile. Were they always to find themselves on the losing side?

Tilly in 1946

What kind of despair and hopelessness did that evoke? Did their appalling situation further cement their determination to make a new life?

Within two years, both Tilly and Inge had left for a new country, each taking a new nationality and adopting a new language. Each woman found a husband to look after her. Was the driving force desperation, survival instinct, or the seizing of opportunity? Perhaps something of all three; both had real fighting spirit. It's awfully hard to untangle motivation in these circumstances. I suspect that my grandmother and mother had something in common neither would ever articulate or admit. They badly wanted to get away from each other and make a fresh start. It was not by chance that they ended up 2,000 kilometres apart.

Lord of all he surveys: 35-year-old Tom in Egerton Park

CHAPTER 9

. . . . .

The wrong man

Tom must have known all about the prison episode. At the end of 1945 he was sent back to Britain to get demobilised, pursuing his courtship from afar. Inge's gnomic notes read: *had to be demobbed – time to think – if you want to then o.k. – courtship as a civilian.* For a man desperate to get married, he seems to have been very conscious of her youth and inexperience. In February 1946, he was back in Brussels. There's no knowing now what form 'courtship as a civilian' took, but the keenness was undimmed. *When do you want to get married? Answer – tomorrow.* Two days later, he had obtained a special licence. The age of consent was twenty-one in those days.

Inge and Tom married on 21 February 1946, one week before his thirty-fifth birthday. He was twelve years younger than her mother. She was nineteen. Inge records the unaccustomed magnificence in four words: *flowers – suite – wedge heel.* She never told us about their wedding and, oddly, there's not one photo of the happy couple. Standing tall on the wedge heels she would always love, she could now obtain a British passport. In her account of her life, Inge says that she was one of the first war brides to enter Britain in 1946 and describes arriving in Croydon by air.

The first member of the Charlesworth family Inge met was Tom's welcoming Aunt Maggy, sister of his mother, Hetty Charlesworth. Offered 'high tea', Inge said no thank you – she had no idea what that was – and waited in vain for dinner. In the pub she drank orangeade. The happy couple travelled up to Birkenhead, arriving in Rock Ferry. Birkenhead and the grim North must have been a shock – the rationing, the shortages, the bomb damage, the dreariness and shabbiness after Brussels, which was now awash with butter and cream.

They were to live in Hetty's rented house in Egerton Park, a pleasant part of town. Inge was greeted by Tom's mother *as if she were Queen Mary. 'Welcome to England, my dear,'* she said in the stateliest manner, and swept her off to see the bedroom. *'This side of the bed is more worn, because Joan* [Tom's first wife] *slept here,'* she announced. Inge makes the sad little note: *wrongly assumed the sisters would be similar.* Inge's trunk had not yet arrived, which caused further snootiness; who was she, Hetty implied, turning up with nothing? Shades of Toni's reproaches in Morocco. When the trunk came with the Dior New Look dresses Inge had made herself in the latest fashion – exuberant skirts featuring metres of fabric – she couldn't wear them. Clothes were still rationed and British women wore pinched wartime garb. She put them back in her trunk.

They honeymooned in Ross-on-Wye. It rained; they looked at the picturesque ruins. This was the only holiday they ever shared. Inge splurged five pounds and nineteen shillings of the six pounds and ten shillings she had laboriously saved up on a marvellous

Demob happy Tom and Inge captured on the boulevards

pair of shoes – for Tom. He had bad feet and always indulged himself in shoes. They were a glorious chestnut conker brown. 'What a fool I was in those days,' Inge said, describing those brogues in detail when, sixty years later, I told her I was going to the nearby Hay Festival.

Soon, the pattern of their relationship was set; he did as he pleased and got whatever he wanted, and she was his eager slave. I never doubted this version while she was alive. But when I think about Inge's uneducated force of character and urge to have babies and Tom's laissez-faire intelligence, I wonder. Maybe they drove each other crazy, as only the profoundly mismatched can.

Everything I know is surmise and hearsay: old stories retold and surely warped along the way by a woman who never forgot or forgave the indignities of those years. She entirely moulded my view of my father, setting certain elements in stone: her innocence, his duplicity, the abandonment. I would later come to question all of these. But I witnessed some things for myself, such as that first memory of a terrible row between them going on downstairs. I know that he only drank milk because of his stomach ulcers, and that he had bad feet. He loved golf, employing his huge intelligence to make others laugh at the nineteenth hole. He played two or three times a week at Upton-by-Chester Golf Club, even when skint. His handicap was 7, which irked him. His solution to the recurring problems of swing or putt was to buy himself new clubs with the latest technical gizmos. From time to time we would caddy for Daddy, enthusiasm waning as the game progressed.

Tom's abandonment of Inge was very tragic. Many decades later, she told me that she was pregnant when Tom announced that he was leaving her for another woman. She said that when he told her he didn't love her, she experienced an electric shock inside, and the baby died. He apparently suggested that he and his new love, childless Flo, would 'take the baby'. What a horrendous idea! No wonder I did so much father-monstering in the novels I wrote later. He was cast as the villain and in our family the parts were inalterable.

Though I held my father to be a wicked absconder, this was never apparent in my behaviour. Whenever I saw him, I fawned on him, hoping to be liked or praised or noticed. And Tom Charlesworth was very amusing: even Inge said so. He had that sharp observant wit that makes people laugh uproariously at themselves. She says that she wanted to go to night school, but he told her not to bother, the implication being that she wasn't up to it. Did he tease Inge in a way that was supposed to amuse, but didn't?

Inge and Tom had much in common: tragic fathers, no siblings, overbearing mothers, and tremendous damage in their past – but I very much doubt that they ever found common ground discussing these topics. She'd chosen an older man, one who I can't imagine being questioned by anyone, let alone a naive teenager struggling with a new country, a new language and a new life. Bright as he was, Tom had no guiding principles, or none I could see. He never applied himself to a job properly. He wasn't interested in children. Years later, when Lorie had her first child, he was all over her boy like a rash. Perhaps we were just the wrong sex.

Born in 1911, Tom had had no fathering of his own to guide him. His father died in a war when he was very young. 'The Boer War', somebody said when I was a child. Perhaps this was a joke. If I had bothered to look it up, I would have discovered that the Boer War lasted from 1899 to 1902. Though later I realised it had to be the First World War, I remained totally incurious. Tom had abandoned us, so nothing about him or his background could matter.

When in 1999 I went on a school outing to the First World War battlefields in Ypres, Belgium with my eleven-year-old son, Jonny, my English grandfather presented himself. To get away from the boys' noise and commotion, I wandered over to the Menin Gate and straight up to the name Private John Charlesworth, Lancashire Fusiliers, engraved in the stone at eye level. That was odd. I photographed the inscription, though I knew he had to be somebody else's war victim. The Charlesworths came from Yorkshire, not Lancashire.

Later that day, our coach went on to the Tyne Cot Memorial at West-Vlaanderen. As we walked along the rows of graves towards the main building, I glanced down. There stood the gravestone of John Charlesworth. This was becoming eerie. I opened the memorial book listing the names of all the fallen, flicking to C. At once his name, rank and Falkland Street address in Birkenhead surfaced. It felt as if he had been waiting years for his family to find him.

My grandfather John Charlesworth went to war in 1914, when his little son was three. Tom can't have had a single memory of his lost father. His battalion landed in France on 30 January 1916 and was disbanded in Belgium on 16 February 1918. Two years in those hellish trenches was a very long time; he so nearly made it to the end. He died aged thirty on 8 January 1918 and was awarded the British War Medal and Victory Medal posthumously. I don't think Tom's mother, Hetty, went to Belgium to see her husband's grave or indeed ever ventured abroad. I found him by chance. Our German grandfather, Arthur, fighting in the trenches on the other side, lost a finger and came home radicalised. I've considered writing a film or novel that would pit one grandfather against the other but have found no way to use this extraordinary but arbitrary piece of history to drive a plot.

I've been sloppy and neglectful. I should have cared more about what happened to my paternal grandfather. I've never visited the Lewisham crematorium where the ashes of Tilly and Heinz were scattered; I've never looked for my father's grave and don't even know if a stone for him exists in the graveyard where he was buried, in Neston on the Wirral Peninsula. As for poor Arthur Rosenbaum, who died in Auschwitz on an assumed date – so much of that final journey unknown – what memorial exists for him?

Approaching seventy and the problematic fact of our own mortality, family history becomes more important. We start to care about these lost souls as we shuffle nearer to their ranks, and we want them to be remembered. If their names are not known and their fates unrecorded, then their lives have no meaning at all. And who will remember us? Perhaps my striving to resurrect these unknowns and tell their stories is a way of procuring some future quid pro quo.

Tom's widowed mother, Harriet Charlesworth née Burley, always known as Hetty, became a state certified midwife. She had no money but made sure that when her only son won a scholarship place at the Birkenhead Institute, the town's premier school, he owned such necessities of life as a cricket bat and football. The school motto was '*Doctus in se semper divitias habet*': The wise man always has riches within. But there were not enough riches for sports-mad Tom to go to university when he left at eighteen. The myth was that he 'decided to play tennis instead'. Lorie sent me a tiny wooden shield with a plaque inscribed Jack Hart

Challenge Cup Runner Up 1931 T B Charlesworth. You can see the shadow where the crossed tennis racquets have fallen off. He wasn't what you'd call a winner. You can also see Tom's shadow in the 1939 list of Old Boys' occupations from Accountancy and Architecture to University appointments (no zookeepers, sadly), where T.B. Charlesworth appears under the catch-all 'commerce'.

On my birth certificate in 1951, the father's profession is 'insurance agent', like John Lennon's dad. Before the war, Tom had managed a branch of Woolworths in Dublin; I learned that from the only letter he ever wrote me when I asked him to tell me about Ireland. Back came a ten-page diatribe about the 1916 Easter Uprising, the Black and Tan constabulary bolstered with British recruits, and so on. Anti-authority and anti-army, Tom wrote extremely well and full of passion; there was not one personal word to me from beginning to end.

I've spent my life hacking through dark German forests; Lorie was always interested in the British side of the family. Her deep instinctive understanding of poverty, of class, of how society works, later fed into her work as an academic lawyer and social historian. A few years back, she had Tom's family traced. That ancestry chain goes back to 1748: steam engine makers and fitters, master plumbers, wheelwrights and carpenters. John Charlesworth came from a long line of respectable Yorkshire folk. Before the war, he was a woodwork machinist. Twenty years after her husband's death, Hetty was still living in Falkland Street with a lodger called Florence Johnson, an unmarried woman who worked as an assistant in a pork butcher's. Life can't have been great, plentiful pork chops notwithstanding, but Hetty found ways to amuse herself. According to Inge, she seduced Tom's best friend – unforgivably and unforgettably – when he was only a schoolboy. This traumatised Tom and he only spoke of it to Inge on one occasion. Straight out of *EastEnders*, said my daughter, Sophie (who has directed numerous episodes), when she read this chapter. Tom didn't abandon his mother, though he might have wanted to. Wherever he went, the supremely disobliging Hetty went too.

The newly-weds' life in Egerton Park was dominated by Hetty, who regularly depressed Inge with tales of the marvellousness of Tom's first wife, Joan, that paragon who died a year after they married. That, she liked to say, had been a real love match. A vocal mini despot, Hetty was firmly set against all foreign muck and would not have excepted impressionable Inge, trying so desperately to please.

What did Tom and Inge do? He taught her golf and soon she played well. He came home for lunch every day and she cooked for him, and then babies came along. Tom had his mother, a compliant young wife, his old friends, his books, Sammy the cocker spaniel and his golf. Love was probably apportioned in reverse order. He was photographed in the garden of the Egerton Park house in a warm embrace with silky Sammy, his favourite child. Another photo shows him and his ubiquitous cigarette in daring proximity to Lorie, safely caged in her playpen. Inge was determined to have a big family and the sooner the better. Many Holocaust survivors felt the same way; having lots of children was their victory over the past. But that didn't happen.

I didn't know that a picture of me with my father existed until I looked through Inge's envelope of black-and white-photographs. There we stand in a tiny deckle-edged amateurish print, father and daughter a yard apart, both nervous and bespectacled. I'm around six.

The only photo of Tom and Monique

By then, Tom was working at Williams and Williams Roften works in Hooton, a site that had been a wartime Royal Ordnance Factory. Lorie thinks it made galvanised steel window frames. Tom did time and motion studies, calculating the exact time it took to make a component and whether this could be speeded up. This can't have made him popular with the workers. Maybe that's why he hung round the office, chatting up the boss's secretary, chic, waspish Florence M. Clarke, known as Florrie or Flo. Lorie has the idea that she protected him when he fought the boss.

Worldly and experienced, she may have been into adventurous sex in a way his new wife wasn't. I have an impeccable source for this speculation. When Inge was eighty-five, she and I were in a taxi driving through Regent's Park – what on earth had she glimpsed? – when she suddenly said, 'Daddy wanted to have sex in public places. He asked me to do it. I couldn't, I was very prudish and couldn't imagine anything like that.' When I pressed her for more, she clammed up. Maybe Flo was up for high jinks. Maybe Tom couldn't stand the babies, our screaming, the nappies, the awful prospect of yet more children. When he left, his mother went with him; that was the only good thing that came from the break-up.

Somebody photographed Lorie and me at the children's party organised by the Roften works that Christmas. Scores of children are seated at long tables enjoying the jellies and cakes. We are dressed in matching pleated skirts and embroidered blouses – every stitch made by our mother – with round paper name tags pinned to our cardigans so we won't get lost. We look absolutely terrified; aliens dropped into a world they cannot begin to fathom.

Tom asked Inge to divorce him and eventually she agreed. I found the ragged piece of paper from the Birkenhead court in

Inge's flat. In this decree nisi of 28 October 1958 'is decreed that the marriage between the Petitioner (Inge) and the Respondent (Thomas Burley Charlesworth) be dissolved by reason that since the celebration thereof the Respondent had been guilty of adultery'. She told me that in court she was crying so hard that the judge (his name was Harold Brown) asked her if she was sure she wanted a divorce. 'Yes,' she said, sobbing, 'I must because he doesn't love me.' He lost us and also the friendship (which he may have regretted more) of his oldest pal, Bunny Benyon. He and Bunny had been schoolboys and soldiers together, but Bunny broke with him, because he'd been 'such a sod' to our mother. Bunny and his wife, Visty, were good and true friends to our mother, who badly needed some, and their elder son, John, always remembered and rather adored Inge. The year of the divorce, Inge took us to Brussels for the World Expo; she would take us to Germany too. Few people in Birkenhead went abroad in the 1950s. I suspect that our mother was wondering about alternative lives, and what on earth she was going to do with hers.

Flo divorced Mr Clarke and the miscreants married the following year. Tom was forty-eight and Flo close to his age. She was skinny and elegant, with fabulous legs, amazing tweed suits, beautiful silk blouses and proper jewellery. I still have her carved jade pin in a small brown leather box part stamped in gold, from Millican Pickerill, jewellers and silversmiths of 18 Castle Street, Liverpool. She spoke in a common voice and specialised in rage. They bought us new dresses for the wedding. Shop-bought clothes were an unheard-of luxury. Lorie's was green and went with her green-hazel eyes. Mine was grey with a large white collar that detached for washing, an exciting novelty. I was thrilled. I seem to recall some sniping about us from my future stepmother in the changing rooms of the chi-chi little shop in the arcades of Chester, to me the Dior of the North West. Of the actual wedding I remember nothing.

From the minute he married Flo, our father was rich. This was bizarre, as if he had somehow always been rich behind our backs. Lorie says he inherited money from an aunt who was fond of him – one of those wraiths we never met, probably in London. He knew people to stay with when he went down south to Vidal Sassoon to train as a hairdresser, a choice of profession as unexpected as their lifestyle. Tom and Flo's fancy big house was full of antiques. It had fitted carpets and central heating and oil paintings on the wall, escritoires and the like, also rather beautiful little miniatures with Tudor figures in ruffs. Not that we were allowed to touch things.

That same year, Inge and her mother were paid their joint restitution money from the German government. Inge said it was 'enough to buy a washing machine', a story to keep Tom at bay. Tom kept equally quiet about inheriting from his aunt: two of a kind. Inge had promised him a car, and he asked if he could still have it, divorce notwithstanding. That seems strange – why on earth would an abandoned wife have given him a car? It wasn't Inge who bought the new Citroën DS on the driveway of Tom and Flo's new house – an unusual choice. The significance of that piece of one-upmanship did not dawn on me until I wrote this book and looked anew at my parents' relationship.

Money was problematic for Tom; he threw it about lavishly but also could be mean. When Lorie was sixteen and I was fourteen, he stopped the small sums he had hitherto sent our mother. His reasoning (as conveyed to Lorie) was simple: 'Now you can leave school and work in the factory and pay your way. That'll be a satisfaction. Then you can have a place of your own.' I wonder what factories in South London he imagined would take two unskilled teenagers doing O levels in a fee-paying private school. Inge was furious, but the only way to challenge child support was through the courts and she didn't have the stomach for it. Tom couldn't be made responsible for his daughters. Later, Flo would tell all and sundry that he had paid for our education, a lie that irritates me to this day.

According to Inge, her awful mother-in-law begged to be allowed to live with her and apologised profusely for her bad behaviour. Hetty must have had a pretty good idea of what wife number three was like. Inge refused; it was, she said, one of the few times in those years when she exhibited some sense. So Hetty landed in the newly-weds' big house at Hooton Crossroads. She got short shrift from Flo; she was never allowed downstairs to pollute the sitting room. The granny I remember was a small ancient person who could have been a hundred for all I knew, topped with swirls of flattened white hair, smelling of talc and sadness. Wobbly jowled, not unkind, she was definitely strange and regularly referred to a mysterious suitcase full of letters on top of the wardrobe that were to be burned the day she died. These must have been from the teenage lover. Hetty died in 1964, aged seventy-seven. We didn't go to the funeral. Children didn't in those days. I imagine that these letters, which must have represented the great passion of her life, were put in the bin with the rest of her belongings.

The six months we spent living with Tom and Flo while Inge tried to sort out a home and school in London were memorable. Lorie and I tried to befriend childless scary Flo. Because my nickname was Monty (powerful King of all the mice), I decided to give her the nickname Minty, a riff on mine. What fun. She really didn't get it, which was painful. Everything was forced and awkward. Maybe she didn't want us to call her Flo – maybe we were supposed to call her Mum? Or Mrs Charlesworth? She didn't want us there. We were daily reminders of her unspoken guilt, and she often took her dislike and resentment a stage or two further. Once she burst into the bathroom while I was having a bath and threw all my washing in the water. 'You're a dirty girl! Wash your own filthy clothes!' At home, my mother did my washing. I was ten, naked and humiliated.

I was ignorant about sex and also feared it. In my first week of primary school, horrible boys had given me the most crude and nasty account of how babies were made. Bullies always sniff out the innocent. Profoundly shocked, I didn't speak for a week. Eventually, my mother worked out what had happened and reassured me that I would never have to do this awful thing. A prude, I never played with boys, never saw a naked man or boy, nor wanted to. Flo sensed that this was the way to upset me.

Flo – and an upscaled version of the bath event – live on in *The Second Mrs McIntyre*, a novel about a glamorous, evil stepmother that came to me in a dream. I had completely forgotten about her when up she rose one night in full force and fang. Flo's usual form of attack was a kind of coarseness – sending me out to the chemist 'to buy S.T.s' and asking me if I knew what they were. Of course not. Everything about her and between her and Tom was somehow mixed up with sex and bodies in a way that scared me. Her nastiness mixed wild flurries – florries? – of rage with what I now see must have been guilt. Attack may have seemed the safest method of defence. I don't remember a single conversation with her: it was silence, sudden barked instructions or reprimands.

Lorie says that Flo was driven – that she came from nowhere and had a dreadful alcoholic father. My sister also informs me that we, unlike Flo, were not working class. The clincher, apparently, is that we ate butter and not margarine. Though we were poor, Inge always lived like a German bourgeoise. Flo thought that we were idle and above ourselves; she probably told Tom that he had to deal with us. Each grey wintry morning at Hooton Crossroads, our father came into our room, flung back the curtains and recited:

Awake! For morning in the bowl of night
Has flung the stone that puts the stars to flight
And Lo! The hunter of the East has caught
The sultan's turret in a noose of light . . .

I eventually found the sultan's turret in the *The Rubáiyát of Omar Khayyám*. I found the poetry amusing but was distracted, worried that the dangling cord on his pyjama bottoms – clearly visible – was his 'thing', which I had no desire to see. We got up and off to school very early. Tom and Flo's big Citroën DS sat on the drive beside the manicured garden all winter while we waited at the freezing bus stop for the slow ride to the Woodside terminal. This huge square, also housing the ferry to Liverpool, was crammed with buses in the blue-and-cream Birkenhead livery. Lorie saw me on to the bus to my primary school in Prenton; she took a different one to Park High and her cohort of friends. In the afternoons I waited, black-tongued, for my big sister in the cafe beside the ferry terminal, slowly unravelling liquorice Catherine wheel bootlaces and sucking sherbet dips. The journey took an hour each way in lashing rain and cold. We did our homework on the bus. When Inge rang on Sundays, we were careful not to express misery, since nothing could be changed, but no doubt she knew what was going on.

I have probably spent more time worrying about the weird meaninglessness of my father's life than he ever did. I'm quite exercised about the irrationality of his choices, and yet more so about the way in which this man drifted from one thing to the next never using his obvious intelligence in any fruitful way. Why didn't he make more of his life? He lacked drive – except on the golf course. All his energy went into his game. He may sound like a stereotypical Scouser, all gabby charm and studied idleness, but he wasn't. A grammar school boy, he sounded and was middle class with a northern accent, not a Birkenhead or Liverpool one. His wit amused Lorie, who spent more time with him than I did. He would speak to her seriously but also mocked her, and she mocked him back. They got on well. His main aim seemed to be keeping Flo happy. In him, ability and ambition were fundamentally mismatched. He indulged himself in pleasurable pursuits as well as shoes and he was awfully good at evading consequences, including his daughters. He didn't seem to lack a sense of self-worth or the ability to think beyond the present, but a slighted daughter is probably not the best judge of character.

Tom remembered every word people said and so could tell you exactly how you were contradicting yourself; he never lost an argument. His knowledge of politics and history was fuelled by the books he devoured. He had an encyclopaedic knowledge of science fiction. He wasn't to be interrupted or spoken to while reading – Lorie is the same and so am I. For him, books were more important than people. I agree, but keep that thought to myself. He expressed himself beautifully but never seriously; politics, ideas and big thoughts were men's work and not to be wasted on women.

Some moments remain vivid, and cars feature in many of them. Tom and Flo did love a nice car; while he was driving the DS, she had a fashionable Mini. I remember him buying a Heinkel bubble car and being absolutely thrilled with it. It was a two-seater; I don't recall riding in it, but Lorie says I did. I remember walking at a snail's pace in front of him in the fog so he would not crash another, bigger and better car. Back then, smogs were so thick, you could not see a yard ahead. I remember that he took us on holiday to Wales once and we were told to look out for the sea. We were in the back of his saloon when we sighted Barry Island and called out – look, the sea! He drove into the car in front and was furious with us. Apart from that occasion, I cannot recall our father ever shouting at Lorie and me.

Flo and Tom shared an inability to deal with children and a gift for spending on beautiful clothes, restaurants and good times. After the big house was sold, they lived in a cute little cottagey bungalow in Neston village. They opened a number of hairdressing salons around the Wirral, which flourished. In the Swinging Sixties, everybody wanted the latest cool haircut. After that training at Vidal Sassoon, Tom became a good hairdresser, known for his cutting skills in every sense. Once he gave me a 'tulip cut', which Inge thought was snazzy. He was great with women clients, didn't schmooze his customers but joked and gently mocked them; yet in many ways he was always a man's man. The salons were full of groovy young women stylists called Babs or Val, who wore trendy clothes and were a lot of fun. Flo managed the staff – she was good at that. But then she got ill and without her, he couldn't carry on. He was much less good at making money and hopeless at holding on to it.

This elegant woman died of cancer and riddled with guilt, believing that this was God's punishment for what she had done to our mother. I didn't see her in that terrible state: I planned on going up north, but she didn't want to be seen. I know – though nobody ever used such words – that Tom truly loved her. And when I reflect upon her pain, physical and mental, all negative emotions dissipate.

I want to praise Tom, if only to flatter that half of myself. On the upside, we inherited his brains; Lorie has his hazel eyes, historian's mind and Inge's excellent memory. Our love of books surely comes from both sides. My drive and love of languages is all Inge. As I get older, I see that knowing how to live in the present – ideally with a small affectionate dog to hand – is a great gift, one I have never quite mastered. Inge was like Tom in that she, too, lived totally in the moment.

The last time I saw my father, I was twenty and at Bristol University. I had spent a pre-university gap year in Hamburg and hadn't visited for years when I took my then boyfriend, Jake, to Birkenhead. I was a woman now, very different to the schoolgirl he remembered, and expecting to be treated seriously. My father was such an intelligent man; I wanted to show him off to Jake, and vice versa. To introduce the two men in my life to each other. But Tom kept asking Jake if he was going to 'make an honest woman of me', like some comedy dad out of *The Liver Birds*. I was disappointed and deeply embarrassed. On the way back, Jake kept repeating the phrase in a mockery of his accent, hugely amused by his own wit. At that moment, it was hard to decide which of them I hated more.

CHAPTER 10

. . . . .

The right man

Lorie and I have done all that we can in Tours. I lug home a suitcase crammed with Inge's family papers, the blue files with her notes on her life plus that envelope with old black-and-white photos. Included is René's file with old IDs, military documents and his will. I'm amassing research material long before I consciously realise that I'm writing a book. Before we leave the flat, I leaf through old photo albums belonging to René's first wife, Renée, which I find at the back of a cupboard. Inge couldn't bear to destroy a single image of him. The sad years after their affair ended look dull and static: René is frail, a lean man in a suit visiting unknowns in sunny gardens. More unknown folk sit round tables smiling for the camera in faded Kodachrome.

Inge probably met the 'two Renés' when Tilly and Heinz came to live with us in Sydenham; the older couples had been friends in Morocco for years. Two years later, at Easter 1964, she sent me off to tour Brittany with them to improve my French. London was swinging. I was thirteen, an innocent in the suburbs of SE26 miles from the King's Road epicentre, wondering if anything interesting would ever happen to me. I was keen on meeting boys, but the only male I met in France was René. Aged fifty-two, he was unlike anybody I knew. Tall and lean, very good-looking with intelligent chocolate-brown eyes, he wore his blond hair long and swept back. He dressed in sharp, expensive suits in fashionable beige and brown. I never saw him without a white shirt; sometimes he wore a silk cravat. He was the man in charge, always glinting with mischief, the alpha male shepherding his female flock.

We drove along the coast and round Quimper, the area where Renée was born, in his DS. He always drove the latest top-of-the-range Citroën. The two Renés were generous and kind. René was mildly provocative and good fun in a sardonic way – the sarcasm was never directed at me. He taught me various moderate swear words and euphemisms and I learned a lot of French. They bought me a casquette, the peaked blue Breton hat fishermen wear, and a traditional blue-and-white-striped sweater, which I liked a lot. A running joke hinged on me being taken for a Breton. I treasured hopes of becoming a thin, sexy French existentialist – Juliette Gréco or Françoise Hardy in a beret and black polo-neck sweater, puffing a Gauloises. Fat chance. In my honour, English breakfast was de rigueur, and by the same token afternoon tea with cake. In one week, I gained five kilos.

We stayed in grand hotels and feasted on serious lunches and dinners. Entering a restaurant, René would tip the maître d' lavish sums to get the kind of service he wanted. He lit his costly Virginia cigarettes with a gold lighter and drank the finest wines. When we weren't eating, we drove through the rain from place to place, admiring the scenery, walking on slippery cobblestones, nipping in and out of shops. On Easter Sunday, it rained with a particular thrumming intensity, and I was told that these were the *lacrimae Christi* and that each year it would always rain on this day. Oddly, it does seem always to have rained on Easter Sunday, wherever I have been. The Cocards were Catholics, but I don't recall them entering a church.

Renée was a large woman with massive bosoms, bleached blonde hair worn in a short bouffant style, always bubbling with laughter. She spent her time in the front seat of the car crocheting a salmon-pink sweater to match my admired English rose complexion, to a truly hideous pattern. Eventually I was made to swap the beloved striped jumper for this appalling garment. She loved shopping and was a magpie attracted to any shiny object, ideally by Limoges. Eternally good-humoured, quick in her retorts, she was mildly frightening in some way I never formulated. I just knew that it was expedient to keep on her good side. She sang very well in the style of Edith Piaf and took little persuading to stand up and perform.

The two Renés came to Sydenham twice at least while we were teenagers; visits back and forth became the norm. Inge would later tell both Lorie and me the story of how she'd fallen in love with René on one of their trips to Scotland. The adults drove round admiring the scenery – eating, staying in nice places – the same format as Easter in Brittany. When she was forty-three (which dates it to 1969), she discovered an irresistible urge to touch the neck of René, driving the Citroën DS. Presumably she refrained, since Renée was always sitting by his side, Inge and Tilly in the back. '*Je vous aime*,' she eventually announced rather formally. All I know about this affair, which took place right under my nose, is what Inge chose to tell me.

Death does not release Inge's hold over me, as her funeral demonstrated. In May we must return to Tours to see the notaire. Aware of how badly I short-changed Inge at the Restaurant de la Gare, I decide to organise a celebration of her life in Tours. A generous lunch will allow Alex (now mended) to say farewell and the friends who couldn't make it to the funeral to gather and exchange stories. Not the true stories, obviously. I miss her so much. I also long to sit her down and ask some searching questions – not that she would ever tell me anything if she didn't want to. A curious mental dance persists, a back and forth between anguish and bewilderment. How is it possible to know somebody so well yet understand so little about their behaviour?

By March I have a venue, the Château de Beaulieu in Joué-lès-Tours, a chic little hotel with a gourmet chef. Our party of twenty-two includes vegetarians and my gluten-free daughter; emails shoot back and forth as we struggle to refine a menu without game and foie gras. I write short speeches in English and French to introduce each set of people to the others, explaining how Inge came to Tours out of love for René and praising her to the skies. I can't find much to say about the epitome of the sexy Frenchman. For years, the two Renés visited us and vice versa – yet I hardly knew him.

Our family assemble on a sunny day in May: Alex and our children, Sophie and Jonathan, Lorie and her younger daughter, Oriel. Many of Inge's friends gather, all so much younger than her. The lunch is delicious and delightful. Inge would have been in her element on the terrace overlooking the garden with a cigarette in one hand and a glass of champagne in the other. For once, it really is her day.

I have come to my senses where her flat is concerned. We will sell. I fret about the title document for the square metre of corridor Inge bought, linking the flat to its adjoining studio when she combined the two to create one apartment in 1998. She mounted a charm offensive with the residents, schmoozing wildly until she obtained permission at the annual general meeting. She imprinted on me that we would need this document when the time came to sell. It is nowhere to be found. Mystified, I am furious when I hear one of the lawyers remark – as an aside – that Madame probably didn't have permission. Madame, I explain to anyone who will listen, was utterly reliable. Inge, as I cannot yet admit to myself, was nothing of the sort. Eventually, we obtain a document at a cost of €1,000. Was this another rainy-day saving? Her beautiful two-bedroom flat in the heart of Tours instantly finds a buyer.

In July 2019 we return to Tours to sign the probate and sale documents. We hire bicycles from kind Franck opposite (who won't let us pay) and cycle along the riverbank. What a liberation to feel the sun on your back, to have the freedom to go anywhere. We eat frites at La Guinguette, an amusing open-air beer garden and dance hall on the river. On a beautiful summer's evening, we wander through streets buzzing with tourists and students. We are meeting René's favourite nephew, Sylvain, and his American wife, Cynthia, for dinner at L'Embellie in the heart of the medieval town. They are both professors, tall and very good-looking ('my favourite giants,' said Inge). Sylvain has René's velvety brown eyes. We drink champagne, order an excellent gourmet menu and plenty of wine. I learn some Cocard family history. Sylvain traces the family tree, explaining which of his five Cocard uncles married whom, and who their children were. He tells us about

René's early years, how he started off working for his father, and that Renée was his father's secretary. She grabbed him very young.

Now he drops a bombshell: the Cocards believe René is our father. To be more precise, they have always known. I'm not eating, I'm craning forward to hear Sylvain's soft voice in the noisy restaurant and scribbling in my book to be sure of getting the exact words. ('Like a Rottweiler,' says my sister.) Sylvain's mother, Madeleine – the youngest child and only sister, whom René loved especially – told Sylvain this *'on dit'* – what people are saying. René's mother also believed that we are his children. They all know that Inge met him when she was a girl of sixteen, and that it was love at first sight for both, though he was already married.

Sixteen? How can that be? In 1942, when Inge was sixteen, she was living underground in Brussels. But Cynthia is certain that Inge told her she met René as a girl, when she went to Morocco to visit her uncle. As we know, Inge was sent to Morocco in 1939, on the eve of her thirteenth birthday. I'm thunderstruck. But of course she could have met René then. I don't know how he got to know Willy in that expatriate community, but they certainly had a lot in common. Though sixteen years apart, both loved women, fast cars and the good life. My mind is racing and calculating. So when he told his mother about Inge, René fudged the ages – as you would when a just-turned-thirteen-year-old gets together with a twenty-six-year-old. My so-prudish virginal mother wrote how when she arrived in Belgium from Morocco, her parents didn't recognise her: *Are you really our Inge?* At thirteen she was a little woman, with bosoms. She must have possessed a full set of adult emotions to match.

As for René being our father – how could that possibly be? Lorie was born in June 1949. But we always knew that as a young married woman, Inge went all the way to Morocco to check out Heinz, the man Tilly wanted to marry. That oft-related tale cast Inge as the marvellous daughter who'd do anything to protect her mother. That trip took place in the autumn of 1948. The dates fit. All this starts to click and buzz unstoppably round my head.

There is more. Sylvain says that René went to England in 1950 to meet Inge 'and you were born'. Bloody hell. Was René around on those occasions when Tilly visited her baby granddaughters? He always travelled widely. Sylvain's mother, Madeleine, knew all about the relationship in the 1950s or 60s because there was conflict between her and her sister-in-law, Renée. Renée wasn't much liked at all, it seems. Sylvain is very sure that 'René always knew wherever Inge was'. He also says that when Renée was dying, somebody said 'tell Inge' – and that she came to see René in Tours then. Even before Renée's death. Maybe the beautiful post-funeral phone call and sixty red roses story I told everyone is also fiction? Did that explain why none of her friends in Tours knew this story when I laboriously explained it at the funeral and celebratory lunch?

I am flabbergasted. After we say our goodbyes and promise to keep in touch, I need a drink. Or to be precise, several rounds. Lorie, Alex and I perch outside the Havana Café, one of the many bars I never frequented while immured in Inge's flat.

'So Lorie – you're half French, half German and wholly illegitimate.'

'Oh please. You can't be illegitimate if you're born in wedlock. I've been saying this since I was fifteen. She's always lied. I always knew it was all shite,' says the learned Reader in Law.

We order more wine and sit on at the Havana, Lorie wistfully looking at the young crowd while I seethe on in a froth of agitated bewilderment.

'I miss being young – smoking, drinking – how cool was that? Does this really bother you? That's hysterical. Who cares?'

Me, obviously. Lorie reminds me of how numb she'd been at the funeral. 'I couldn't cry,' she says, 'because I felt liberated from the rage.'

Rage? I didn't understand what she felt then – just as I didn't understand the real cause of our estrangement for so many years. Now my rage has arrived. My head throbs with it. This goes much further and deeper than father anxiety. All my life I believed that Inge adored Tom and that his absconding destroyed her life until René came to rescue her. My inner world is constructed on this myth of sacrificial virginal mother, untrustworthy absconding father. This somehow coexists with the understanding that fathers are special and to be adored. Lacking trust, needing to please Inge, I formed no relationship with my father. And I never had a proper relationship with René. In so many ways, some good and others not so good, the bad-but-special-father construct shaped my attitude towards men and family and parental duties.

I am consumed by fury. And yet – and still – no matter how I turn this revelation in my mind, I find it impossible not to believe/trust Inge. The brainwashing runs too deep. The contradictions clash and whirl round my head unstoppably. The world swirls for hours. At 5 a.m. I get up and start typing out my notes. I record everything Sylvain said, as if staring at the words on a computer will make them comprehensible.

Later that morning, the notaire fires up her computer, bringing up the official probate document, which must be signed off online. Lorie, Alex and I sit at the large table looking at the big screen; up comes the title MADAME INGEBURG ROSENBAUM VEUVE [widow] COCARD. Omitting Tom, the seemingly superfluous Mr Charlesworth, this description indeed depicts the trajectory of Inge's life. I scoffed at the way the worldly French seek the illegitimate children under the Napoleonic code because all must inherit equally. And now we – the legitimate but possibly also illegitimate children – sit waiting for the tax bill. Incredibly tired, I am also hyper alert, pulsing with fury and angst. This weird inner maelstrom will torment me for months.

The probate process reflects the ethics of the Republic, but it is also supremely practical. Once the notaire has sorted out who the heirs are, the value of the estate is agreed and the property is put in their joint names. That way, everyone is tied in and equally liable for tax. Egalité and fraternité! There is a get-out. The heirs can choose to repudiate the estate if, for example, liabilities and debts exceed assets. Egalité, fraternité and liberté!

While the notaire does her calculations, my frenzied mind is turning on the liberté angle. What is my real inheritance? After our dinner of revelations, Lorie and Sylvain are happy to do DNA tests, but don't have my burning need to know. It will take months for me to have certainty about our parentage. I dig deeper. Sleuthing through the boxes of Inge and René's papers and scrutinising photographs for clues throws up different versions of my mother's life. So many of the facts I'd casually accepted are wrong. As I question and rewrite the past, I am also rewriting my narrative of myself. Many of the memories of my youth – so fixed and seemingly inalterable – need to be re-examined.

Inge – somewhat economical with the truth – claimed in her account of her life that the affair began in 1969: *Do I start at the age of 43, when after living 17 years on my own I fell madly in love with a gorgeous, elegant, exciting Frenchman who already had a wife?* Something was surely going on in 1967, two years earlier, when we holidayed in Spain. That red-hot summer, our Triumph Herald broke down north of Madrid. We were marooned for nearly a week in a grotty hotel in the middle of nowhere, waiting for spare parts. Two German engineers building a road, sick to death of the place and bored silly, hit on me and Inge. This amazed Lorie, unused to playing the gooseberry. They took us to a local bullfight, plying the three of us with sour thin wine poured from a height out of bottles made from goatskin to get us drunk. And they succeeded. Inge batted her suitor away. The other bloke snogged me in our shared bedroom while Lorie lay on the other bed, terminally bored, reading her book. Aged sixteen, I was desperate for some experience.

When she discovered me canoodling with that man, Inge was horrified. She was spending her time in a phone booth down the road with a bag of coins making international phone calls, in a flap about getting back to her job in London. We were on no account to miss the ferry. Once the car was fixed, Inge drove hell for leather across the dusty plains in boiling heat. Lorie lay on the back seat reading, with her feet sticking out of the window. I sat in front, navigating. A flip-flop flipped. Inge refused to stop, but we had to: the miscreant had no other shoes. We turned back. The car crawled along the hot road. Words were spoken. Eventually, we found the flip-flop. After that, Inge drove and drove. She got so tired that she started driving on the left, nearly killing us all – which she hotly denied. At one in the morning, she stopped for black coffee. After three cups, she drove on through the night. In this way she got us to Loudun, where the two Renés lived and where – no talk of the ferry now – all urgency disappeared. She must have been desperate for a few days with her lover. We noticed this discrepancy but said nothing. Or rather, nothing she responded to. Inge didn't encourage questions. How could I have been so blind?

Psychologists have studied inattentional blindness: when we fail to see something that we don't expect. In one entertaining experiment, students were told to observe film of two teams playing basketball and record the number of passes made. Intent on their task, half of them failed to notice a woman in a gorilla costume walking through the middle of the action. Well, I hadn't even counted the passes. Blocking my vision was her grand confection: that she was a one-man woman, who'd loved my father madly for years after the divorce. Meanwhile, the gorilla was thumping its chest and doing cartwheels.

My chief witnesses, Sylvain and his wife, Cynthia, belong to the other 50 per cent, the ones who see what's going on. The two professors bonded with Inge over finding love at the age of sixty. Inge often told me how much she liked them, and she was thrilled to welcome Cynthia to the Cocard family. None of them judged each other; they were mature people who understood that lives take many different turns. They, like René, always knew that Inge was German, and it didn't matter a fig. This unbuttoned trio had talked, really talked. What a release for Inge, after years of politesse and pretence with friends and acquaintances. At the restaurant, Sylvain said en passant that he once mentioned bondage – and Inge replied, 'I miss that.' When he saw the expression on my face, he smiled. 'She was a normal woman!' he said. 'Very elegant and there was something sexy in her.' Whereupon Lorie helpfully found this to add: 'The submissive holds the power.' This made me yet more queasy.

Corroboration comes: Inge told Lorie's elder daughter, Siobhan, that she fell in love with René before she met Tom. She told her granddaughter that she was fourteen, 'and thought him the most handsome marvellous man she had ever met'. Even here she fibbed, adding an extra year to her age. In response to questions, Siobhan emails from New Zealand, remembering her exact words: '"But he was a married man" – and with a shrug of the shoulder, she implied that he did the right thing.' Which was, presumably, not sleeping with the nubile Inge? Or?

Writing *The Children's War*, I had numerous conversations with Inge about Meknes. She described what fun she and her Uncle Willy had in the garden and with the dog. She never mentioned René. I look back through those rough notes she made for her autobiography to double-check. Not a word. The child who arrived in Meknes in 1939 on the eve of her thirteenth birthday must have been a more complex creature than the innocent victim of war I depicted playing in the beautiful garden while her uncle watered the lawn. She told me how Willy would make the spray of the hose arc high into the air and threaten her with it, daring her to run across the courtyard. He would soak her, helpless from laughing too much, from head to foot. Then, I wrote, she ran to scramble into another dress in half a minute because they were going out to dinner, and she wanted to look her best. All very girlish and charming.

The film winds back in my head and this time it plays with three people in that scene. Tall, gregarious Willy, with his bright eyes and hair of reddish gold, is joined by his handsome friend René Cocard, twenty-six years old, blond hair swept back, all naughtiness and charm. Maybe Toni is preparing cocktails for him and his wife, Renée. They are heading out for dinner with Willy's teenage niece, just as soon as she gets a pretty dress on. The child I imagined wearing a sunhat and summer dress is rather taller, with bosoms. What was young Inge feeling and thinking during this wet-T-shirt moment in that shimmering iridescent green? She must have been exhilarated. No wonder *I had never had so much attention in my whole life.*

The treats I gave her in my version – cinema visits, ice creams, Coca-Cola at the pool, those baguettes stuffed with chocolate – pale compared to romantic ecstasy and the first throb of sexuality. For six glorious months, Inge lived a dream of amour and happiness, sunshine and attention. Now I get her lifelong outrage and sense of utter betrayal at being sent back to grim Europe and her sorrowing desperate parents who had no means of looking after themselves, let alone her. Her life would have been so different. She would have remained close to René. She would never have met Tom.

The solid certainties of my life – and Inge's – are melting, reforming themselves into something very different. In old age, Inge also told my niece Siobhan 'how awful it was waiting for her sister to die so they could leave Germany'. So she did know what was going to happen. Our mother never expressed such feelings to us. This chilling blend of dread, anxiety and guilt surely explains why she never tried to know her sister – that was too sad. Instead, she blanked her out. Fleeing German hell, she emerged into a heaven free of tormented Jews. Willy and René larking about in the garden were kind and great fun. These blond supermen were up for dares and teases with a freedom and physicality unheard of in the grey regimented life she'd left behind. At thirteen, Inge already understood the fundamentals of life and its dangers. Morocco must have been pure pleasure, an unforgettable explosion of light, colour and romance.

What did René see in that garden? A blooming young girl, madly in love with him and flirting outrageously. She was always complimenting men and schmoozing them. 'Oh Monsieur le Générale, you're so very intelligent,' she would say to the rather formal neighbour we met in the street in Tours, all smiles, warmly pressing his hand. Inge did not merely love; she worshipped. And René was susceptible, sexually available and looking for diversion from the disappointments in his life.

CHAPTER 11

· · · · ·

'Mon roi, mon amour'

René married the woman who shared his name – the wrong woman – in 1937, just two years before he met Inge. The two Renés met when she was working as his father's secretary in Tours, and when they married, Renée was twenty-three to his twenty-five, young but highly manipulative. 'She had always been on the make; she wanted to be seen as a bourgeoise,' said Sylvain. On the wedding certificate, René's profession is *'entrepreneur de carrelages'* – tile entrepreneur like his father, Achille, who ran a successful business making tiles and mosaics from various buildings along the Rue Bernard Palissy. René was the sixth and last son of this enterprising father who, according to Sylvain, 'knew more women than there were days in the year'. More colourful gossip would follow: 'Do you know he had only one testicle and his right leg was shorter than the left one?' This hopalong philanderer spent his time and money in the Continental and Univers bars in the Place Jean Jaurès in Tours. His children were well educated. René learned German and English at the Lycée; he played the flute to a high level, attending the Conservatoire in the Rue Jules Simon. His was a bourgeois world.

The Cocard family didn't much care for this lower-class wife on the make. Sylvain's mother, Madeleine, talked freely about her sister-in-law with little love lost. And their feelings were reciprocated. On their honeymoon, Inge told me, Renée had slept with René's best friend. According to Inge, she was completely without scruples. If true, this extreme behaviour must have been devastating; I think back to how shattered Tom was as a schoolboy when his mother slept with his best friend. After that, the two Renés apparently did as they pleased. His wife's behaviour explains why René chose never to have children, having, as he later put it, no way of knowing whether they were his. Renée's affairs were common knowledge. No doubt René also amused himself elsewhere; and then of course Inge entered his life.

I trawl through René's papers and the war records that show him going back and forth between France and Morocco throughout the 1930s. In 1934, aged twenty, he was in Morocco, working as a 'representative', perhaps to get away from the family business and his oversexed, overbearing father. In 1937, the year he married, he was evidently back in France in the family business. Then the young couple moved to Morocco. Perhaps he needed to escape from France, where everybody knew or suspected something. Perhaps it was the lure of a better job. The land of muezzins (and those hole-in-the-ground toilets Inge so feared) was a great place to be a French expatriate.

René was always a refined man with tremendous pride and dignity. What was it like to be married to a woman like Renée? Appearances mattered greatly to him. If a jacket didn't have an

Armani or Hugo Boss label, it wasn't worth considering. No French designers for him (Yves Saint Laurent didn't do menswear in his day). His raincoat had to be a Burberry, his ties silk, his cufflinks 24-carat gold. To me he seemed arrogant, sexy and fun and very much in charge, but the total breakdown he suffered when he and Inge broke up reveals a more complex and tormented character. As a young man he had his freedom, sexually at least, yet his situation must have been painful.

He and Inge had a good deal in common. Both were sad and disappointed – but also full of energy and vitality, yearning for pleasure and love. What a refreshing thing it must have been for this worldly man to meet a child-woman who adored him. But after six months Inge was gone, and war broke out. René's call-up papers for service in the air force were issued in Rabat. In his nine-month military career in Morocco he rose in the ranks, going up four grades to sergeant: how unlike Tom. When France surrendered in May 1940, René was demobilised.

The two Renés returned to France. In Tours, René's deals on the black market with German officers got him into trouble. 'René had been arrested,' said Sylvain, 'and so Renée "sacrificed herself" with the police chief to free my uncle.' Very film noir. One wonders quite how much of a sacrifice this was for a woman who enjoyed both power and sex. According to Madeleine, he could never divorce his wife because 'she knew too much about his behaviour during the occupation'. Later, René ran a good line of business with American officers at the military base near Chinon dealing in cigarettes, cigars and whisky – just like Tom, with his lorryloads of fags. They were pretty much of an age too: Tom was born in February 1911 to René's December 1913. Both men loved cars. Inge really did have a definite type.

In September 1945, René and his wife flew from France back to Morocco, which was virtually untouched by war. As Catholics, they would be married forever. Stateless Inge was trapped in Belgium. There was no question of returning to defeated Germany. Marriage to a victor was the only route to a better life. This explains why Inge gave Tom serious consideration. I reread those gnomic notes, which she never fleshed out. *(Tom) went to Germany – more letters, made me an offer Jane Austin* [sic] *accepted – mother's comments – no permission – no fraternisation – wrote said no (like in Emma, Harriet did) reasons – dreadful tales of girls who had gone to America – I said he is OK mother not a man for you – selfish – (only 10 years difference with mother). He came again he made me another offer – thought of estal. Yes.*

In this sub-Joycean stream of consciousness, the crucial word I still cannot decipher looks like 'estal'. Could it be short for establishment – as in 'one of my own'? Estate? Statelessness? The ironic reference to Jane Austen's novel is clear enough. My mother, the autodidact who read for hours each day, particularly enjoyed *Emma* and the self-deception of its heroine. In overlaying her memory of her teenage years with Emma's bad advice to her friend Harriet, who is told to refuse a proposal and then regrets it, Inge puts Tom's proposal, or rather *offer*, into the category of a marriage transaction, the sort that is crucial to save the heroine from penury – as Jane Austen's readers well understood. It is wholly practical. No love. No *gorgeous, elegant, exciting Frenchman.*

I start to feel sorry for my 'OK' father. That is a novel emotion, upending everything I had always believed. Persistent Tom must have been very much in love. He waited for Inge and Tilly to serve their six-month prison sentence. He went back to Britain to be demobilised, saying that he wanted to give his teenage beloved time to think, so she would be certain. He returned in 1946 as a civilian and proposed again; he didn't want to take advantage of this innocent girl.

Inge's decision was a sober one. Passionately in love with René, she couldn't have the man she wanted, but here was somebody not unlike him. Tom was entrepreneurial, he would take care of her. They were both tall, slim, older men. Maybe she thought that Birkenhead, with its industrial past and attractive countryside, bore a resemblance to Mülheim. Did she even think about this place she was going to? I doubt it. She always was wildly impulsive. At the age of ninety, she bought a flat without bothering to look at the plans properly, because it was 'her day' and because the excitement of a property transaction energised her. In 1946, she was choosing to escape from her mother and her situation; Tom came along at the right moment.

Did she ever love our father – or non-father – at all? I doubt it. Her intense, sensual, and wholly reciprocated love for René was in a category all its own. Did Tom have his own suspicions about another man? Does that explain why he was never interested in his two girls? Why we weren't allowed to learn French? How painfully this rewrites my childhood and everything I was brought up to believe.

Among Inge's papers I find a 1957 application to Germany, written in German, requesting reparations for the loss of her education. She signed this at the German Consulate in Liverpool. Four years earlier, the German government had introduced the first law enabling compensation to be paid and Tilly was applying from Morocco. This piece of paper states that Inge's passport was issued on 16 August 1946, in Liverpool. Six months to issue a passport for a new citizen sounds about right.

'My feet – yes, I know.' One of the photographs Inge must have sent to René

So this must be the document Tom obtained for her, and which she used to travel to Britain.

But nothing in my mother's life is what it seems. Going through the photographs I took from her flat, I find a cheerful photo inscribed May 1947 showing Inge on the beach at Wenduine, where her friend Nina lived. She is standing in a slightly pigeon-toed position and has written on the back: *Mes pieds – oui oui, je le sais – Photo prise trop tard de changer de position. Baisers Inge. My feet – yes, yes I know – Photo taken too late for me to change position. Kisses Inge.*

Inge always dated her photographs, and this date gives me pause. Did she leave her new husband and return to Brussels fifteen months after the wedding? That seems unlikely for a newly-wed at a time when travel was difficult. Or did she drag her feet after she got her passport in August 1946, not leaving for her new home in Birkenhead until the summer of 1947? That's also possible. All I know for sure is that this black-and-white message of intimacy and familiarity cannot have been sent to Tom, who didn't speak French. If it was given to her pals, Nina or Menousch, why was it in her flat in France? The most likely explanation is that twenty-one-year-old newly married Inge sent it to René, and he kept it all his life. *Baisers Inge* indeed.

Another set of pictures show her on that Wenduine beach with teenage girls and boys. Dated 1943, they must have been taken during the German occupation – were these also sent to René? All smiles and fun, she's curvy in shorts and halter necks. No inhibitions there. No hardship either.

I can't reconcile this with the stories of hunger and the oven that wouldn't light (though I remember Inge telling me that she was always bloated from eating nothing but sugar beet).

Inge with teenagers on Wenduine beach: no sign of wartime privations here

The photo that really gives me pause was snapped on the boulevards in Brussels by a street photographer during the Nazi occupation. It must be 1943 or 1944. Inge (aged seventeen or eighteen) and Tilly are both smiling, and Tilly is carrying what looks like a nicely wrapped piece of cake. A German officer strides a few paces behind them and close by is a young woman also wearing a German uniform. Tilly is chic in a fur-collared coat and trim little hat.

Is this the cat's fur acquired after the illegal shenanigans with the cheques? They look well fed. They look as if they're having a good war. The lens shifts just a little, and the picture is more complex than it at first appeared. I'm happy for them – and I can also see why the neighbours later accused them of collaborating.

In August 1947, eighteen months after her wedding, Inge was in Rock Ferry, Birkenhead. The photo with that date shows an incongruous pair: Inge in her short white beach outfit beside Tom's mother, Hetty, seemingly dressed in deep mourning. Then aged sixty, she looks as ancient as the hills. This photo too is inscribed 'Bon baisers', the ungrammatical 'good kisses'. It's an odd picture to send to your lover, but perhaps it was all Inge had. If writing to Tilly, she would have written in German – later photos of us as babies have German greetings on the back. This must be another from René's collection.

At this time, Tilly was settling in Morocco. I find and read a paper, dated September 1946, in which Willy Lindemann formally declares to the police in Meknes that he is able to support his sister, the widow Rosenbaum, for a visit of six months. This enabled her to obtain a visa for Morocco and travel papers, even though she was stateless. Rather than making the journey from Meknes, Willy sent his good friend Heinz Steinberg from the

Brussels: despite the German military presence,
Tilly and Inge look as if they're having a good war

Legion to pick Tilly up at the airport in Casablanca. The girl from Lintorf, whose eventful life held excitements she had never dared dream of, fell for Heinz instantly. She married him and settled in Morocco. He was fifty, she was forty-seven.

I need to know more about Inge's fabled trip to Morocco in the autumn of 1948 after a year (or perhaps two) of Tom and the ghastly Hetty. Lorie and I were told that twenty-two-year-old Inge headed for Morocco to vet her mother's suitor in an altruistic quest. Fortunately, as Inge used to tell us, she'd liked Heinz (another Jew) and given the match her blessing. And so the marriage went ahead. Maybe she transmitted this romantic dream of camels, palm trees and middle-aged people finding happiness to bolster the myth of family unity, which in Sydenham needed a helping hand. But the crucial element in her story isn't true. Tilly had married Heinz Steinberg in Casablanca over a year earlier, on 19 July 1947; I find their wedding certificate among Inge's papers. It was René Inge went to see. She must have concocted this tall tale as her excuse for Tom, and the story subsequently took on a life of its own, as such inventions often do.

This was an enormous distance to travel for civilians in those days. If you had the money, you could fly BOAC from the new Heathrow Airport to the USA, Australia and South Africa with stopovers. You could probably fly to North Africa too. But I think she went the cheapest way, by boat and train. Plenty of time en route to think about your British golf-mad husband, his grim mother, and the worn side of the marital bed in cold Birkenhead. She probably travelled across France, in multiple trains, across the Pyrenees and down to Gibraltar, then from Gibraltar to Algeciras by passenger ferry. That would take a good three days or more. Inge excelled at geography – she could draw a map of Europe,

Africa or the whole world with every capital marked. I remember her talking about Algeciras, and Fez, and Gibraltar. The slow boat to Africa from Algeciras to Tangier across the Strait of Gibraltar takes three days now. That whole trip might have taken about a week. The excitement and anticipation must have been overwhelming. Then as now, the boat to Tangier docks in the heart of the old town, next to the Hotel Continental and the medina. Within half an hour she could have been sipping a café crème in the main square, the Grand Socco, heart beating fast. I bet she took those beautiful New Look dresses. Did she take a train to Meknes or Rabat? I don't think so. Somebody came in a fast car to collect her.

When they met again in the autumn of 1948, after (I presume) an interval of nine years, Inge was twenty-two and René rising thirty-five. He had just landed the prestigious job of running the Compagnie des Boissons Hygiéniques de Casablanca 'Coca-Cola'. Among his papers is the contract, which he signed on 11 August 1948. His salary is a princely 14,000 francs a month, which in Morocco went a long way. The Coca-Cola headquarters were at number 1, Boulevard Victor Hugo, Casablanca, then as now a major street. The two Renés must have had a wonderful apartment, a car, chauffeur, the works. Of course he would have had the latest Citroën. Sylvain mentioned en passant that René had bought the last Citroën model 15 CV made in the 1950s and exported it to Morocco.

Perhaps René played chess with Heinz, a master of the game, under the palm trees in those elegant French cafes on the broad boulevards. I can see the jolly group of the two Renés, Inge, Tilly and Heinz, Willy and Toni meeting at the best restaurants and dancing in nightclubs. How incredibly exciting the moments of passion and stolen kisses must have been. Mr Coca-Cola was a connoisseur of grand hotels and the best restaurants. A man who lived his own life while his wife lived hers would have known where to take his twenty-two-year-old lover for *'le cinq à sept'* – the hours of 5 to 7 p.m. when a Frenchman visits his mistress.

These scenes play out in my mind like *Casablanca.* The women are wasp-waisted and behatted in that sharp light, the men manly in their broad-shouldered suits. Rapturous months in the sunshine flew by. Then Inge discovered that she was pregnant – did she know whose baby it was? There's a thought to panic a woman. She needed a husband. Living with her mother and step-father was never an option. René was not an option either; much later, he would say how greatly he regretted the decision to stay with his wife. Charming though he was, he did not have Inge's strength of character, that steely determination.

An ultimatum came from Britain. Irritated by his young wife's long absence, Tom wrote to ask when she was coming back 'and if you're not home by Christmas, don't come back at all'. His deadline was Christmas Eve. Tom told this story to Lorie and said that Inge turned up on Christmas Day and told him they were expecting a baby. Cutting it rather fine. It's hard to believe that Tom knew anything about René. But he knew something was up, according to my worldly sister. Lorie remembers two (conflicting) stories Inge told her: the first was that she was pregnant with a boy and miscarried in Morocco. The second was 'you travelled to Morocco in my tummy'. It seems that the baby story took on certain necessary confusions as Inge elaborated her tale, keeping both men happy.

Lorie, born on 25 June 1949, weighed 4 pounds 12 ounces. Maybe she is Tom's and full term – and maybe not. I have no way of knowing the date of Inge's departure for Morocco. She could be René's and born prematurely, like me. Both Inge's babies were light in weight. Maybe Inge didn't know. She was deceiving Tom – or René – and possibly also herself. Is this why she made such a fuss, calling little Lorie 'the professor', always saying she was the image of her father, for which she was punished in her teens? Was she trying to convince Tom that Lorie was indeed his after her Moroccan escapade? How sadly that backfired. Sylvain had told us that René came to England to see her in 1950 – and in 1951 I was born. When she lay in hospital pregnant with me, crying over *War and Peace*, was it really the hopeless passions of Pierre and Natasha that held such resonance?

The colonial regime in Morocco survived until 1956, when Moroccans fighting for independence kicked the French out. Willy – soon to be on the wrong side of history – lost his wife, business, house and all his money. Toni, who presumably still had Polish nationality, chose to stay on. Inge once mentioned that this fascinating and opportunistic creature had remained for the rest of her life in Meknes, living with a woman. The two Renés returned to France, where René took over a fruit and vegetable business owned by a farmers' cooperative that was going down. He saved it, dramatically boosting exports to Germany, where he had several acquaintances. Then he took over a major *champignon de Paris* mushroom canning factory in Loudun, near Chinon, where he also bought a bookshop. That was where 'Monsieur Champignon' was living when I first met him in 1964.

I fret a good deal about the chronology of this relationship and how often the lovers met. When we were children, Inge went away from time to time, leaving us with neighbours or friends – we never enquired or were told where. We were also sent to spend odd (indeed, very odd) weeks with Tom and Flo. Around 1967, Inge began working in schools as a domestic bursar; she used to slip away in the long school holidays. I remember her always working. For weeks on end in the summer, she was absent; Tilly looked after us. I never asked what she was up to or suspected a thing.

Their affair was certainly in full flow in 1967, the year of our Spanish flip-flopping adventures. In May 1968, when the student revolution erupted in Paris, Inge was there (Zelig-like), meeting René. On 25 April that year, lovely Heinz had died suddenly. This was a tremendous shock. When you went for a walk and Heinz wanted to say something, he would stop to talk, as if you couldn't do both. I thought it a mannerism, but there was something else going on. Heinz exercised every morning vigorously; he had a wonderful muscular figure with a broad chest and narrow hips. He seemed super fit but had a heart condition. Apparently, he had asked the doctor what exercise he could do; the reply came: 'Walk at the speed where you can see the grass growing.' If only he'd had the sense to let it grow. He regularly mowed the grass on the sloping side garden with our ancient machine and this brought on the heart attack that would kill him, aged only seventy. On 1 May he was cremated in Lewisham, an inappropriate resting place for this exotic man.

Shortly afterwards, Inge and Tilly visited Willy in his old-age home near Paris to tell him in person that his brother-in-law had died; the two men had remained close ever since their days in the Legion. Inge must have peeled off to meet her lover. She told us that she had donated blood, insisting that her rare blood type, B rhesus negative, only be given to the students and not to the police, who, in their helmets and shields, looked exactly like the SS. On the flight home she was so glowing and alive that the steward asked if she had been to the fashion collections, a compliment she related to me. Innocent that I was, it never occurred to me to wonder why the blood-giving bearer of sad news was so ridiculously elated.

She and René probably met three or four times a year en famille, either in Tours or on those long drives up to Scotland, plus a couple of illicit trips to Paris or elsewhere. The French song endlessly played on the Sydenham turntable was Georges Moustaki's 'Le Métèque': We'll make each day an eternity of love, which we will live even if it kills us. It's about illicit passion and the right to be different and wayward. I still didn't twig. Inge had a way of deflecting questions and launching into another topic that made it very hard to get anything out of her. It's that gorilla again: you can't see a thing you can't conceptualise.

When Lorie left home, the overheated frenzy of our all-female household calmed perceptibly. Inge became visibly happy. In the summer of 1969, I was despatched to Hamburg with unseemly haste. Because I adored my wonderful German family, it took me decades to wonder why I was foisted on to them at a time that suited nobody. Now I have my answer. The photo is labelled 'France 69'. Inge adopts one of her extravagant rapturous poses. She's wearing a white skirt, black top and straw hat, and she's jubilant and radiant. There's the Citroën DS and behind her a smiling René, unusually clad in white vest and trousers. Goodness, it must have been hot! My grandmother is in the picture, all smiles. I am sure that Tilly knew – how could she not? But I can't imagine my mother ever confiding in her. Just another tricky element to manoeuvre in their complex love-hate relationship.

The affair must have reached a dizzying intensity. In December 1970, Inge, Tilly and I met the two Renés with a couple of their

Summer of love: René, never seen without a shirt and tie,
is uncharacteristically unbuttoned while Inge adopts a pose.
What did my grandmother Tilly (centre) know?

Inge and René dance into the New Year in Badgastein, 1970

friends in Badgastein, Austria, for a skiing holiday at a spa hotel; I was the only one who actually skied. The hotel put on a lavish New Year's Eve party. Inge wore a Pucci-style dress she'd made and danced constantly with René; in the photos, she could not be happier. I noticed this but, concentrating as I selflessly was on a good-looking Austrian boy, I failed to realise what it meant. René, always wildly generous, paid for the whole shebang.

I find a photo dated three months later inscribed '*Inge en folie douce*' – Inge in sweet madness. René and Inge are doing an impromptu dance in the Cocards' living room on 4 April 1971, Renée's birthday. As you do, when you can't keep your hands off each other. This picture must have been taken by Renée, but the writing on the back is his. His wife's birthday was their celebratory excuse for the regular Easter get-together.

My fellow student of French and German and lifelong friend Tricia remembers the two Renés visiting our student digs in Bristol around 1970. Tricia has wonderful recall: 'We bought Jamaican Blue Mountain coffee which we couldn't afford and cleared up the flat in their honour; they drank the coffee and we all went out to a restaurant.' Tricia picked up the tremendous excitement in the air; she saw what I didn't. 'They and Inge [christened Mummy Two by Tricia] had something very special and amazing between them. There was something about her aura that forbad questions and evoked admiration and adoration. She kind of commanded these in a way I found thrilling. I was delighted to admire and adore her.'

Tricia had always found Inge dramatically glamorous and beautiful in a way she felt her own mother wasn't. 'Inge always wore lipstick, her hair was nicely done, she always wore smart clothes and she cultivated her stylishness.' No point in dwelling

'En folie douce'

on how deeply I envied my friend her distinguished academic mother and diplomat father, her four close siblings.

When René offered to leave his wife, Inge said no. She wouldn't do to another woman what had been done to her. That is the story she told me. Renée, who had sung and crocheted her way through so many holidays, was not to be abandoned. I don't believe that this is the truth. But something must have occurred to disturb their regular meetings. Did Renée have some way of blackmailing her husband when he said he was finally leaving her – if indeed that ever happened? At some moment, the lovers must have understood that they had no certain future together. Each had a breakdown, but René did not recover as Inge eventually did. He took to his bed and remained there.

I think hard about him, trying to understand him better. He was a man of great pride, who couldn't stand shabbiness or anything second rate. His snobberies about clothes and restaurants seem terribly French and faintly risible. But these underpinned his life, as did his romantic obsession. In his fantasies and pleasures, in his inner life, he was utterly concentrated and serious. His love for Inge and the stories he told his family about her (and us) created a far happier dream life than his actual one and when he wasn't able to continue that fantasy, something in him broke.

In 1971, Tricia and I were spending the year in France and Germany that our joint degree in French and German required. We'd spent a term in Aix-en-Provence supposedly writing our dissertations – actually picking the grape harvest, making rare visits to the library, dieting furiously and mooning over our boyfriends back in the UK. I had met Alex and was helplessly besotted. The ratio of dissertation to love-brooding hours was one to ten. We spent our time planning, speculating, and soaking raisins to expand them (one orange and a small handful of raisins was the meagre ration Tricia permitted for lunch and dinner).

Two thin and rather spotty femmes fatales returned to the UK that icily cold Christmas. Inge told me about the affair and that René was terribly ill. All communication between them had ceased and she was desperate to know how he was. She only confided in us because we were returning to France to complete our 'studies' and might be persuaded to divert on our way to Aix. Her distress and need were evident. Her request was deadly serious, but also felt like the most exciting kind of adventure. Weren't we lovesick too? We threw ourselves into this quest with great enthusiasm. Our plan hinged on some simple timing; we would pretend we were stranded so the two Renés would have to put us up. We spent hours hanging around at Montparnasse station in Paris then took a train to Tours. We rang up from the station with the unlikely story that we had got on the wrong train and were stranded. It's hard to believe that Renée bought it, but she came and picked us up and drove us to Loudun. In the car she explained that René was very ill.

Their house in Loudun at Porte de Chinon had a big garage and gate and rooms all on one floor around a central courtyard. The kitchen, dining and sitting room were to one side; René was on the other, in a bedroom hidden from view. We were taken into his bedroom to say hello, then rapidly ushered out. We had decided that the best course of action was for Tricia to keep Renée busy while I tried to talk to him on my own. Tricia followed her into the kitchen and fiddled with the kettle, chatting away. As soon as they were out of sight, I scurried back into the bedroom. René knew why we were there. They both must have. In a short time, he told me that he loved Inge; we embraced, he said I was to tell her that he loved her, and she was his great love. And he gave me a big banknote; I was to buy a large bottle of her favourite Chanel No. 5 perfume.

Tricia did a sterling job of keeping Renée in the kitchen; she literally hung on to her. My dear friend remembers every detail vividly: 'Renée grew excited and excitable and very dramatic. "We must telephone Inge at once! What a surprise!" she announced in a very false way. She picked up the phone and rang Inge within hearing of her husband. "What a surprise, Inge! Your daughter is here! René is far too ill to come to the phone. My dear Inge, you must know how terribly ill he is. The girls are stranded, they will stay for the night." It was torment of the most agonising kind. On and on she flowed, giving no information at all, and we had no way to tell Inge between the lines that things were all right or that we had a message for her. Phone calls were expensive and special in those days; Renée milked this one for all it was worth. I had thought the two Renés were a kind uncle and aunt, but now I saw what she was like.'

We telephoned Inge as soon as we could to tell her how René was; I don't think I wrote. The need for secrecy had been impressed on the amateur sleuths. I search in vain for that letter among the many bundles, for Inge kept every letter and postcard I ever sent her. I bought her a large bottle of Chanel No. 5 eau de cologne, which was far cheaper than perfume, and pocketed the change. She cast one look at it and said, 'He always bought me perfume.' So I pretended that I didn't know the difference.

Writing this now produces a familiar flush of shame. Decades later, en route to Inge, I remembered my incredibly shabby behaviour and sent a salesgirl searching through a parfumerie until she found a bottle of Chanel No. 5 so huge it looked like one from a display. Thrilled, Inge pestered until I told her what it cost. She enjoyed informing her visitors exactly how much I'd spent. This came far too late. Perhaps if I'd realised in 1971 that he was the great love of her life and that their affair had been going on for thirty-two years, I'd have behaved better. I took this huge bottle to the morgue, to spray perfume on my dead mother; Lorie says that I was like a mad thing, and unstoppable. She has it now.

After this visit, a new complicity arose between Tricia and Inge. Tricia: 'Inge knew that I knew, and she told me that it was with René that she had learned the meaning of *une nuit blanche* – a white [sleepless] night of lovemaking. She also told me that on her birthday he had sent a number of red roses that was phenomenal – I think it was a hundred.' I have no memory of these birthday roses, which would have caused quite a stir in Sydenham. Perhaps this was a special confidence between Inge and Tricia.

René and Inge were the master and mistress of the grand romantic gesture. Their story was operatic in its extremes of love and anguish. The pain was all the greater because Inge had made her heartbreaking decision and because there was no hope, and now he was so ill. Tricia completely got her need to end the affair: 'It's not that you don't love them – it's that you have to save your soul and get away.'

From 1971 to 1986 there was silence. Or so I was led to believe. When I send Lorie this chapter, she tells me something odd. Her best friend Ilka Zimbehl (a family friend from Germany) ran into Inge and René one summer in the late 1970s. Ilka was on holiday in a French market town with her husband and three children when they saw a woman who, from the back, looked just like Inge. Indeed it was. Inge introduced René; there was a third person with them, but Ilka couldn't remember who – it can't have been Tilly, whom she knew well. The lovers weren't dramatically sundered, as I was told; their affair just got sticky and complex. Did Inge nobly reject René, honourably insisting that she could not cause another woman such pain, reducing him to a wreck? I doubt it. This was a lovely story to tell her children. It seems likelier that she issued some kind of ultimatum, telling him that he had to leave his wife or else – and meant it. *Once I have started with A no matter what, I continue right through to Z.* Inge always said that his illness was her fault and she never stopped blaming herself and feeling guilty.

A banal and more likely explanation might be that the two Renés rubbed along together in mutual dislike and mild resentment, as long-shackled couples do, until (prompted by Inge) a hint at divorce threw a spanner in the works. Perhaps Renée did have a way of blackmailing her husband into staying with her. Sylvain said that there was some dodgy business between the two of them, and not just in wartime with the black market. The Cocard family thought so too. There always was something sinister about Renée. Perhaps the social opprobrium of divorce was too great. Perhaps, much as he loved Inge, René didn't have the balls to go through with it. Either way, the age of frequent jolly holidays together came to an end. They both suffered. René was ill when Tricia and I saw him and only partially recovered. Inge later told me that she'd had a complete breakdown. Absorbed in my own life, I never noticed it. Or was that another of her myths? Wouldn't I have noticed something that extreme? I don't know. This could be more of that unintentional blindness on my part.

The Cocard family albums in Inge's flat show him as frail but up and about on excursions through the 1970s. Then again, one doesn't take photos of a sick man in bed. René consoled himself by seeing Inge sporadically, but it wasn't enough. They were so completely besotted with each other. Inge once told Lorie that René could never divorce because he promised Renée's father he would always look after her and a Frenchman never broke his word. This noble promise sounds about as likely as her noble sacrifice.

In January 1986, Renée died of a heart attack. Off Inge hurried to France – or perhaps, depending on who you believe, off she hurried just before Renée's death. Their reunion must have been extraordinary.

I felt nothing but joy that my mother was marrying '*l'homme de ma vie*', 'the man of my life', an epithet I never took literally. I did wonder at the time how he explained this rapid remarrying to his family – it never occurred to me that his mother and siblings had known all along. How very French. They wed on 28 July 1986 at the town hall in Tours. Inge was sixty and René seventy-two. The wedding had that feeling of unreality the rest of their life together would have – that something unattainable long dreamed of and yearned for was happening and almost couldn't be true. The emotion was overwhelming.

There were very few guests: two of René's dearest friends, Sophie and me. We stayed in a romantic little chateau, its woods carpeted with rose-coloured wild cyclamen. The celebratory lunch was lobster and champagne. That weekend, it was visibly an effort for the elegant groom to hold himself upright and to keep going. René was weak and ill, a hypochondriac who suffered from agonising headaches and a host of other complaints. After their marriage they began to travel, always with an immense suitcase containing his medicines, and in March 1988, when our son Jonny was born, they came to London. Tricia, who was visiting,

The wedding felt unreal, as if this longed-for event couldn't really be happening

remembers Inge perched on René's knee, giggling like a little girl. That summer, they spent a week with us in Lacoste in Provence. René had little of the swagger and dash of before. Inge was sometimes sad that after sharing such incredible passion he was so diminished.

When I visited, it was hard to connect with either of them. Inge could not sit still. She dashed hither and thither asking how he was, and could she get him anything, *'mon roi, mon amour'*, my king, my love? No, my queen. There was no possibility of a proper conversation when there was always a cigarette to light, a glass of wine to fetch, some little chore to do. It was both touching and weird to watch them in their bubble, her wreathed in smiles, acting the beloved slave. Inge indulged her joy in adoring him. He never took his eyes away from her. Once, visiting Tours, I noticed him looking at me very intently. What was it? 'René thinks that you should wear lip liner,' my mother said. And, absurdly, that is the only specific remark of his (or should I say of hers) that I remember. I can't say it was particularly paternal, but perhaps it displayed more than a passing interest.

More pertinent was his offering to adopt us shortly after the wedding. He was sending a message; one we were primed not to hear. Inge didn't explain why (how could she?) so I took it as a sign of his love for her, which made it even more charming. Mildly taken aback at the time, Lorie and I said no thank you. I remember saying that, at thirty-two, I was too old to be adopted. Inge had given us to understand that under French law, two children would receive two-thirds of his estate: far better, we thought, that she should not have to share with us. Not for one moment did it occur to me that this was a serious offer or in any way connected to paternity. But now, looking through his papers, I find his will, one handwritten paragraph, tucked away at the back of the file. And I see that he left everything to Inge and specified that if Inge died first, we, not his many nephews and nieces, would inherit.

As far as he was concerned, we were his, always. I'm beginning to hope that we are.

Speaking of inheritance, I've always disliked my name and used to ask Inge why she called me Monique. There is no way Tom would have chosen a French name. 'Be grateful I didn't call you Toots,' she always said. 'That was my first choice.' Hey Toots! That was what GIs used to shout at girls on the boulevards. She clearly thought this obfuscation very funny because she said the exact same thing to Lorie about her name, despite its obvious source. I was never 'Monique' in the family – always Monty (of mouse kingdom fame). French-hating Tom called me Mont.

On the warm July night when we met Sylvain and Cynthia at the restaurant, he mentioned his cousin Monique. My ears pricked up. She is the daughter of René's elder brother Ange, who died young of TB around the age of thirty: a charming young man whom everybody loved and missed. Monique was perhaps eleven or twelve when I was born. I now think that Inge picked this name – which Tom would have heartily disliked – to please René and honour the memory of Ange. She named me for her secret love, recreating the sunshine and joy of her French-speaking fantasy world. This perhaps also reassured René that I was his. The fact that Inge taught both of us French as babies until Tom put a stop to it reinforces this idea.

How many veiled ways did she have of talking about her lover – calling her child Monique, extolling the virtues of the Citroën DS? Did she regale Tom with stories of the glory days in Morocco? They clearly struck a chord, even if on the surface he knew nothing. Why else, after the divorce, did Tom buy that Citroën in what looks like very pointed one-upmanship? I can't believe that Tom knew about the affair with René, because I think he would have mentioned it in subsequent years. He would have discussed it with Flo, and she would have said something mean to us. He was an adulterer himself – perhaps he had his suspicions.

Again, the template of my life shifts. Every time Inge looked at Lorie, she thought of tragic Hanne Lore – but I was her constant, secret reminder of René. I was set up to be the favourite. René really did claim us, I belatedly realise. He is the one who told his mother and sister Madeleine those stories about Inge, his lifelong love; there's no other source for Sylvain's knowledge. He wanted them to understand that he always knew where Inge was and that he had fathered Lorie and me. He wanted them to know that he wasn't what he seemed to be – a man with no children in a loveless, sterile marriage. And they – disliking his wife, Renée – wholeheartedly colluded. Inge's romance had to be secret, but his was proudly worn.

I wish I'd had the chance to understand all this and to have known him better while he was alive, given how much I yearned for a father to love. But Inge had created so many myths about Tom. She built a high wall to fortify her position of moral superiority that could not be torn down without awful damage.

She and René were married for seven years until his death; they came to London, and we visited Tours. These visits had an artificial feel. René was ill and didn't talk much; ebullient Inge carried the conversational burden between her constant acts of devotion. In Tours, Inge was living in the marital flat the two Renés had shared and chose not to change things too much in case this upset René. It didn't feel like her place; I was not surprised when she moved after his death. Daily life revolved around lunch and dinner, the afternoon sleep, the ingestion of innumerable medicines at specific times. Inge shopped and cooked. It was weird to see her in this old-fashioned decor, tending the huge white cat, Blanchette – soon put on a diet by dog-loving Inge. She went on using Renée's cutlery and plates, producing multi-course lunches on the dot of noon like a good French housewife. She'd never lived that sort of life. I thought the strangeness was because I wasn't used to her living with a man; in hindsight, I see the elephant in the room.

We spent many hours and days together and never talked about these things; it must have been most peculiar for René to be with daughters who didn't acknowledge him. That's a sad thought. What on earth was going through Inge's mind as she simultaneously danced around looking after him – my king – my great love – always making sure the topic of fatherhood never arose? René couldn't speak of it if Inge didn't allow it. He adored her and took his cue from her. He was always so very kind to Lorie and me. I wonder, is it possible that René perhaps even loved us, in his own way? By the time they married, he was too tired and ill to think about anyone but himself. Like Tom, he had spent years of his life doing nothing very much. Unlike Tom, he laid claim to two daughters.

When René was dying in January 1993, Inge wouldn't let me visit. This was something she had to live through with full intensity and bear alone. Did she perhaps worry that he might want to say a final fatherly farewell? This is an upsetting thought. His funeral was bleak. We drove to the crematorium at Esvres, where Inge too would be cremated. She was frozen in a grief so profound she could barely function. She insisted that there would be no prayers, no religion, no people, nothing. A void. She and I sat in an empty room with the coffin. No music. Inge was sunk into herself, waiting in agony for the coffin to be taken away. Then we went to a room at the side and sat for hours until his ashes were brought out, still hot. She was too distraught even to light a cigarette. We scattered them in the garden of remembrance and then drove back to Tours. It was utterly dreadful.

Even as I write this, it's extraordinary to realise that my mother loved René Cocard for nearly eighty years: forty-seven years before they married and then another thirty-two years until her death. And that he truly adored her. To be half French and half German and the daughter of this generous, passionate man would suit me very well.

Inge never assumed that her beloved René would live forever. She possessed her grief alone, hugging it tight, as she had possessed her secret passion. His photos were on the dressing table, his books in the bookcase. His manicure set, embossed with the initials RC, sat beside her bed. He was everywhere and nowhere. How delicate he was at the end, so very frail. Their beautiful passion had dwindled to the tiniest wisp of smoke and white ash.

CHAPTER 12

. . . . .

Back to the Heimat

For months after that summer evening with Cynthia and Sylvain I remain obsessed, living inside my mother's life and past. Her lying enrages me so profoundly. I wake in the night as furious and upset and sad as if all this has only just happened.

But I am my mother's daughter – she isn't the only one prevaricating. Inge died not knowing that I was hotly pursuing the German citizenship she so firmly rejected. Germany's 1949 Basic Law guarantees an absolute right to citizenship to those persecuted under the Nazi regime and their descendants. Like many Brits of German and Jewish descent, I discover the existence of Article 116 laying out these rights because of Brexit. Right away, a technical legal problem arises: the child's claim goes through the father – Tom not Inge. Those born after 1953 can, however, claim through the mother. I am too old by two years. This is outrageous. Even setting aside the murder of my grandfather and his relatives in the camps, I speak German fluently. I have lived in Hamburg, written novels about Germans. My love of order is such that I am regularly chastised by my husband for attempting to organise the queue in Tesco. As a proud Brit (which I also and forever am), I feel this rejection by the Heimat deeply. It is the tiniest taste of Inge's trauma.

The charming women running the Legal and Consular section at the Embassy do their utmost to help. They feel the unfairness of these rules. Angela Grossman tells me that a foreigner living abroad like me can take a different route and apply for discretionary naturalisation if she speaks reasonable German, has strong ties to Germany and can prove her naturalisation serves the public interest. Far from sure about the latter, I nevertheless set about gathering papers and strengthening my case.

As I don't have a death certificate for my grandfather, I email the archive in Mülheim an der Ruhr to ask whether they have one for Arthur Rosenbaum. Archivist Annett Fercho replies instantly. To my astonishment, she has been looking for Inge and for us, the Rosenbaum grandchildren. Just two weeks earlier, the town set two commemorative brass plaques called *Stolpersteine* – the word means 'stumble stones' – for my grandparents at Eppinghofer Straße 134. This is the down-at-heel street where Tilly and Inge fetched up in one room in 1939. It was from this wretched place that Inge was sent away to Morocco; from here that Tilly and Arthur left at night to walk over the border.

I am sent a photo of two brass plaques, each the size of cobblestones, set in the pavement side by side:

'Here lived Arthur Rosenbaum born 1892. Resistant/ Communist Party. Frequently arrested. Flight 1939 to Belgium. Interned in Drancy. Deported 1942. Murdered in Auschwitz'.

And:

> 'Here lived Mathilde Rosenbaum née Lindemann born
> 1899. Flight 1939 to Belgium. Survived with help'.

Annett Fercho sends biographies of Arthur and his brother Otto
(my great uncle), who also died in a concentration camp. These
documents are astonishingly detailed and tell a very sad story.

Frau Fercho explains how this came about. Under the aegis
of their wonderful history teacher, Frau von Bancels, a group of
students at the Gymnasium (high school) in Broich decided to get
involved with the nationwide Stolpersteine project. With the help
of the archive, they delved into the mass of material available. Two
students in particular, David Bakum and Angelina Mehler, wrote
the biographies. They chose the Rosenbaums because the family
story was harrowing and because there was a surviving Rosenbaum
to tell the tale, ninety-year-old Hans-Joachim Rosenbaum. Inge's
cousin! I am stunned. To possess a putative cousin in Sylvain is
already remarkable – to find a second seemed miraculous.

Hans's very survival is a miracle; he lost his father, sister and brother-in-law to the death camps; his elder brother survived but his life was destroyed. Their father, Otto Rosenbaum, had followed where his big brother Arthur led, joining the Communist Party and resisting authority. He too had an Aryan wife, Luise. They had three children, of whom Hans, the latecomer, was born in 1929; all were raised as Protestants.

Like Arthur, Otto was placed in 'protective custody' as soon as the Nazis came to power. Incarcerated in numerous prisons and camps, he ended in Gross-Rosen Camp, formerly part of Germany, now Rogoźnica, Poland. His name was on the list of prisoners due to be transferred to the 'Euthanasia Institute Bernburg' when in March 1942 he died during the night. The village of Rogoźnica now has a population of 856; during the war, 40,000 prisoners perished here.

Otto's middle child, twenty-one-year-old Edith, married with a baby, also suffered a terrible fate. As an eighteen-year-old with an Aryan boyfriend, she had been prosecuted for the so-called crime of 'race defilement'. Determined to emigrate, she was living in a camp near Bielefeld, where she met her husband. Both were working for Siemens in Berlin when the Wannsee Conference took place in 1942, sealing the fate of the Jews. Soon after, they were rounded up and deported to Auschwitz. The Gestapo also took the Jewish nanny. Neighbours who heard little Judith crying broke in and discovered her alone in the flat. Fortunately, there was an address on the table. The two-year-old was rescued by her grandmother, who rushed to Berlin and brought her back to Mülheim an der Ruhr. It was the story of little Judith that so touched the Broich Gymnasium students.

The archive gives me a number and I telephone Hans-Joachim in Mülheim an der Ruhr. An astute and with-it ninety-year-old, he remembers my mother, his first cousin, very well from early childhood. He tells me that they met up a few times when he was in London for work, but then she disappeared. He subsequently looked for her in vain. I tell him about her life in France and her French second husband; there is no need to dwell on quite how firmly she exorcised her German past. Later in the year I will go to Mülheim to meet him and see for myself where we come from.

You knock and a door opens. I found my (assumed) English grandfather by chance in the battlefields of Ypres. And now I've stumbled on my German grandfather. The Stolpersteine record the last places where victims – Jews, communists, Roma, gays or disabled – lived before being deported. The project originated with Gunter Demnig, an artist based in Cologne, who fixed thirty-one plaques to Berlin's pavements illegally. The idea took off. Over seventy-five thousand brass plaques have now been hammered into the pavements of more than twenty European countries. It is comforting to think that the past cannot be forgotten when the very stones speak to honour the dead.

Thanks to the archive in Mülheim an der Ruhr and to impressive German bureaucracy, I will discover far more than Inge ever knew about her difficult and stubborn father. The local Gestapo knew Arthur Rosenbaum extremely well; their files (which I later receive from the Nordrhein-Westfalen archive) run to over 560 pages. In January 1939 he was in 'protective custody' in Dachau, having been arrested shortly after Kristallnacht the previous November. Tilly obtained his release on the grounds that he had been a Frontkämpfer, a 'front combatant' in the First World War. The Gestapo let him go out the understanding that the Rosenbaums would emigrate. Arthur never actually lived in

Eppinghofer Straße. Fearful of being arrested, he stayed underground. A few months later, Inge left for Morocco.

The Gestapo fully expected the 'Rosenbaum couple' to follow. But Arthur didn't want to leave Germany. Despite persecution, despite years of imprisonment, he clung to his Heimat and worked against fascism until he was driven out. Heimat for a German is the place you come from and where you belong forever. The landscape and country built into your bones and blood both cradle and shelter you. The Heimat is the smell of the coffee, the texture of the bread, the jokes that don't work in another language; it remains forever part of you, even if you have been rejected.

This is why, after the divorce, Inge seriously considered a return to Germany. She thought about emigrating to Australia or New Zealand but knew nobody there. So in 1960 she went back to Germany to stay with her childhood friend Willy Zimbehl and his wife, Liesel. He was the kind man who adored Tilly, who'd given little Inge chocolates and told her he was her friend. Before the war, he'd been a trade unionist. Afterwards, somewhat mysteriously, he was Krupp's Labour Director with an industrial town, Zimbehlstadt, named after him. Married to red-headed Liesel, with one son, Jochen, the family's showpiece ultra-modern house behind electric gates on a lake in Rheinhausen is actually a private estate with beautiful gardens and its own island. A little stream runs through the indoor-outdoor eponymous 'chimney room', shining with polished copper. Photos show thirty-four-year-old Inge looking young and thin and anxious in her cute black-and-white-striped skirt with a cherry pattern and neat bolero. Dressed to kill, she is nervously sussing the place out.

When she visited Mülheim an der Ruhr, the old fear and revulsion came surging back. She later told us that she threw up

A nervous Inge in Rheinhausen at the Zimbehls' modern house in 1960

in the street outside the school where the teacher had victimised her. In her account of her life, she would write how strange the visit was, the place simultaneously familiar and alien.

On these visits to Germany, Tilly reconnected cautiously with her family, the Lindemanns, who had turned their backs on her as persecution of the Jews intensified. Inge was initially charmed by Tilly's second brother, Otto, an uncle with a selective memory; he loved telling rose-tinted stories about how he used to look after little Inge. But on one visit Otto reminisced about Hanne Lore, always everyone's favourite, drunkenly proclaiming that 'the wrong one died'. Outraged, Inge walked out, dragging her mother with her. Chaos ensued, and Inge could not be placated. She refused ever to see that uncle again. When eventually news came of his death, she said that *for me he died long ago*.

When Inge took us to Germany, we never went near the Lindemanns. We sat in the back of the Zimbehls' vast Mercedes driving down to Lake Titisee in the Black Forest, roaring past innumerable similar cars on the Autobahn. Germany was a country of smooth roads, new houses and well-tended gardens. The ancient forest was magical, with pure clear water, sunshine and birdsong. We slept in a tent, the Zimbehls in a caravan. German holidays were about being close to nature, fresh air and cold clean lake water. Jochen brought a friend and we wandered through the forest for hours on sun-dappled tracks, soft, thick cushions of pine needles underfoot. Sometimes we sang old German marching songs: 'This is how the farmer walks through the mud-mud-mud!' Walking and singing were baked in, like salt grains on crunchy pretzels and sugar on succulent Streuselkuchen. We carried baskets and Liesel Zimbehl foraged for mushrooms, showing us the bad ones to avoid. Liesel was very kind, always joking that Willy had married her as second best after Tilly.

Inge made us stop taking sugar in the milky tea we drank in huge mugs, because it would ruin our teeth. A painfully shy child, I was made to go to the camp shop on my own and buy things using new words. Self-improvement was in the air. When we returned a few years later, we acquired dirndls – mine was red and blue with a white apron printed with fine blue patterned lines. Lorie's was green to match her eyes, with a black apron, and we both had a sexy little white bodice with a drawstring. I still have my apron, made of the sort of crisp linen that lasts forever. Fetching though we undoubtedly were with our near-perfect teeth and little white blouses, we never became proper German girls. Germany was for holidays – not a place to settle.

We were able to settle in Sydenham thanks to the money the German state paid for the persecution of its Jews. The German government enacted three separate federal compensation laws, in 1953, 1956 and 1965, called the BEG (BundesEntschädigungsGesetz). The Germans used the word 'Wiedergutmachung' to describe this (literally meaning: 'making good again'), which was of course impossible. The dead would not rise. Still, these laws had considerable consequences for us and many others. The stinginess of the BEG was well known in the 50s; the proceedings were slow, the methods stony-hearted, payment of any sort of reparations was unpopular inside Germany. But – all credit to them – payments were made.

Writing from Morocco between 1954 and 1962, Tilly claimed compensation in categories ranging from 'Damage to Freedom' to the Orwellian category of 'Damage to Life'. Her lengthy correspondence with the Mülheim Restitution Office and subsequently with the Düsseldorf District Court survives on tissue-thin yellowing airmail paper; Heinz, a good typist, made carbon copies. He had been the director of a large ladies' hat factory in Berlin with a salary of 1,000RM per month (well over £100,000 per annum today) and was claiming for 'Damage to Professional Advancement through Persecution'.

When in February 1955 Tilly returned to Germany for the first time in sixteen years, the Restitution Office asked her to supply a death certificate for Arthur Rosenbaum – the very document I still lack. She wrote to the Allied High Commission for Germany International Tracing Service at Arolsen asking them to confirm the date of death of 7 September 1942 they had logged for Arthur Rosenbaum, and they did. More months passed, and nothing happened.

As Tilly sent birth and wedding certificates, lists and descriptions of furniture and objects, back came more forms and requests for further and better detail. At various points in this process, the authorities demanded that she withdraw her claims as lacking sufficient proof. Tilly persisted and carried on pointing out their errors.

In 1957, a first ruling came on 'Damage to Freedom'. The restitution authority added up all the time Arthur had spent in prison between 1933 and 1938: three years, nine months and twenty-five days, to be precise (and they are always precise). BEG rules allocated 150 DM for each full month (or thirty days) of imprisonment and, as it helpfully pointed out, this sum could be inherited by the widow and children (some damages couldn't). For the 'damage to freedom' of Arthur Rosenbaum, Tilly would receive 46 x 150 = 6,900DM.

'Compensation for Damage to Professional Advancement through Persecution' mingled bureaucracy with some interesting calculations. The court added the period of imprisonment from 15 May 1940 (Germans march into Belgium, Arthur is summarily rounded up and deported) to 7 September 1942 (Drancy to Auschwitz deportation date). That made five years and one month for which compensation was due. They estimated his work as a former coal merchant and independent bread driver to be the equivalent of that of a civil servant in group 2 of the middle salary table. This enabled them to work out what compensation would have been awarded, had said civil servant missed five years and one month of pension provision.

But the BEG dealt in lump sums, not pensions. Their final calculation (taking into account a 20 per cent surcharge for each of the missing years of pension provision in old age) multiplied the figure of 3,600 Reichsmark by five and one-twelfth (let's not forget that extra month) and so they arrive at 18,300RM. At this point in the calculations, I'm totally lost. Where does the figure of 3,600RM come from? I think (but cannot be sure) that that was a forty-year-old pen-pusher's annual salary in 1933. Or perhaps in 1942. Converted to DM at the ratio of 10:2, this comes out at 3,660DM.

Throughout 1957 and 1958, Tilly sent descriptions of her dark oak bedroom furniture and leather chairs, the Adler sewing machine and washing machine, the twelve-piece porcelain set and everything else she had lost. She detailed shop fittings: the Krupp till, glass counters, Berkel scales and three-wheeled delivery van. The authorities demanded to know how much each item cost and what she had received from their sale and here, unusually for her, a touch of annoyance enters the correspondence.

'I can't tell you what things cost,' she wrote. 'My husband Arthur bought them at a time of high inflation, he was gassed in

Theresienstadt.' (It was in fact Auschwitz.) 'Nor do I remember what we received because we had to sell in a hurry for ridiculous prices.' The BEG, slowly grinding through its process, did not take account of such factors. Everything had to be proved.

At one point, Tilly wrote desiring the court to ask Herr Kolk, 'the ex Gestapo chief in Oberhausen now residing in Kettwig/Ruhr', to confirm that he personally ordered her to leave Germany if she didn't divorce the Jew. This is the man who presided over years of persecution; if Tilly in Morocco knew where Herr Kolk now lived, surely everybody in Mülheim did. But there is no further mention of him. I have no doubt that the Düsseldorf court also knew Herr Kolk; they had access to all the Gestapo files. Perhaps they had a nice chat.

A decision on 'Damage to Property' came on 18 March 1959. In the absence of receipts, prices for items bought between 1922 and 1930 were estimated. These estimates were reduced by 3 per cent per annum for depreciation plus 25 per cent for wear and tear. As a married couple owned their furniture and belongings equally, the final sum of 2,600RM was divided in two. At the very end, Reichsmarks were converted to Deutschmarks at the usual rate. The sum of 5 per cent was then added, in accordance with the generous spirit of §56 of BEG law 2. In this way, by a thousand cuts, compensation for all Tilly's personal belongings came to 273DM. A rather higher rate of depreciation of 10 per cent per annum was applied to the shop fittings and delivery van, which Tilly owned outright. The total for the flat and shop added up to 568.31DM – £50 at the 1959 exchange rate of 11.74DM to £1. This would not quite have bought Inge that mythical washing machine; the Servis Mark 17 cost £59 10s in 1958.

The calculation of 'Damage to Life' came on a pre-printed letter from the State Pension Authority of Nordrhein-Westfalen with numbers filled in by hand, stapled to a buff-coloured ancillary page with handwritten calculations working out the pension a civil servant in middle group (2) would have received if the state hadn't happened to gas him. On the basis of Unfallruhegehalt (a kindly portmanteau word meaning taking retirement because of an accident), they calculate an entitlement of 238.91DM per month, of which a widow would receive 60 per cent. But the calculation has to be based on the 'retirement period'. This presumably means the number of years worked. Tricky, given that my grandfather was murdered aged fifty, but the number crunchers had their ways and means. The pensionable period is stated as being between 1 June 1945 (end of the war generic-death date – not the real 1942 date of the previous calculation) and 31 July 1947. Why 1942? Why 1947? I don't know. Arthur would have been fifty-five that year; was that the statutory retirement age for (non-gassed) middle group (2)?

There hadn't been much pensionable activity in Inge's young life, but she made a claim for her lost education. On 9 April 1957, a year and a half before the divorce, she deposed her sad little document at the German Consulate in Liverpool. I reread the blurred carbon copy. She describes her wartime hardships and explains that she received no education after the age of thirteen. Her claim was merged with that of her mother.

Tilly won compensation in every category, barring that of health. Sent to see the wonderfully named Dr W. Spickernagel in Lima, this gentleman decided that her ailments, ranging from 'arthrosis and spondylarthrosis, duodenal diverticula, vegetative dystonia with spastic colitis to neurotic symptoms' were caused by normal wear and tear and 'old age'. She was sixty-three. Tilly eventually received a total of 18,926DM, then worth £1,612. Heinz, who had to employ a lawyer to track down former employees in Berlin, received 40,000DM in compensation for his career. Between them, the total came to £5,000. This did not compensate for intense persecution, the murder of a husband, loss of all belongings and ejection from the Heimat. On the other hand, it did enable Tilly and Heinz to give Inge half of their joint restitution, £2,500, for that newly built two-bedroom Wates flat.

In Sydenham, I grew to love all things German. Given that Inge's Heimat is all misery, persecution and penny-pinching bureaucracy, it is curious that I hold such a romantic view of her lost paradise. My childhood fascination with Jews soon translated from books to people. I did my absolute utmost to befriend the only Jewish girl in my year at Sydenham High and she put up with me with very good grace. Her elder brother would become my first serious boyfriend.

After school came that gap year in Hamburg. My new Heimat was revelation and liberation. The gap year, which had opened off-puttingly in an empty house, turned into a glorious and rather wild adventure. Nineteen-seventies' Hamburg in the era of Baader-Meinhof was very exciting for an eighteen-year-old bent on discovering life; the Che Guevara types at the university, themselves bent on revolutionary change, were a decade older and most willing to assist. I went everywhere, explored the Reeperbahn and nightlife, wandered up and down streets named Große Freiheit and Kleine Freiheit (Large and Small Freedom) where the prostitutes displayed their wares in shop windows. I sang with the Hare Krishna tribe, who provided delicious vegetarian food for free if you stayed to the end of their chanting sessions, stayed up all night and gathered armfuls of tulips in the early morning flower market.

I also got up to less fragrant adventures, some of which I was too naive to realise were insanely dangerous. One of the people I hung around with used to tell me he was a spy for the Stasi in East Germany; at the time I thought him a fantasist. Now I believe him. There were 40,000 spies embedded in West Germany and he was a weak character with a dark side. Once, he tried to get me to help him break into a very grand house near the Alster because there was something 'he needed to get'. This episode did not appear in my countless letters home. I had the good sense to refuse and soon he disappeared from my life. There was much talk among student radicals about shocking the bourgeoisie and taking violent Aktion; I listened and nodded and forbore to mention my pampered life as an au pair in the affluent suburb of Blankenese.

I was living in a mansion; a beautiful home with deeply cultured and charming people, a Steinway grand piano in the music room and an atmosphere of wit, tolerance and joy. I acquired wonderful substitute parents and dear brothers in my Hamburg family. The parents loved each other madly, providing a charming and novel picture of what married love and a happy family looked like. They went to every play and opera and were kind enough to take me with them; we would study the libretto before outings to the new State Opera auditorium, where Rolf Liebermann was the resident god. I grew deeply to love the adorable mother in particular and this upset mine no end. Later, I would try to underplay this lifelong relationship to minimise the pain. Inge often mentioned that she wasn't jealous at all; code for the reverse. Infuriatingly, I used to congratulate her on this marvellous self-control.

I had stepped into a new world and become a different person, just as my mother had at that age. When, in the summer of 1970, I headed off to a childcare job in the South of France, I felt myself to be a true woman of the world. I was confident, pretty much trilingual and ready for university. In Germany and France, I found those parts of myself that I liked most, and there I felt truly alive.

This was quite a trial to Inge, who had sent me away to grow up and mature but didn't care for the result. She was particularly vexed on the beach at Théoule-Miramar (not far from Cannes) where I was more interested in flirting than making tea for my mother, the arrival of her Triumph Herald with the camping stove a major embarrassment.

The German odyssey Inge set in train had consequences beyond acquiring savoir faire. Becoming Jewish some seven years later was far and away the worst thing I ever did to her. For some years her refrain was that Alex would never marry me because I wasn't Jewish. She had nothing against him personally, she said; wasn't it a pity, mind, that my youth was passing, and I was wasting my life. I was twenty-five.

Alex and I met in Bristol when he wandered into the kitchen of the house in Goldney Road I shared with seven other girl students and devoured a huge bowl of tomato salad I had made. What excellent taste he had! Or was it simply that he couldn't tear himself away? The salad orgy wasn't why I fell for him so massively and instantly, but it helped. It would transpire that he had acquired a tapeworm during his global gap year travels.

My husband was born in India, where his Polish Jewish parents met after the war. We had no idea that so much history connected us, but children of survivors are often drawn to each other without knowing why. When I told Inge that I was converting to Judaism and we were getting married, she took me away for a week-long holiday in Sables d'Olonne. Cold Atlantic breakers rolled in as we took long walks along the sands, expressing our feelings. That didn't go well. 'As far as I'm concerned, you are walking into the gas oven of your own free will,' said Inge flatly. She tried desperately to persuade me out of it. Though my relationship with her depended upon my being a good obedient girl, I was obdurate. Madly in love, I wouldn't listen to her. That trip was in 1976, after she and René had broken up. She was heartsick and crazy for love herself, but we didn't talk about that. The stages of our life had some eerie similarities. And here I am writing my life story at just the age when she wrote hers. Was I – the supposed favourite – in fact always her stumbling stone (or Stolperstein)?

On our wedding morning, my mother sewed me into my dress – it was an evening gown and daringly open down the front – herself wearing a singularly ugly dress in brown. She's never worn brown since. The nearest she dared get to black, it must have been a form of mourning. It was the first time she had ever set foot in a synagogue. She, my grandmother Tilly, Lorie and her three children came to the wedding. Alex and I invited friends, though nothing like as many as my mother-in-law. My new father-in-law, Simon, was desperately ill with pancreatic cancer and this was a last opportunity for him and my mother-in-law, Hanna, to meet friends in celebration and farewell; he died two weeks later.

As part of our service, I had asked our lovely rabbi, Hugo Gryn, to say a kaddish (the traditional prayer for the dead) for Inge's father, Arthur. This gesture reduced her to a frenzy of tears; how stupid of me to have seen it as a delightful surprise. I had somehow imagined that this would help her to connect. But Inge could not possibly enter into the spirit of this gesture; a person can't align herself with a group she doesn't want to belong to. At the reception, generous Auntie Myra – so often a conduit to Inge's inner feelings – presented us with her gift, a pair of aluminium spaghetti tongs roughly wrapped in tissue paper. 'This is the most useful item in my kitchen,' she said insouciantly. They looked as if she'd grabbed them from a drawer on her way out. But she was right, and I have them still.

The Judaism I adopted was modern and evolved but still alien to Inge. All her experiences of her father's religion and home town were negative. The descent of the Rosenbaums is easy to track through the town's directories from 1900 to 1940, which Lorie obtained in the archive years back. The address book for Mülheim and surrounding area lists residents alphabetically, giving address and occupation. As early as 1910, our great-grandfather Salomon Rosenbaum (dealer in coal, bottled beer and mineral water), living in his big house at Josefstraße 37, had a telephone (number 812). The E beside his name stands for Eigentum (possession), meaning that a house belongs to the named individual.

Firms and individual traders are listed by name and additionally by profession alphabetically (coal merchant, conserves, corsets). The street directory portion of the book does as its name suggests, setting out house numbers on both the even and odd sides of the street, with lines to indicate where adjoining streets cross. Each house number lists inhabitants and their professions, adding that E where appropriate. There was no hiding in this orderly society, which put great emphasis on knowing who people were, and where to find them.

In 1920, Salomon Rosenbaum's widow is still living in the big house at Josefstraße 37 with her second son, Otto, and two other individuals. By 1927, the era of high inflation, six individuals (or households) share the house. In 1929, Arthur is a bread driver living in Cheruskerstraße 43 and by 1933 he is living at Schreinerstraße 6 – the nice flat that Inge loved. By 1936, things are going downhill. Arthur is listed at Sandstraße 71, living above the bakery; Mathilde (Tilly) appears as proprietor and Arthur as driver. By 1938, Arthur was in prison and Tilly forced to move to a single room in Eppinghofer Straße, but the address book places both in the Sandstraße, with Tilly as proprietor of the business.

These directories were not official but (rather like the Yellow Pages) compiled from registers of inhabitants by independent printing companies; they cannot be precise as it took time for these companies to catch up with changes of address. Nevertheless, by cross-referencing names with the street directory, the downwards trajectory of the Jews, including that of the Rosenbaums, is clear. By 1940, both Tilly and Arthur are gone; Otto (then in Sachsenhausen camp) is listed as living in the wretched Hindenburgstraße, where the Stolpersteine for him and his son, Helmut, will be set.

Close examination of Jewish names shows them increasingly confined to certain streets in the worst part of town. After 1942, all Jewish names disappear. The story is simultaneously written large and totally hidden, just like fascism and its workings. What a dizzying descent Inge experienced, from her nice family flat and secure life to one wretched room. The safe place became dangerous; her sister died and then she was expelled.

When the homeland in which you are secure rejects and ejects you, something very complex and alienating happens. Germany was a rough teacher and some of that brutishness echoed on down the decades: *The wrong one died*. And 'the wrong ones' did die, in their millions. You never get over something like that. When, for whatever reason, you are forced to abandon your first language, you lose a part of yourself forever. Exiled Germans all suffered, the writers particularly so. When the language in which you think and dream is rightly vilified as an enemy one, this is a second kind of death.

The only language Inge spoke perfectly (without an accent) but also imperfectly (knowing very little grammar) was German. It belonged to the self she hated and the self she did not understand. Her parents mostly spoke the local dialect, Mölmsch, and in Morocco then Brussels she learned French, the first of her exile languages. Everything must have been so distressing and confusing, a kind of permanent hollowness where the loved place used to be.

There were many contradictions in her life. She hated Germany, yet sent me there. She seriously considered returning to live in the Rhineland, but the place made her vomit. She watched me learn to love her mother tongue, yet for decades never spoke one word of German to me. She expressed herself best in English but was constantly frustrated by her lack of erudition. When years later I introduced her to the witty and muscular German of Kafka and Roth, those Jews of the Austro-Hungarian empire who wrote so beautifully, she grew to enjoy the language of her birth. But what was the language of her soul?

CHAPTER 13

. . . . .

Governed by emotions

In August 2019 we escape to the serene green hills of Umbria for the first holiday since Inge's death. In that lovely place, I calm down. For the first time, I start to think seriously about my part in this *galère*. As Inge liked to say, it takes two to tango. This isn't just about her. Is my obsessive recording of anecdotes and revisiting of ancient family stories therapy or revenge? If, each time we met, Inge projected her conflicting emotions on to me, what was I projecting on to her? Not the love and adoration she craved, but perhaps something more passive-aggressive. Maybe a two-way *sub-voce* needling was always going on. Maybe the mere sight of me evoked doubts. When I reassured her that she was a great mother, how convincing was I? Why didn't I ever tell her what I really thought? There had to be a reason why we wearisomely went on galloping round the same track. The tension in those visits to Tours came from both sides. Reliving Inge's childhood (and mine) is exhausting but I can't stop.

I am also recovering from the death of my dear mother-in-law, Hanna, three months earlier. For twenty-five years, Alex's mother lived in a flat we created for her below ours, where she felt safe and secure. She was ninety-nine; both our mothers reached extreme old age. Born in 1920 in Warsaw, Hanna escaped from the Warsaw Ghetto and was saved and sheltered by the great courage and kindness of the Kierszniewski family. In the doomed August 1944 Uprising, she went in and out of the shelters, risking her life to forage provisions for the old people and children trapped there. Rounded up by German soldiers, she and a friend were marched through the devastated burning city. Hanna escaped again from Pruszków, a transit camp outside Warsaw for the survivors of the uprising – an antechamber to the extermination camps for a Jew like her. Red Cross nurses working at Pruszków lent girls their capes and encouraged them to walk out through the gates as though heading for the hospital. For these acts of goodness and mercy, the Nazis shot fifty Red Cross nurses. Accompanied by a friend, Hanna then walked 150 kilometres through the countryside to a farm that belonged to her friend's uncle.

Fifty years later, she wrote a memoir of her life:

'That journey took us almost a month, working mostly our way on farms. Sometimes the marching took us through a forest and enchanted us with the rays of early sun filtering through the tall fir trees, the freshness of the scent exhilarating. We walked there unafraid and feeling free and almost happy. We were like the birds let out of a cage and in these moments forgot about the war. Our shoes gave away and we walked barefoot until someone took pity on us and gave each of us a pair of shoes, not too comfortable either.

'But we learned many things which stayed with us for life. We learned about courage and hope, we practically lived on it. We realised how much more one is capable of enduring than one thinks one is. Also how one clings to unnecessary possessions, when without them you are mobile and it's easy to deal with life's changes. We found out how important money can be when you are short of it, but equally it is not everything, while human relationships are. How wonderful it is when you can be truthful, but how, regretfully, one has to deviate from it when in a dangerous situation. Last but not least, how beautiful is the countryside, and how rewarding friendship can be even in difficult circumstances.'

Hanna lost her entire family in Treblinka, bar one sister who escaped to India. In Bombay to visit her, Hanna met Alex's father, Simon (born in the village of Zółkiew), who had fled the Nazis through Russia via Japan and Burma just before Pearl Harbor and got to safety in India. His life, like that of Hanna's sister, was saved by the fictitious visa given to him by Dutch industrialist turned consul Jan Zwartendijk and the transit visa he was given by Japanese consul Chiune Sugihara in Vilnius, Lithuania. Inventive and brave, these noble men saved the lives of many Jews fleeing east. Zwartendijk is estimated to have saved between 1,200 and 1,400 lives and Sugihara 6,000.

Secure in her Jewish identity and always an optimist, my mother-in-law was joyful in spite of – or perhaps because of – all she had survived. This great lady had experienced so much and her death from extreme old age was very beautiful. She breathed her last peacefully in her own bed, surrounded by her family, with her son holding her hand. Do we die as we live? Everything about Inge's death had been extreme; Hanna's was the reverse. With double grief came the trials of double probate.

In Italy, I begin to reflect about our dual heritage of grief and survival and what it means for us and for our children. Sitting among the olive trees, it comes to me that despite my supremely happy life of writing, a wonderful marriage and the great joy of my children, anxiety is always thrumming away somewhere deep. I was a sunny child, but my childhood taught me that the world was not safe. I knew something awful lay underneath. The mind uses many tricks to conceal what it knows, but the body holds ancestral memories and fears that destabilise. Are these things temperament, character, choice, inherited trauma? It's hard to untangle. I long ago overcame childish delicacy and shyness. I hide my anxiety well. We build our carapaces, and we protect ourselves. But, however well concealed, anxiety remains.

Writer Eva Hoffman says that the children of Holocaust survivors carry 'a supercondensed pellet of primal information' taking on despondency, panic and the impossible duty of rescuing their parents. She describes the homes of survivors who (like her) were told nothing as being full of secrets and silence, withdrawal – or suffocating over-attention – great anxiety and unresolved pain. The second generation feels so much without knowing why. We felt but could not understand our involvement in an event we had never experienced. And we two sisters in that tense Sydenham flat dominated by a migraine-afflicted mother were not unique.

As Hoffman explains, 'whereas adults who live through violence and atrocity can understand what happens to them as actuality – no matter how awful its terms – the generation after receives its first knowledge of the terrible events with only childish instruments of perception, and as a kind of fable.'

Eva Hoffman is a Pole who emigrated to Canada at the age of thirteen, and in her memoir, *Lost in Translation*, and a subsequent meditation on the aftermath of the Holocaust, *After Such Knowledge*, she writes brilliantly about the dual legacy of immigrants and second-generation survivors. The very notion of being part of a 'second generation' is something she came to with 'a slight recoil of displeasure' at being a sociological phenomenon – yet she describes also feeling 'a surge of recognition, curiosity, even excitement' at the commonality with others (all quotations from *After Such Knowledge*). I entirely understand this.

Like her, I didn't think of myself as being part of that second generation until much later in life; and, like her, I wanted that commonality. I tried hard to find other second-generation Jews in our part of South London, and later of course I found Alex. My over-involvement with Inge's past propelled me in a positive way towards Judaism, and to remaking my identity. Loving my German grandparents and the language, I never hated Germans as some did – though I remain capable of the occasional rant.

Children react in many complex ways to their persecuted parents, whose victimhood does not guarantee saintly behaviour. As Eva Hoffman writes, 'Even those greatly sinned against are capable of greatly sinning.' Looking back, I see that as a child I was always trying to remove my mother's pain and make her safe by providing comfort and love. The task was impossible, the burden of guilt long lasting. No wonder I find it so hard to accept guilt –

whenever I am blamed for anything, my snap reaction is always to blame others. I'm not proud of this. For all its sadness, Inge's life fuelled creativity in both Lorie and me. My mother's complexities stimulated my writing and for this I am forever grateful.

Inge could never unpack the death of Hanne Lore, the Holocaust, the deaths of her father, uncle, aunt and cousins in the camps. She was too preoccupied with the first-level problems of being a foreigner, a single mother and a second-class citizen. Hoffman, who writes so well, evokes what it means to inhabit a language and society in which you are not yourself but function, involuntarily, as an amateur anthropologist, gradually accruing sense from what you see and hear. As you absorb the things that people embedded in their culture take for granted, you first unmake and then remake yourself. Even for someone as self-aware as Hoffman, a woman of dazzling intellect, this was not easy.

How impossibly hard then for Inge, who had no education to speak of, yet remade herself in Brussels, then England, and finally in France. What might she have achieved, if she'd had a proper education harnessing and refining her native intelligence, energy and industriousness? I can only wonder what sort of woman she would have been if she'd been happily rooted in a Jewish or German identity – an impossibility obviously, given her background. In the last decades of her life, she reinvented herself as bookish English Inge, teaching and reading and even for a time studying with the Open University. But she never overcame deep feelings of inferiority at her lack of education and at who she unavoidably was: the refugee, the Mischling. I don't think child refugees ever get over the horror of being ousted from their homes, their safety, their language. But there are ways to manage and deal with trauma; Inge never tried any of them.

We now know that early traumas such as severe illness, disability, divorce, bereavement, sexual and other abuse, known as Adverse Childhood Experience (ACE), cause physiological and neurological distortions that affect adult life, mental health and memory. Such experiences affect how the brain develops and the way the body reacts to stress. Adverse experiences also put children at risk of cancer, liver disease, substance abuse and depression in later life. Inge's ACE score is at least 6; adults with a score of 4 or more points are at serious risk with an 80 per cent increased risk of premature death compared to those with none. What strength she possessed to survive to the age of ninety-two.

Inge was affected in many ways, all of which she felt deeply, none of which she understood rationally. She became the victim, not the agent, of emotions she was unable to control. Her self-help recipe was quite a cocktail. Avoid and deny. Swerve and suppress. Her continual swerving from one topic to another wasn't exactly willed. Her mind – that pained and elaborate construct of contrary notions, emotions, confusions, thoughts darting every-where and never reaching a conclusion – was fragile and needed constant propping up.

When you can't stand being German, be English. Create a moment – bring on the champagne. La la la! Madame la Marquise sang and laughed through pain. She pretended the bad thing wasn't happening. She was a party girl who wanted to have fun and be loved.

Underneath lay terrible pain and doubt, but the exterior she'd constructed carried her through the day, every day. Alone within that maelstrom of emotions, Inge remained in some respects forever a child with no way to trust adults and no way to control what she felt.

A huge amount of work has been done in mental health to help people 'mentalise' and define their emotions, thus mastering and redefining themselves. With such help, Inge could have been an entirely different and I think happier person, a woman understanding rather than *governed by emotions*. But she would have died rather than ask for it.

This interior struggle also gave her incredible rigidity. She'd evolved her own set of rules on what was right or wrong, what she could or could not do. She thought that changing your mind was very bad for children and so she stuck to her last, even when she came to regret decisions that had been rather cruel. She knew that she had made some terrible mistakes. The theme of regret circled and circled, perhaps because I forced it on her in those afternoon discussions in Tours when we were supposedly talking about Tilly and her bitterness surged up anew. I tried to make her see that in every relationship there were always two points of view. And this prompted her fear: 'Was I a bad mother?' In her old age, she kept asking this. I always reassured her how brilliant she was because I couldn't face the fallout if I didn't; perhaps that was my way of keeping control over her.

She was tough on herself too. When it rained, this tiny person took her wheelchair down to the garage, pushing open doors so heavy I could barely shift them. Then for an hour she would walk to take her daily exercise. One day she decided to read all the labels on the pills she took and discovered that she was on antidepressants. Her doctor had put her on them nineteen years earlier after René died, when she could not deal with her unassuageable grief. Furious and outraged, she resolved to taper off the drugs. And within weeks she had weaned herself off them. She either simply refused to let the side effects happen or pretended they weren't happening.

By the end of her life, Inge was on a cocktail of medications: heart stuff, the puffer for her shallow breathing – innumerable strong painkillers and so on. 'Good news, darling! My lung capacity is now 51 per cent!' Her voice rang out joyfully. The lung doctor had got her to breathe into his instrument several times – it was arduous, but she'd managed it. She'd gained 1 per cent more lung capacity over the previous year and claimed this as a triumph. That's what a lifetime of smoking does for you – seventy-six years from that first fag with Nina in the air-raid shelter in Brussels. She kept going on willpower and a refusal to give in, invigorated with a hot seasoning of rage. All credit to her for that. I admire her resolve and her absolute refusal to let anything get her down.

I have another moment of epiphany during that Italian holiday. While talking to my daughter, Sophie, about Inge, I wonder how tough I actually am on myself. One dark circling thought is the notion that I too have been hiding in plain sight all my life. In my work, I am always showing off about my languages and trying to impress. When I wrote my novelistic version of Inge's war, I created my own straitjacket by insisting on using only wartime histories and contemporaneous diaries. I sought out personal and unmediated accounts of civilian life in Germany and France and went to extraordinary lengths to verify every detail, from the weather on a certain day to the exact names of streets, shops and cafes. I spent days poring over old photographs. It was a novel, not a PhD; it was set in France and not Belgium, so who cared? On top of this giant pyramid of factual research (most of which I then submerged) balanced my story of a sensitive young girl growing up alone in exile. My Ilse wasn't Inge, though she shared some of her experiences, and I deliberately sent her on a different path to my mother's.

Was this to justify the appropriation of my mother's story? I'm a research fiend; it was incredibly important to me to get it right and I couldn't set about it in any other way. But I wonder if it was a sort of smokescreen of the kind I like to create, mostly bamboozling myself. In a book, emotional truth and intelligence are what the reader cares about, and they rise from the interior not the exterior.

I give my sister the first six chapters of this book to read and discover more about my so-called facts, and how sometimes the things you are most certain about are the least true. The details are small but telling. The rockery at our council house, number 15 Boswell Road, was built with the help of local men including our father, not abandoned plucky Inge labouring alone. Tom remained with Inge for longer than I thought. He was still living with us when he announced the divorce outside the library in Borough Road. My vivid recollection of him visiting and taking us out to deliver the bad news and then having to deal with two sobbing children at the bus stop was imagined.

I've forgotten the time when the four of us (five with Hetty) lived in Boswell Road. I was probably five when he left. How much more self-serving (and dramatic) to create that vision of the three-year-old aghast at the top of the stairs with all that screaming going on as my only memory of living with my father. Something like that may have happened, but that's not the point. Every encounter with him was refracted through the dark lens of Inge's suffering and my highly selective memory; no wonder my father and I never connected.

CHAPTER 14

· · · · ·

Charlie's wars

Two days after we return home from Italy, a letter brings War Office records I requested months earlier. Time to revisit the story of my possible father, the cruel abandoner. These records confirm all Inge's tales of his inglorious antics, promotions and demotions; his not turning up for parades, his regularly going absent without leave, forfeiting pay and being given up to fourteen days' detention. I admire his bolshiness.

In 1942 he was posted to 30 Corps: Signals and sent off to the desert war with the Eighth Army, arriving in Egypt on 5 July 1942 with the 8th Armoured Division Signals. He must have been part of the Second Battle of El Alamein, a protracted, bloody and messy affair in intolerable heat, the victory against Axis forces achieved at the cost of enormous casualties. I know that he absolutely hated General Montgomery. But he found the desert amazing; he told Lorie that once it had rained and left a sea of flowers, and that he had enjoyed watching a dung beetle working very hard.

Tom moved from the Mediterranean Expeditionary Force to another theatre of war with British North Africa Force (their area was Algiers to Tunis). In November 1943, after more of the usual failures to appear on parade, he was sent from Sousse in Tunisia to Home Forces and back to the UK. In February 1944, after more misdemeanours ('forfeits one day's pay for AWOL 15 hours 46 minutes'), he received the Africa Star, a new medal awarded to those who had served in the winning fight in North Africa. Inge said he drank his way through Italy, but I didn't find these joys in the record. In June he was sent to north-west Europe, first to northern France and then on to liberate Brussels and our mother. When the signals division moved on, he was reluctant to. He must have been completely mad about her.

Inge also said that he went AWOL with a vanload of cigarettes to sell, driving back to Brussels while the rest of his regiment were fighting the Germans. His friend Gerry rushed all the way from the front on a motorbike to take him back before he got into trouble. There's no reason to doubt this. I read his qualification certificate as a wireless operator and his release testimonial dated 13 December 1945. Thomas Burley Charlesworth has given 'very good service'. 'Has recently been employed as a clerk and this he has done efficiently. Willing and trustworthy.' All's well that ends well, then, in war if not in love. Off he sped to Brussels, eager to claim his 'underage' nineteen-year-old bride – that is the wording on the wedding certificate. They married on 21 February 1946, a week before his thirty-fifth birthday and three weeks before his official release to the Territorial Army Reserve on 17 March.

Tom told Lorie that Inge never loved him. He thought that she had married him because she was stateless, to get a British passport. I always dismissed this as complete nonsense, a divorcé's insult. Now I believe him. By the time that conversation took place, Lorie was eighteen and he was long married to Flo, who, for all her faults, undoubtedly adored him. He had no need to justify or explain ancient history. He wasn't that sort of man anyway. Tom also told Lorie that when he and Inge split up, Heinz took him aside and said that there was no need to get a divorce – why didn't he just keep a mistress? He was appalled. This man believed in love and marriage; he married three times. He did so out of love each time. I was so wrong about him.

After Tom left to live with Flo he returned to Inge, but after a few months she threw him out (this was most unusual in those days) because 'she couldn't stand him loving a woman more than her'. Inge told me this more than once as proof of her devotion. And I bought it. But the truth is that she got rid of him. Then she made everything right with us by casting herself as the perfect abandoned wife. Never a word about René. All those frenzied nights of sewing Inge did in Boswell Road weren't some sort of displacement activity because she was broken-hearted about Tom: she was a gifted seamstress and wanted to look fabulous for her lover.

Flo and Tom married in Chester in 1959, the year after the divorce. Things went wonderfully for a while. Lorie, who stayed in their snug house in Neston on the Wirral Peninsula, remembers reading in the kitchen (which had a big wood-burning stove and one wall painted crimson – very 1960s' cool) because they were in the sitting room and always needed to be à deux. Just like René and Inge. Flo, always chic, had memorably brilliant clothes, including an amazing raffia skirt.

The illness that struck her was horrible: some kind of sarcoma of the lungs, which she chose to believe was a punishment from

God for her adultery. Tom sold off the hairdressing businesses and looked for a place where they could work and live so he could look after her. In this way he came upon the confectioners and newsagents at 109 Greenway Road, Tranmere, a business for which he was ill fitted. Flo suffered terribly. Her spine collapsed because of the treatments and the steroids, and she was put into some kind of plaster corset; no wonder she refused to be seen. She died in 1970 while I was completing my gap year adventurings in Théoule-Miramar in the South of France. Living in a hovel beside a luxury hotel, I was busy looking after a small boy abandoned by his young mother, working on my tan and flirting with hotel staff. When grey sad news of Flo's death filtered through, it felt far away. I don't remember dwelling on how my father would feel. He didn't get in touch. We weren't asked to go to the funeral and I had embarked upon my own life with all the callous egotism of the young.

Lorie tells me that Tom ran the shop with Micky, his dachshund, as his only companion. After Flo's death, he started seeing Lorie more; she used to go over on Thursdays with her firstborn, little Antony, to watch *Star Trek* on his colour TV. She says that he was fond of the baby and nice to both of them. Aged sixty-one, he died of the pneumonia he had not bothered to treat.

I track his descent through the blue Smiths News shop diary of 1972. This is a large format hardback diary with space to record daily orders and returns of magazines, as used by every confectioner and newsagent. It records his orders of *Bunty*, *Twinkle*, *Sandie*, *Judy* and *Jackie*, *Tiger*, *Valiant*, *Mandy*, *Hotspur*, *Hornet*, *Valentine*, *Mirabelle*, *Lamb Chop*, *Scorcher* and *Knockout*. He never fills in the weekly sales chart, but makes notes in the diary part, adding or subtracting *Reveille*, *Woman and Home*, *Jack and Jill* and, harbinger of changing times, *Disco 45*. There are lists of tobacco to order: Silk Cut and Guards, Rothmans and Dunhill 20s. In tiny writing in pencil: Virginia one oz. Or Virg. Half an ounce. He was half-inching his stock. One thing he and Inge always had in common was their habit. But Tom smoked roll-ups, which were even worse for you.

Punctuated through this book in his neat italic writing, always in fountain pen, are notes on his lessons with his coaches, Gene O'Brien, or Peter, and details of successful rounds. May to August 1972 is full of densely inked golfing insights with one entry *IMPORTANT NOTES*. 'I have decided to write down every detail in order to improve my game.' And off he goes: 'Rained like hell, couldn't play but at 1 o'clock had a lesson. Peter found a basic fault, I hope it's the root of all my troubles. When I think I am square to the target, my feet are wide open, therefore I swing out to in and, with irons, full-hook. When I think my stance is closed then it is square. But I have never attempted to play with a closed stance. Therefore I must always be open when I think I'm square. After adjustment I hit a lot of good shots.' These are described at length. Like me, he needs to record the important matters in his life. But he's no plutocrat, devoting his life to golf. The man is running a sweet shop from dawn to dusk, smoking a lot, lonely, eating badly. No holidays, not much money, and no future.

On 27 August, a 'slight change in method' is 'highly successful with long straight drives'. 'Relax everything and swing hard' is written in his neat slanting writing in dark-blue ink. Also: 'Stop *New Scientist*' and 'Add *Express*'. After this, his golfing life ends. No more notes about drives and swings, just orders in pale biro. The pages are lighter and emptier, as if everything is ebbing away. The last entry is on 19 December: order *Materials Reclamation,* cancel *Man and Woman.* If he couldn't play golf, or wouldn't, what was left?

Was he ill during those final months? Tom always had a bad chest and smoking can't have helped. He didn't bother to see a doctor: I don't think he wanted to die, but he was tired and overworked and heedless. He was undoubtedly depressed, but might not have thought in those terms. As always, he didn't take himself very seriously. On his death certificate, the cause of death is 'Bronchopneumonia'. My understanding is that the paper boys came first thing, and he hadn't opened up. It was 31 December 1972, an awfully sad day to die alone. The three women he employed part-time in the shop really liked him. They worked hard and made their own wages plus £7,000 – rather more than he ever did – in the year of the probate when they ran the shop without him.

His death came as a huge shock. When we drove up north, I saw how things stood. Before, he'd had nice houses; here, he lived above the shop. He'd been happy with Flo and here he lived alone. The whitewashed building was crooked and unprepossessing. It was the remnant of an ancient manor or farmhouse, apparently the oldest building in Tranmere. His flat above the shop was quite small but neatly kept with furniture and objects I remembered. I went up to the bedroom, saw the crumpled bed he died in and a solitary roll-up lying on the sheets where he had coughed himself to death. The half-drawn curtains, the unmade bed, the Rizla papers and green tin of Virginia tobacco and the musty smell imprinted themselves on me. I felt like an intruder. It was the saddest and most intimate moment we had ever shared.

Alongside upset, a bad feeling arose. His life had ended without my having known where or how he lived, without my ever understanding him. Birkenhead should have been familiar from my childhood but felt alien. Daddy had paled in importance compared to Hamburg, my student life, and my strong need to be somebody else. But he had been real and physical; the bed held the shape of his body. I remember staring at Inge's white Triumph Herald parked outside – surreal here, because for me their two worlds had always been separate – with that awful lump in your chest you get from shock and disappointment. Most of all, I was disappointed with myself.

I had never stopped hoping for something from him, despite the letters he didn't write, the allowance he wouldn't pay, the general lack of interest. Two years after we'd moved to London, no card came on my birthday. Turning thirteen – finally a teenager! – I was terribly upset. In the afternoon, a bunch of freesias was delivered. I danced round the room, ecstatic. 'You see! He didn't forget! You see!' All my life I have loved their delicacy, their strong peppery smell. Years later, Inge told me that she had phoned him up and told him I was inconsolable, and he had to do something. But I can't stop loving freesias. I always buy the first bunch I see in the spring.

Inge, Lorie and I went to the funeral. I wasn't expecting other people to be there. In fact, I'd never been to a funeral and so had no idea how it would be. Flo's sister Gladys had arranged it. The church was in Neston, where he had previously lived and run a popular salon, and because he was well liked, the churchyard was packed, with a long queue stretching from the gate right along the main road. We queued outside – Inge with her hair done and super glamorous in a big fur coat and heels – until she suddenly saw some of Tom's old friends, and hers. She fell into the arms of Lal Grierson, who had been her great buddy when they were nineteen or twenty. Everything shifted. People moved out of the way. Suddenly we, the family, were whisked through and to the front. Inge was the star of the show and revelled in the attention, waving, greeting old friends. I watched the pall-bearers carry the coffin into that traditional church, visibly having trouble. I remember thinking that he must have put on weight. It was so long since I'd seen him that I no longer had an accurate vision of him. That was painful. Were there readings – a eulogy? I don't remember them. The image of the unsteady coffin has stayed with me. That he was incredibly well liked, and the turnout so huge, did not register at the time.

Inge organised the probate because there was nobody else to do it. This was an education. She claimed arrears of maintenance of £300 plus one quarter of his estate. He had left his money – such as it was – three ways, between Flo's nephew Robert, Lorie and me. The law was changing; divorced women were going to be entitled to claim a share of their former husband's estate within a few years of probate. I remember sitting in the smart office of Walker, Smith and Way in Chester (Tom played golf with one of the partners, Don Diamond, his executor) and my mother being asked on what grounds her claim was made – and her saying well, she made a claim, and it was for them to say why she couldn't.

There was a definite froideur in their response to this. Eventually, a carefully expressed letter came from the solicitors saying that Mrs Charlesworth was claiming a quarter and we three were asked to decide if that was OK. It was. She was entitled to claim a portion of the estate, and I entirely understood that this was of great importance to her; she was also getting even. Inge received her £300 arrears of maintenance plus a quarter of what remained. She told us that she was claiming it from Flo's nephew's portion (something I could dimly see was impossible) and would divide this money with us, but she didn't.

The lawyers asked us all to make a gift to the nice women who'd run the shop (and made the money). Lorie suggested that we gave them full redundancy pay (they worked part time and were not entitled to it) and we agreed also to give something extra to Mrs Davies, who'd put in so many hours running the business over the nine months until it was sold. Without them, there'd have been very little. Tom had neglected his accounts and the charges for the accountant, solicitors and running the business came to the best part of £1,000. I put the £1,079.92 I inherited, my quarter share of what remained, towards the deposit on the little flat I bought in Christchurch Avenue, Kilburn in 1976, which cost £11,250. That was the great thing Tom did for me.

There was one further legacy.

He was sixty when he recorded his 'Random Thoughts' in a cheap lined notebook with a picture of a blue tit on the front, cost 4p. No doubt this too came from his stock. He wrote the date: 30 May 1971, five months after the death of Flo. I read it years ago and noticed only that I wasn't mentioned. That hurt, because when a man records his thoughts about his life and his wives, you imagine he'll also remember that he has two daughters.

I read it again and find a direct conduit into the mind of a rational man.

'60 years old. I don't think much about death although it plays an ever-increasing role in my life. It seems the conventional view that it is a greater tragedy to lose a wife when one is young than later in life. I don't agree. I have lost two wives through death, one at 29 (my age) and this one at 59. Attempting to leave aside the question of which one I loved the greater, I think the second one was the greater blow.

'It is hard to remember all the details of Joan's death although I have a vivid recollection of walking down Waterloo Road, Manchester, with tears streaming down my face after being told by the doctor that she would never come out of hospital, the following months before she died are confused in my mind but I remember later how grateful I was to be called up into the army within a month. There was a great feeling of loss and I remember going to a Christian Scientist church with Joe Hitchener in the wild hope of receiving a message from the other world. What a fool I am! It was a Spiritualist church, not a Christian Scientist.'

(Spiritualists try to contact the dead; Christian Scientists believe that prayer best heals disease.)

'However I don't remember feeling that my life was over, or that I could never meet anybody else. I have never been very sentimental and can't remember ever believing that there was only one person with whom one could be genuinely in love. I think that outside circumstances can influence very strongly the act of falling in love, there are times in life when one is much more vulnerable than others – for example when one is lonely, feels friend-less, or even bored. This is a different subject and one in which I am deeply interested. Shall I go on? That means abandoning my present theme before I've really got into it. No, I shall go back to the original subject and hope that I can be bothered coming back to this one on another occasion.

'To return. At 29 it is impossible to feel that life is finished but 59 is a different proposition altogether. First of all I must try to make allowances for the fact that Flo has been dead for only five months, that I am still living in the same circumstances, that maybe in another year I may be a different man. Strangely enough, for the last few weeks before her death I did not feel like this at all. She always said to me that I should marry again and this I agreed with.

'Even immediately after the shock of her death I still thought of re-marriage. When did this attitude change? I think it was, first, when I began to make an assessment of what a new wife would have to live with, and secondly, the character of Flo herself and my relations with her also what I thought of her and she of me.

'The first point. What woman could possibly blend with the life I lead? Take my normal day. Up at 5.15am. In the shop until 8.30, sleep until 9.30. Second breakfast then mess about until 1pm lunch, intending to go out but rarely doing it and then always at the last possible moment. Sleep from 2 to 4.30 then shop until 7.30, tidy up, supper finished about 8.30 then television and read, feed and walk dog, bed any time from 11.30 (rarely) to 1am (often). What a day! The interest in this routine is heightened by worrying about all the urgent things I have to do and which never get done.'

And there the diary ends: four and a bit pages. Another thing he didn't get done. What woman could possibly blend with the life he led? Late in 1971 or early in 1972, our father took our mother out to lunch at the Blossoms Hotel, Chester and asked if she would marry him. She was utterly scornful when she told me the story. I don't know how evident or enjoyable her display of scorn was at their lunch table. I understood that, for him, remarrying was a transaction, balancing what you had to offer with the services you require. Eighteen-year-old Inge in Brussels considering her 'offer' had been similarly unmoved by emotion.

Reading it again, I linger on his sorrows over two wives who died, on his 'unsentimental' belief that there isn't only one person with whom one could be genuinely in love. He is 'deeply interested' in the different ways that people fall in love, 'for example when one is lonely, feels friendless, or even bored'. Tom, never friendless, was sad and lonely when he died. The unsentimental man did have feelings.

He doesn't say anything about Inge, but perhaps he still cared for her? He told Lorie that he'd thought they might rub along nicely and be comfortable together. Both my parents were capable of great passion. I wish Tom had written something more about 'the character of Flo herself and my relations with her also what I thought of her and she of me'. I wish he had written some of his thoughts about Inge.

Micky the silky dachshund got a mention, the adored child hand-fed with steak or chicken breast. I minded terribly at the time that he didn't mention us, and I still do, but I understand him better now. He was a rational man, and we were not the subject. We were never part of his definition of self, and he would never have written in a way that was sentimental or fond. If he had doubts about our paternity, he never breathed a word of that. In his own way he was a decent man; he would not have wanted to distress us.

When Flo died, all the stuffing went out of him. This highly intelligent man was getting up at 5 a.m. on four hours' sleep, organising newspapers for the delivery boys and selling sweets to children – a man who disliked children and only wanted to read (and smoke) and play golf. All that remains of him is the blue Smiths diary, that exercise book, the little wooden tennis shield minus its racquets and Flo's jade brooch, plus some letters he sent Lorie – with whom he did have a relationship. He had been very much loved and now, with nobody to care for him, there was no point going on.

Looking back, I see that Tom is not the villain of the piece. Since Inge's death, I have learned how little I knew and understood him. He was a clever, witty, popular individual and a kind father to Lorie. I could have tried harder to know him, had Inge's emotional baggage not barred the way ('If you are not for me, you are against me'). I projected my ambition and my urgent wish to be something in the world on to him. He was perfectly happy as he was; to improve his game of golf was the limit of his aspiration, with maybe a new set of irons. And, like Inge and like all of us, he so needed to be loved.

CHAPTER 15

• • • • •

First and final journeys

We rush to France in October 2019 under the threat of a Halloween Brexit. Nine months after Inge's death, her flat in Tours is being sold. Nobody knows how Britain falling out of the EU will affect passports, or rights, or goods being transported. What if we aren't permitted to bring her things home? We order a man with a van and book the Eurostar. The SNCF is expressing its liberté by holding wildcat strikes across France and nobody can say which trains might run where or when. The journey takes twice the usual time, it rains ceaselessly and is freezing cold.

I unlock the door to Inge's flat. It still smells of smoke; the carpets and soft furnishings are impregnated with it. Silence, cold, a place frozen in time. The electric shutters roll up, revealing a mini lake brimming on the balcony where the overflow pipe is blocked. I make coffee with the Nespresso capsules Inge bought for me. Alex and I sit quietly on her old cream sofa. Each object is held in place by the power of her personality and her insistence that nothing be moved. Objects, emotions and decisions: all fixed. These ley lines are as powerful as ever.

The interior is a curious mixture of familiar objects from childhood and the unfamiliar, courtesy of René. Her books line the study. His collection of gilt and leather-bound classics lives in its own bookcase, which is never opened. His vast old-fashioned mirror is fixed to the wall of the shower room. The whole arrangement is imprinted by the hours of boredom, irritation, love and anomie spent here. In my mind I can still draw the jar of shells in her bedroom, the arrangement of family photographs, the blue Delft bowl on the coffee table, the little dish her pencils lived in – elements as fixed as the order in which she lit her lamps at dusk.

By the end of the weekend, Inge's home and possessions will be gone, whirred into the unreliable blender of memory. The issue of the square metre of corridor was solved by recruiting a surveyor to measure up. The work had been done thirty years before; nobody disputes that. I defended my mother to the death and indeed beyond, insisting on her probity and correctness, making a fuss nobody else understood. The eye-rolling young notaires were right: Inge hadn't bothered to get her permission regularised. Instead, she'd impressed the importance of that square metre on her compliant servant. Why pay when Monique will sort it out later? How much more sensible to keep your money for that rainy day.

All Saturday, Alex and Lorie and Oriel and I wrap and pack and tape, helped by Inge's friend Martine and her husband, Jean. This unravelling is sad. As soon as furniture is shifted and pictures come off walls, the ley lines dissolve. It feels like a second death. What do you keep of your mother's possessions when even her ashtray is simultaneously precious and worthless? It feels horrible to throw everything away, yet foolish to bring it home.

I take the Marcel Falter painting of horses my great-uncle Willy bought from a social-realist artists' collective in 1951, the picture that passed to Heinz in lieu of various debts. The two carthorses straining to pull their load of hay hung for years in Sydenham. Inge always wanted me to have this in memory of her adored but unreliable uncle. I sneak in a few doilies remembered from childhood, cross-stitched and embroidered by Tilly, that I will never use but cannot bear to leave behind. I find that I 'need' two brown fringed napkins adorned with llamas Tilly brought back from Peru. They have no meaning for anyone else, but then nothing does. I take Inge's ancient black polo-neck cashmere sweater with leather elbow patches she sewed on by hand. Her wedding ring now lives in my office in her absurd porcelain bowl, a red and gold concoction from Austria featuring two children in colourful peasant garb. I take her stamp collection, all remaining papers, and albums of photographs. I will spend further hours searching for clues on her activities, generally in vain. Who are those women she was corresponding with in the 1960s, signing themselves 'les Parisiennes' and sending scores of new, brightly coloured stamps?

Homes are cleared, objects given away, stuff flies into a skip. Instantly, you and your busy life are unrecorded history, your loved ones' photographs mouldering in a dump. When we come to sell my mother-in-law Hanna's silver cutlery and objets d'art, all deeply unfashionable, the treasures she polished for decades are valued by weight. In Tours, nothing goes to waste. After we leave, dear Martine ensures that every single usable thing Inge possessed goes to a charity supporting refugees. Each remaining book will find a good home.

Leaving books behind is painful. I take a brown box into the study, intending to take the minimum. I fill three boxes, and that takes considerable restraint. The top shelf of Inge's library, accessible only by stepladder, holds the German books she didn't want her French friends to see. I find a 1938 German novel in Gothic script with an image on the cover of some sort of church and a congregational-type gathering. Called *Verwandlung der Herzen (Transformation of Hearts)* by Kurt Ziesel, it is inscribed in my father's writing: For Menousch, with thanks for your extreme kindness and understanding, Charlie 31st October 1945.

Everything about this intrigues me. If Tom (Charlie was his wartime nickname) gave Inge's friend Menousch a German book, then she must have been a German refugee too. No wonder the girls were so close. What exactly did Menousch do in the way of kindness and understanding – perhaps while Inge and Tilly were in prison? Did he acquire this pre-war bestseller in Germany, where his war was ending? It's not the obvious choice for a war-hating soldier, but then he couldn't read it to know. Ziesel's book, which sold 350,000 copies, is quasi-religious and though it starts as a doctor/nurse story, it's actually a Nazi propaganda vehicle with some soldiering thrown in. I can't force myself to read more than a few pages. It opens with a quote from the eighteenth-century German romantic poet Hölderlin, calling for heroic death in battle. 'Do not count the dead! For you, sweet Fatherland, not one too many has died.' Indeed. This poem, by a sometimes bonkers visionary and Napoleon fan, is not what it seems. It is actually a call to revolutionary youth to overthrow tyranny, but was appropriated by the Nazis. Maybe Tom chose it for the romantic-seeming title, because he wanted Inge's heart to turn to him? But why is this book here if it was given to Menousch? It must have had special meaning if Inge (the woman who probably destroyed her wedding photos) kept it for seventy-five years.

On that high shelf I also find Renée's leather Bible inscribed with her initials and swollen to twice its size with prayer and communion cards, paper ephemera with bright pictures of Jesus, saints and nuns and many pious sentiments. Adultery and frequent confession are perfect bedfellows for a lifelong Catholic with a taste for other people's husbands. I take this and a super-trashy epistolary novel – *Mon Amour* by Elisabeth Trevol, which I do read (after a good deal of bonking, it doesn't end well) – that can only have belonged to Renée. I leave behind the typescripts of my novels, still sheathed in their original brown envelopes. Inge wrote Monique Novel on them and occasionally the words VERY GOOD. I never was knowingly overpraised.

When we break for lunch, I ask Martine what she knows about René, curious as to what, if anything, Inge confided. Martine tells me that Inge fell in love with René when she was very young. There is no longer any doubt. Until the DNA results come, I can't know for sure, but the notion of René-as-father has progressed from shocking through possible to desirable. I have also begun to appreciate Tom. He was a true romantic, as was Inge. To lose one wife is a misfortune; he loved deeply and lost three.

It is time to go home on such trains as might run. Crossing Paris, our taxi is hit by an English mother and daughter stupidly perched à deux on an electric scooter; it nearly ends very badly for them. The taxi is damaged, the driver shaken, and considerable drama ensues. All the Eurostar trains are delayed. We stand for hours in a queue snaking several times round the Gare du Nord. The driver is so upset that he has inadvertently put his own rucksack with wallet and ID along with our suitcases in the boot of the second taxi we hailed. He is traversing the giant station desperately looking for us to recover his documents. Luckily, we are reunited just before passport control. It is all miserable and strange and perfectly suits my mood.

We return home to interesting news. The German Ministry of the Interior has brought out a catchily named discussion document, which I loosely translate as *Naturalisation of Descendants of German Citizens Forcibly Excluded from Citizenship during the Nazi Era*. This suggests that a form of discretionary naturalisation might be available to close the loophole excluding people (like me) rejected under Article 116 Section 2. The legislators are good people; the door stands ajar. Angela Grossman at the German Embassy is encouraging. She sends over a long form to fill in and a list of original documentation required to prove parental/grand-parental former German citizenship: birth and death certificates, passports, persecution, details of any restitution made, and so on. We will require current police checks. I gather and annotate my documents – eventually they will number fifty-two – and turn my thoughts to the archive.

CHAPTER 16

• • • • •

A small town in Germany

In January 2020 Alex and I fly to Mülheim an der Ruhr, the hated place that made and unmade my mother, the town she never forgot yet could not abide. Both curious and full of dread, I don't know what to expect. Perhaps a rerun of Rheinhausen – a small affluent German town in an industrial zone surrounded by lovely countryside. We have two rendezvous. The first is with Hans-Joachim Rosenbaum, my mother's first cousin, the second with Annett Fercho, the archivist who has done so much to commemorate our family. We fly over flat green land, watching rows of neat white houses emerge from the cloud as we land in Düsseldorf.

It takes the taxi all of twenty-one minutes to reach the town, which lies in the centre of a ring formed by Duisburg, Essen, Oberhausen and Ratingen. I see the turn-off to Lintorf, the village on the edge of the ancient forest where Tilly was born, and where my grandfather wooed her. Towards the end of the war, a crime was committed here: the bodies of executed anti-Nazis were discovered in the forest. Lintorf subsequently became the site of a displaced persons' camp, housing Ukrainians, Poles and Yugoslavs awaiting settlement. Heading along the motorway towards the Ruhr, so many place names are familiar: Krefeld and Kettwig; Breitscheid, where one of the aunts lived and an uncle had an inn; Broich, where Inge was born. What do you call nostalgia for a place where you've never been? Germans have the great word *Fernweh* (the opposite of *Heimweh*, homesickness), which means a longing for far-off places. *Ostalgie* is the witty name for that curious post-Wall yearning for East Germany. Maybe neo-nostalgie. Or no-stalgie. Whatever you call it, it is unsettling.

I am not expecting the elaborate blue dinosaur scene graffitied on a motorway underpass, the Tattoo Parlour and Max Hair Lounge Anglicisms. Where is the charming little town of my imagination? We pass numerous businesses selling the caravans and camper vans Germans adore. An appealing piece of land dotted with gingerbread houses straight out of Grimm belongs to a purveyor of 'garden houses' like the one Inge's Tante Nelly once owned. The only old house we sight is a peeling ruin. Where the road meets the river, a couple of old brick factory buildings appear, signalling an industrial past. They have been tarted up and converted to trattoria. All this is decidedly downmarket: not a place for Sunday jaunts through the countryside dressed up in your best clothes.

On the night of 22/23 June 1943, the first serious RAF attack on heavy industry along the Ruhr set fire to the centre of Mülheim and the area around the Kirchenhügel, leaving the old town in ruins. The ninth-century castle of Broich survived but Mülheim had forever 'lost its face', as the official history puts it.

Two schools were destroyed and others partially so; the council moved into the undamaged part of the girls' Mädchenrealschule in the Von-Bock-Straße, leaving no space for lessons. Yet worse, most of their teachers were injured, some severely.

That August, the (Aryan) children of Mülheim assembled at the railway station beside the cement works of the Friedrich Wilhelms-Hütte, where a special train was waiting. Nearly three hundred girls and boys around Inge's age were evacuated to the countryside. They and the teachers accompanying them travelled to a safe haven, the Reich's new eastern territories of Bohemia and Moravia (now the Czech Republic). Hitler believed in training and indoctrinating Germany's youth from the earliest age. They would remain here for two years, enjoying a secure life in the countryside in modern buildings with daily roll calls under the flag, lessons on politics and open-air excursions.

Later, many of these young people didn't want to return home, where the bombings had continued unabated, halving the population and reducing survivors to bombed-out cellar-dwellers. It's a moot point whether Inge would have survived, had she remained. After the war, the town hall with that smooth square where she loved to roller-skate would be rebuilt, as were the half-timbered medieval houses around the Leineweberstraße. The rest had to wait. A million cubic metres of rubble needed to be cleared. Seventy-one per cent of the buildings were damaged. This was an industrial town, not a tourist one. The centre was rebuilt slowly and in a singularly depressing 1960s' style.

We go for afternoon coffee with Inge's cousin Hans-Joachim, who recently turned ninety, and his wife, Inge (another Inge Rosenbaum, but a Catholic one), in their handsome modern house in the well-to-do green suburb of Menden, to the south of the town and backing on to the river. They are a charming and touching couple and utterly devoted. Both are incredibly bright, with astonishing recall. Born in 1929, three years after his first cousin Inge, Hans was raised as a Protestant, which did not spare him from persecution. He spent his life in the Thyssen steelworks as a senior engineer. The Ruhr coalfields are among the world's largest, which is why Germany's heavy industry was concentrated here. The town prospered through Krupp and Thyssen, Siemens, AEG and affiliated businesses. Now one steelworks remains, with 500 to 600 employees. Mülheim's last mine closed in 1966. The decline is painfully visible; as Hans puts it, 'The town is dead.' When he tells me the story of the tragic deaths of his family members and the rescue of his niece Judith, he refers to the Gestapo as 'the men in leather coats'. And for him, the men in leather coats are never far away.

He is a man of science and has no wish to dwell on the persecutions of the past, but events so overwhelming cannot be suppressed. The past rises up with its ghosts and sorrowful questions, its unbearable freight of sadness and loss. A film or television discussion can trigger an exhausting sleepless night. And then he asks himself: how could people do such terrible things to their neighbours and friends? I don't ask why he chose to stay in Germany; he raises the question himself and offers the only possible reply. 'I answer with one sentence,' he says. 'This is my Heimat.'

The harrowing story of little Judith and the Rosenbaum family aroused the compassion of the students of Broich Gymnasium when they embarked upon their Stolpersteine project, encouraged by their history teacher, Frau von Bancels. She and Mülheim an der Ruhr archivist Annett Fercho understand the need for the young generation to research for themselves, to learn, and to remember. The students made a documentary and a drama film, both still on the Mülheim archive website. In London, I had the surreal experience of watching these strangers discuss the lives of the Rosenbaums online. As the camera panned over the documents, they lingered on the names of Arthur and Otto. The film ends with the laying of the shining Stolpersteine to commemorate Otto and Helmut, Inge's uncle and first cousin. It quotes the Jewish expression '*Der Mensch ist erst vergessen wenn sein Name vergessen ist*': A person is only forgotten when his name is forgotten. This is the leitmotiv of the Stolpersteine initiative.

Breakfast in the friendly, decent Hotel Kocks am Mühlenberg tastes of the Heimat. The wonderful fresh rolls and butter with cheeses, home-made jam and good filter coffee carry me back to my grandmother, who, according to Hans, I greatly resemble. The morning is cold and grey. It is a long walk to Hindenburgstraße 132, the last place where Otto and Helmut lived before being deported. Paul von Hindenburg was the German president after whom the airship was named, a man of multiple disasters during whose presidency Hitler came to power. This road has been renamed Friedrich-Ebert Straße (for an earlier and less contentious president of Germany) and bears no trace of a residential past. A four-lane ring road slices through an abandoned industrial zone. A vast factory lies shuttered and closed. Nothing shines in this no man's land. It takes us a while to spot the Stolperstein because the brass is now so darkly patinated and because there are no buildings on this side, just an electricity substation. It is hard to imagine a more abject spot. 'Here lived Otto Rosenbaum, murdered on 25.3.1942 in Gross-Rosen. Here lived Helmut Rosenbaum.'

I write up my notes in the pleasant hotel bar over pretzels and a glass of Mölmsch beer (the local equivalent of Cologne's celebrated Kölsch, Mölmsch being the local dialect). A group of business folk sit chatting. One young woman is from Vietnam and the group falls easily into good English, talking about the Ho Chi Minh Trail. The waitress can't work out from my accent where I came from – maybe Essen? I can't guess hers. She is Sicilian, her family long established here though she still loves to go home to Agrigento.

That bad old Germany doesn't exist. And the pleasant town Inge knew, with its ancient history and medieval heart, has gone. People worked in local industries and earned well; the town was affluent and now it is hollowed out. Not one old house remains in the Schreinerstraße, where Inge kept her handbag collection filled with nonsense words and carefully laid her dollies to rest, safe from germs, on the bed. Sandstraße 71 exists but the bakery has gone. Half the street is an industrial zone and the rest is modern houses thrown up on the cheap, most empty and shuttered. Hans's wife, Inge, says that this was once a nice area of little boutiques run by their owners; if you wanted a department store, you would go to Essen or Duisburg. Otherwise, she said, Mülheim 'had everything'. Now it has nothing.

The next morning we go in search of the Stolpersteine laid for my grandparents, Arthur and Tilly, at Eppinghofer Straße 134. It is a dual carriageway, a big main road. Then, as now, it is a very poor area of town. A Turkish supermarket and fish shop jostle a conglomeration of cheap stores. We see mostly old people, many evidently in bad health. Today, numbers 132 and 134 are combined in 132, a featureless block of ugly flats. The two shining stones are easy to spot: later, when we visit the archive, student

David Bakum, who co-wrote my grandfather's biography, tells us that he and his sister polish the Stolpersteine (Mülheim an der Ruhr has laid 168) when they go out.

'Here lived Arthur Rosenbaum born 1892. Resistant/ Communist Party. Frequently arrested. Flight 1939 to Belgium. Interned in Drancy. Deported 1942. Murdered in Auschwitz.' I know that Arthur, living as a 'submarine', never even dared to sleep here. 'Here lived Mathilde Rosenbaum, née Lindemann, born 1899. Flight 1939 to Belgium. Survived with help.' On the cold pavement, I find myself weeping for them and for the wretchedness of this place. What a memory to take into exile. Poor little Inge, numbed by a succession of tragic events, was here severed from the Heimat, parting from her mother for the first time in her life, unable to shed a single tear.

The stones speak, but not everyone chooses to hear. The first reaction to the Holocaust was silence and denial. In the late 1940s and 1950s, nobody spoke of it; people accepted collective punishment as they rebuilt their lives out of the rubble. They blamed Hitler for everything. They bitterly resented the unfairness of de-Nazification, which often punished the small fry more than active Nazis.

There was a shortage of professionals, of trusted men; the American occupiers wanted no truck with ex-communists or resistance fighters. The former Nazis were reliable and hard-working: much more their type. In the civil service, police, universities and the law, former Nazis quietly returned to their posts. The 1960s was an era of growth and prosperity and rebuilding, looking to the future. Germany was a civilised country, where human rights were enshrined in the new constitution and the horrors of the Nazi past taught in every school. The status quo was not under threat. Then the next generation grew up to challenge the collective silence and Baader-Meinhof was born.

In 1969 I attended the sixth form of a good girls' Gymnasium in Hamburg Blankenese for a term before going on to the university of Hamburg. My silent class sat listening to the terrifying radio speeches of Goebbels, all frothing hatred. It was impressive to see the country confront its Nazi past. We were given facts, figures, pictures of the camps, and we listened to many broadcasts. Years later, it occurred to me that the emphasis on propaganda was one way of getting around the problem Hans spoke of: how to comprehend that your own fathers and mothers, your grandparents and uncles were complicit in this horror? Better to believe that they too were victims, their minds poisoned by propaganda and the ravings of maniacs.

The generation just ahead of me, safe in their affluent lives, listened to these stories in school and asked their parents why they had never spoken of the past. The answers were not satisfactory. Trouble brewed. The Paris 'events' of 1968 were harbingers of more to come. German students rose up against their ex-Nazi professors, against the war in Vietnam, against the silence of their parents. They rose up in solidarity with all the oppressed and suffering peoples in the world, making their cause an international one. It would eventually come about that – irony of ironies – young German guerrillas would be trained to kill Jews by Palestinians in camps in the deserts of Jordan. Taught by men who were fighting the Jewish state of Israel, they eventually came full circle, adopting the anti-Semitic rhetoric of their parents.

I remember that youth explosion and the wild Baader-Meinhof years. Ulrike Meinhof lived in Blankenese too and her first 'Aktion' – a year or two before my time there – was to trash the handsome bourgeois house she lived in. The terror attacks, executions and kidnappings terrified Germany. In the heavily fortified Stammheim court built for the express purpose of bringing them to justice, Baader, Meinhof, Ensslin, Meins and Raspe refused to recognise the right of the legal system to try them, when so many Nazis had never been punished. A huge majority of young people saw their point. When polled, the youth of Germany announced that they would shelter rather than denounce the terrorists if they knocked on their door.

Apart from the military war crimes tribunals held in occupied Germany, transcripts of which are relatively unknown, public transcripts exist of three trials in German history: Nuremberg, the SS men at Auschwitz and Stammheim. The latter can be found on the Hamburg University website, as yet only in German. Despicable and violent though they were, the murders and crimes committed by the Baader-Meinhof gang were by no means comparable with Nazi ones. But they held Germany to ransom and dominated headlines. Emotions – pro and against them – ran high. When Helmut Schmidt went on TV to say that the terrorists would not win and Germany would prove it was a democracy, three-quarters of the nation tuned in to watch him.

Germans use the word *Vergangenheitsbewältigung*, to mean working through or dealing with the past. They use this specifically for the agonising process of coming to terms with the dreadful deeds of the Nazi era. The concomitant convulsions, recriminations and anguished self-examinations are too complex to go into here, but the word stuck. East Germans now speak of their own *Vergangenheitsbewältigung* when dealing with the Soviet era. When Alex and I visited the infamous Stasi prison known as the Berlin-Hohenschönhausen Memorial, a former inmate showed us round; it soon transpired that explaining what had happened to him was as important therapeutically to him as it was educationally to us.

After reunification, the 1990s signalled a new period of remembering, with commissions for big museums and memorials and a plethora of anniversaries. The one-man Stolpersteine movement developed upwards rather than being imposed top down and is accordingly all the more rooted in German culture. That a small town like Mülheim an der Ruhr, lacking the resources to build memorials, chooses to deal with and remember its past does the town great credit. In this process, the archives play a valuable part.

On our last afternoon in Mülheim, we visit the archive, housed in an airy modern building in a green area; unfortunately, the archivist Annett Ferco is unwell, so we don't get the chance to meet her and thank her in person. We are, however, met here by David Bakum, part of that original group at Broich Gymnasium. He spent much time here and in the Duisburg archive with fellow student Angelina Mehler, researching the Rosenbaum biographies.

The very first document we view, Arthur's birth certificate of 1892, offers a disturbing snapshot of Germany's troublesome past. The certificate is a printed form, names and details written in elegant copperplate. On the left-hand side of the page is the addition: 'The person designated here has additionally adopted the first name "Israel".' The registrar (for it must be a man) has signed the addition, which is dated 10 March 1939. The name Israel was also added to Arthur and Tilly's wedding certificate on 13 March 1939. Nazi bureaucrats trawled through the local registers, writing in the 'additional' given names of Israel or Sara for

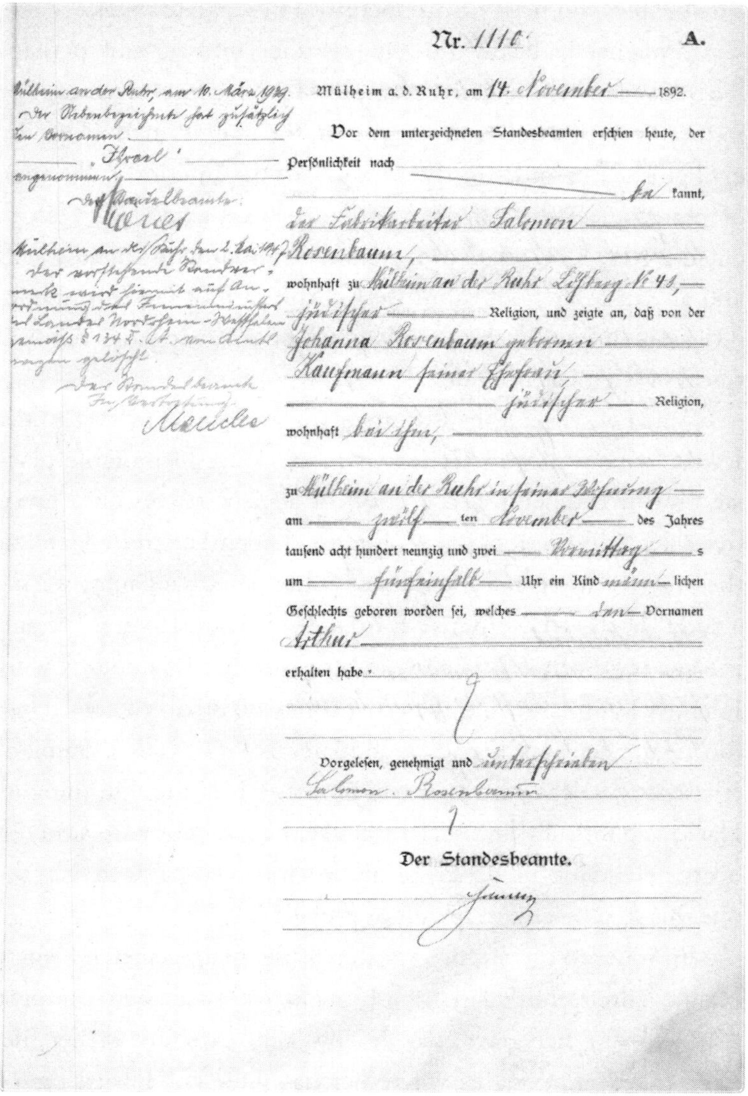

Nr. 1110. **A.**

[left margin, handwritten:]
Mülheim an der Ruhr, am 10. März 1929.
Der Nebenbeamte hat zusätzlich
den Vornamen
Karl
aufgenommen.
Der Standesbeamte:
Merer

Mülheim an der Ruhr, den 2. ... 19...
Der vorstehende Beamte
wird hiermit auf an-
ordnung des ...
... § 14 ... ... vom ...
... ...
Der ...
... ...
Maneles

[main body, printed with handwritten insertions:]

Mülheim a. d. Ruhr, am 14. November 1892.

Vor dem unterzeichneten Standesbeamten erschien heute, der Persönlichkeit nach _bei_ kannt,

der Fabrikarbeiter Salomon Rosenbaum,

wohnhaft zu Mülheim an der Ruhr Eißtraße Nr 41,

jüdischer Religion, und zeigte an, daß von der

Johanna Rosenbaum geborene

Kaufmann seiner Ehefrau

jüdischer Religion,

wohnhaft bei ihm,

zu Mülheim an der Ruhr in seiner Wohnung

am _zwölf_ ten _November_ des Jahres tausend acht hundert neunzig und zwei _vormittags_

um _fünfeinhalb_ Uhr ein Kind _männ_ lichen Geschlechts geboren worden sei, welches _den_ Vornamen

Arthur

erhalten habe.

Vorgelesen, genehmigt und _unterschrieben_

Salomon. Rosenbaum

Der Standesbeamte.

[signature]

Jews. This had become law on 17 August 1938: in order to persecute people, you need first to identify and separate them.

Immediately below this, in a rather messier and perhaps hurried hand, is an early example of 'Wiedergutmachung' or restoration. A second note states that 'the margin mark is hereby extinguished by order of the Minister of the Interior of the state of Nordrhein-Westfalen in accordance with section 134'. It is dated 2 May 1947. Safe in this modern room with friendly staff and an atmosphere of calm, we feel the chill of Gestapo meticulousness alongside the impossibility of removing the physical traces of what has been done.

When we've seen the documents, David walks us over to the Jewish cemetery. Well tended, it is the most memorable place we find in Mülheim, a collection of ancient stones on a green tree-filled hill overlooking a pleasant residential street. Here, at the grave of my great-grandfather Salomon Rosenbaum, we say a kaddish, the Jewish prayer for the dead that celebrates life and the greatness of God. Here we see the graves of Salomon's wife, Johanna Kaufmann, and their first son, who died as a baby. Here too are the graves of David's grandparents, for he is of Ukrainian-Jewish origin. The past is alive in him, as it is in me. Multilingual David is politically and socially active; he has chosen to study in Scotland and his life already occupies a much larger stage than the one this small German town can provide.

En route to the airport, we stop at the main cemetery, where Hanne Lore is buried. I have brought the small buff-coloured map showing her grave, which Tilly kept carefully all her life. A crayoned cross marks where her daughter was buried on 14 April 1938 on Feld II/3 in an area directly opposite the chapel: '*Your plot is in the area marked with a red cross.*' We know what to look for. Among Inge's photographs was one of her sister's grave that must have been taken in the 1950s or 60s, showing a simple piece of granite with her name lettered in gold and the dates of birth and death. It is beautifully tended and planted with flowers. Tilly must have arranged this in 1955, when she went back to Mülheim for the first time after the war. It had mattered tremendously to her that the beloved child be buried here, and not in the Jewish cemetery.

An old set of railway lines runs past the entrance to the cemetery and there is something about the lines of the building and the closeness of those railway lines that makes me shudder; this is not Auschwitz, however, and I am far too fanciful. Over the road at Kocks Blumen we buy a large pot of pansies in a beautiful dark purple that the florist assures us 'will last'. Two hundred years old, the cemetery is extensive and handsome, with fine copper beech hedges and an alley of elms. But it lacks graves, just as it lacks visitors on this grey January day. Feld II/3 is strangely empty, with very few graves around the edge, and those few are modern, planted with heathers and evergreens. Interspersed are handsome plant displays discreetly advertising the firms that look after the graves. We walk everywhere but cannot find the grave.

How can this be? We go to the office to enquire; it is closed on Wednesdays. Eventually, we find a man with a van whose shovels tell us that he is a gravedigger. He explains that every twenty-five years, the stones are cleared out. When this happens, notice is given in the town. The 'row graves' in the centre are no longer there – the 'edge ones' can be bought permanently. People discover this, he says, and yes, they tend to get very upset. Some make representations about their relatives being cleared away, but most people choose to buy urns now. I wonder if I can find out from the office exactly where my aunt once lay. 'Good luck with that,' he says. 'As far as they are concerned it's all done and dusted.'

How ironic that the Jewish cemetery has survived with its ancient stones and history intact and not the 'safe' Aryan one. We choose a spot in the big empty space of Feld II and leave the flowers in that solitary place. I tell Hanne Lore who we are, and why we have come, and that she isn't forgotten. I tell her that she has descendants: Inge's five grandchildren and many great-grand-children. I know that I'm speaking to a void: this place has been ruthlessly cleared of its memories and its emptiness is distressing.

Hanne Lore Rosenbaum died eighty-five years ago. Of her existence, two objects remain: Tilly's green plastic wallet with that curl of auburn hair and the studio portrait of two little sisters I never saw during my mother's lifetime. Hanne Lore inclines gently towards Inge and their heads of shiny hair touch. I see them every day from my desk. Inge never cried for her father and sister. Yet when she visited Israel in the 1970s and went to Yad Vashem, she suffered a meltdown so devastating that she had to go outside and be comforted and still could not calm down. The shock and pain were too great. 'You know me and my extremes of behaviour,' she said. On this occasion, the wall she had built to protect her tender inner self was breached with devastating effect.

I've always been afraid of going to Auschwitz, but after Mülheim I know that we must. *Ein Mensch ist erst vergessen wenn sein Name vergessen ist* – a person is only forgotten when their name is. Saying a kaddish for a dead person makes the name live on. Flowers die but stones remain. And papers too.

I think that there is nothing more I can learn from Germany about my mother's past, but I am wrong. Later that January, a disc arrives with copies of all documents relating to Arthur

Rosenbaum held by the central Duisburg Nordrhein-Westfalen archive. Two substantial Gestapo files run to 560 pages. There are 100 pages of court judgements. There are in fact so many papers and repetitions that the Duisburg archivist suggests that a judicious selection should suffice. Judicious is the word; Arthur Rosenbaum spent two decades in and out of court.

Arthur existed thus far in a few anecdotes, a couple of photographs and some official documents. But he survives in the statements he made in court, in his many attempts to avoid prison and in Gestapo interrogations. His is the voice of a difficult stubborn man committed to political change, by violence if needs be. The disc will fundamentally change my view of my grandparents and the child they made.

Gestapo mugshots of Arthur Rosenbaum
courtesy of the Nordrhein-Westfalen Archive:
all acknowledgements are on page 306

CHAPTER 17

• • • • •

What we inherit

In my eyes, my courageous doomed grandfather was a heroic Nazi victim. The historical record tells a different story. Arthur Rosenbaum was a firebrand, street fighter and troublemaker with a considerable criminal record.

The Duisburg archive holds all the records for Nordrhein-Westfalen, Germany's most populous state. It includes the cities of Cologne and Düsseldorf, Dortmund and Essen, the largest urban area in Germany. Lengthy files from the regional courts record eleven convictions for Arthur even before Hitler came to power in 1933. After that, everything escalates. Two thick Gestapo files record searches, offences, arrests, interrogations, imprisonment and constant surveillance. I get in touch with the national Bundesarchiv for the sake of completion and am amazed to discover that the infamous Gestapo headquarters at 8 Prinz-Albrecht-Straße in Berlin also kept a file on my grandfather. He was an enemy of the state and far more significant politically than I realised.

The Berlin file reveals a reason for the focused persecution that ruined Inge's childhood. In 1937, Karel Lodewyk Diepgrond, a Dutch national living in Amsterdam, denounced 'the Jew Rosenbaum' in Mülheim an der Ruhr as the main liaison between illegal communist cells and central offices located abroad. The file suggests that the information came via an émigré communist colleague of Arthur's, one Sloty, also from Mülheim, who had turned informer. The Gestapo say that Arthur brought communist propaganda into Germany and disseminated it. He fomented agitation and was a linchpin of the left, the network they were determined to smash. This explains the frequency of the raids that so terrified Inge and perhaps also why he was often released and followed: they wanted to catch him in the act and capture his associates.

In the buff-coloured Duisburg files, three Gestapo mugshots depict Arthur in profile, full face and wearing a cap. They were taken in 1936, when he was forty-four. In the workers' outfit of striped collarless shirt and dark jacket, he looks like a Russian revolutionary. He has a strong lean profile, frown lines between wild eyebrows. Pale eyes (probably blue like Inge's?) stare defiantly ahead. He has jet-black cropped hair. These official forms offer abundant space to describe the detail of ears, brow, nose, mouth, teeth, dialect plus such characteristics as tattoos, scars, knock knees and pigeon toes. The masters of eugenics were keen to record the innumerable physical and moral defects of the underclasses. Yet in each file relating to Arthur that page is blank, bar a massive black J for Jude stamp. Was that usual? Was being a Jew sufficient to damn a man? Or was he so well known that no description was needed? He has great intensity and a set of the mouth that brooks no opposition. This is a face that knows how to take a blow and has taken many.

Constant letters and reports on 'the Jew Rosenbaum' fly back and forth between the Gestapo in Oberhausen, the local office covering Mülheim an der Ruhr, the regional HQ in Düsseldorf and Berlin. The Gestapo files are dense with notes, abbreviations and official stamps, with further dates and references inked or pencilled in on thin paper, typed on both sides. Show-through makes some pages illegible. Notations and remarks made by unknown hands in blue pencil between the typed lines have blurred to unreadability. But the files are impeccably organised in date order.

In 1935, a typed report running to several pages sets out his background: 'Rosenbaum has been politically active from 1918 until [Hitler's] seizure of power in 1933. During these years he held leading positions in the terror organisation the KPD [Communist Party of Germany] and manifested himself as one of the worst political aberrations in Mülheim an der Ruhr, as his many previous convictions for breach of the peace, etc, clearly attest.'

My English grandfather died in the First World War; my German grandfather emerged from the opposing trenches alive and set on destroying the system that had sent him there. Arthur left the army aged twenty-six with an Iron Cross and 'front fighter' status, minus that finger lost at Verdun. His burning sense of injustice was shared by many. Three million soldiers had been killed and innumerable others crippled. To what end? The defeated country was humiliated and impoverished, burdened with enormous debt. Defeat came so suddenly and unexpectedly that the myth of the '*Dolchstoß* or dagger blow arose; it was said that the brave soldiers on the battlefield had never been defeated, but stabbed in the back by politicians, socialists, and above all Jews. This terrible lie led to social unrest with obvious consequences.

In post-war Germany, paramilitaries ran amok; war had legitimised violence. Joining and taking sides was already deeply rooted in German culture. Most citizens' lives from cradle to grave revolved around clubs and societies for work and leisure, whether attached to religion or political parties. Veterans flocked to join military associations, both left and right wing. Communist veterans like Arthur went into the Front Fighters' League; the Russian revolution of 1917 had lifted their hopes. There were hundreds of thousands of armed men: gangs of thugs openly fought on the streets.

Arthur the 'front fighter' combatant relished these turbulent times. He joined the USPD (Independent Socialist Party of Germany) straight after the war. He joined the Communist Party (KPD) as soon as it was founded and became the local treasurer. He was pushy, gritty and very resilient. Inge wrote that *all the Rosenbaum children had had a tough upbringing*: she heard someone mention that the girls (her aunts) had carried sacks of coal during the First World War.

Ostensibly a coal merchant running his widowed mother's business, Arthur was always pursuing something dodgy and illegal on the side. Those eleven offences between 1921 and 1932 attest to that sod-them attitude. He spent many short periods in prison for inciting others to disobey the law, for assault, riot, 'gross mischief', receiving stolen goods, driving with false number plates and other minor misdemeanours.

In February 1922, two months before his wedding, Arthur, his brother Otto and two other men were had up for handling stolen coal, driving with false number plates, not paying traffic fines and various other minor offences. Arthur, the ringleader, avoided a prison sentence of up to three months (which would have derailed the ceremony) by paying a fine of 500 Marks. A further fine was imposed for an offence in March; he and Tilly married on 8 April. That October brought another fine, and another offence. In January 1923 he was sentenced to six weeks for disturbing the peace, singing communist songs. From the outset of their marriage, roustabout politics held sway and that did not change.

How surprising that my calm grandmother chose to marry this man. But when a powerful and determined man comes calling, few can resist. Arthur was a maverick with little respect for authority and women are attracted to this type. In this violent era when it was every man for himself, there were thousands like him, wheeling and dealing. Most would later decide to invest their energies in Hitler. But Arthur was a contrarian, unusual in his doggedness and that crazy courage, in holding his beliefs to the very end.

Tilly must have known that the young man bicycling through the deep forests in Lintorf already had a substantial criminal record. That bucolic scene takes on a less innocent flavour in hindsight. Inge told me that her mother married Arthur (*the Jew*) because he was well-to-do, determined and (neatly trashing both their characters) because *one man was as good as another*. This cynical take cannot have been the whole truth. Tilly was a beautiful woman who attracted many men, and she was no fool. When she spoke of Arthur to her angry and troubled daughter, she was rewriting and refining the script. Better to depict yourself as a self-seeking idiot rather than actively complicit in the disaster.

Inge also had a taste for bad boys. Both Tom Charlesworth and René Cocard went in for black-market dealing in their different ways: in occupied France, René would trade with first Nazi and later American officers. Tom ran a profitable venture with stolen cigarettes during the war and had no compunction about going AWOL whenever it suited him. As far as I can tell from the records, neither he nor René ever got near a fight. Arthur was made of stronger stuff.

Germany was sliding into further chaos. French and Belgian troops occupied the Ruhr to seize the coal the German government was supposed to provide as part of war reparations. Inge would later wonder whether she should start her life story with the extraordinary sight of French troops marching through Mülheim an der Ruhr. The country could no longer afford to buy gold to repay its colossal debt. To regain control of its crucial industrial zone and get the foreigners out, tremendous efforts were made to renegotiate the terms of the debt. Even so, it would take ninety-two years for the last payment to be made on 3 October 2010.

The economic situation worsened as inflation and then hyper-inflation set in. A kilo of rye bread cost 163 marks in January 1923 and ten times more in July. By October, that loaf cost 9 million marks, and a fortnight later 233 billion. Daily life took on a desperate quality. Shops hoarded food in anticipation of hourly price rises. While some profiteered, ordinary people lost their cash, savings and investments in government bonds. Crime, theft and barter swept through Germany. Arthur seems to have been adept in all three. To this day, Germans have a horror of insecurity and households like to save around 10 per cent of their disposable income. The word for debt – *Schuld* – also means guilt and the two remain entwined in the German psyche.

Fuel shortages were severe and Arthur's yard and industrial coal business, supplying local factories, was affected. In July 1924 (nine months after Hanne Lore was born), he was back in court with a lawyer, appealing against a conviction for handling stolen coal. Busy lawyers used thick red or blue crayon to underline dates or passages they wanted to reference in court. Several of Arthur's statements show this crayoning – he could afford lawyers and for this appeal employed Dr Koenigsberger. Arthur had been called in to serve a jail sentence owing to a (perhaps understandable) confusion about which fine applied to which particular sentence.

His witness statement is blunt and truculent. On the subject of the stolen lorryloads of coal, he denies any illegality and has a pretty good go at incriminating Schröder Junior, from whom he had bought various loads of coal and who was also commissioned to sell these loads in Dusseldorf. 'I didn't trouble myself with the formalities for this delivery, this was the job of Schröder who went along himself.' 'As to whether Schröder or the driver had a heavy goods vehicle licence I wouldn't know, that wasn't my concern.' Perhaps the lack of coal to deal in (or steal) drove the decision to go into the bread business; he had a wife and child to support.

Two years after this conviction, in 1926, Inge was born and the family moved several times. By 1928 Arthur owned the bakery at Sandstraße 71 and appears in street directories as a 'bread driver' or 'free bread driver'. Was it safer or more profitable to be in the food business or was this part of a political game? He used the daily bread round to distribute red literature and communicate with comrades. Arthur became founder and technical director of the Roter Frontkämpfer Bund (RFB), the Red Front Fighters' League. When that was dissolved, he became leader of the Kampfbund gegen den Faschismus (Fighting League against Fascism) and member of the Internationale Arbeiter Hilfe (International Workers Aid) and Rote Hilfe (Red Aid). He was also a member of the works council of the Friedrich Wilhelms-Hütte foundry and head of Relief for the Unemployed. All this intense activity is documented in detail by the Gestapo. No wonder Inge had few memories of her father playing with her.

The Wall Street Crash of 1929 and the Great Depression that followed raised the number of German unemployed to 6.1 million. Streets filled with hordes of unemployed men with placards round their necks, desperate for any kind of work. The communists mobilised the unemployed, proclaiming 'red districts' and beating up the Brownshirts. As fewer than 10 per cent of party members now had jobs, the class struggle abandoned the workplace for the street, spreading into neighbourhoods. Parades, demos, hunger marches and prolonged clashes with the police became the norm.

In 1930, Arthur led a group of sixty to eighty of his black-shirted communists – men whose shirts he'd personally funded – into a punch-up with a small group of 'Stahlhelme', a set of paramilitary First World War veterans, which resulted in another arrest. The 'Steel Helmets' were nationalist, monarchist anti-Sem-ites who enjoyed marching about in uniform, led by a veteran called Biel. Several witness statements tell the story of a proces-sion of communists happening upon the Steel Helmets at 10.30 at night, both sides fresh from meetings in their various drinking halls. 'Rosenbaum stood at their head; he told Biel they needed to talk "man to man". He shouted, telling the group to "hold their discipline" and "stand firm".' Herr Biel, who was badly beaten in the fray, was known to Arthur. Perhaps they had served in the army together? Despite numerous witness statements, it could not be proved that Rosenbaum had struck anybody. The court decided to blame him anyway, asserting that his shout to 'hold discipline' was a coded way of telling the commies to lay into the other lot, whom they in fact grossly outnumbered. They held Rosenbaum to be entirely responsible. Arthur's appeal was rejected so it was back to prison, with costs.

Nothing stopped him from agitating, nor from seeking to expand his influence. The following year, 1931, he was elected to the city council of Mülheim an der Ruhr representing the KPD and spoke in several debates. That year, he also spent five months in prison for various offences: inciting disorder and illegal behaviour, traffic violations, grievous bodily harm, rioting and 'aggravated mischief'. As the bureaucrats would later establish, between 1933 and 1938 he spent three years, nine months and twenty-five days in prison or in camps.

Tilly never spoke of Arthur and these tumultuous years; I wish I had known more and asked about him. She had no interest in politics and it's hard to visualise her managing this combative forceful husband. Puzzling through these papers, I saw a very different side to the mild-mannered domestic woman I knew. It is notable how active Tilly was in Arthur's defence, visiting the Gestapo, visiting him in prison, obtaining letters of support, organising marches in the streets. While holding the household together, she constantly strove to get him out of prison. A lengthy letter in the files dated 1931, written by the owner of the Styrum Bread Factory, Karl Nie, offers a glimpse of their domestic circumstances. This letter begs for a reprieve from Arthur's latest sentence, explaining that Tilly has been keeping the business going as best she could while he was in prison. '*Rosenbaum assures me that he will in future remain distant from every kind of political agitation . . . He made this promise when I gave him my word, that I would intervene on his behalf.*' Nie provides a glowing reference. Tilly must have used all her allure to obtain this letter, knowing perfectly well that Arthur had no intention of giving up politics.

As Inge wrote, her father's priorities were *first the party, and then the party, and then the family.* The bakery was put in Tilly's name and she ran the business full time.

When Hitler came to power in 1933, Inge was six and any stability in the Rosenbaums' family life was wrenched away. Communists were rounded up. Arthur and his brother Otto were put into 'protective custody', released, then rearrested. In February 1933, Arthur was let out. At once, he set about distributing anti-Hitler material and even, outrageously, targeted the police. In March he was arrested for distributing copies of the *Red Star* and other seditious material in the letter boxes and under the doors of policemen in Oberhausen, where the local Gestapo had its head-quarters. The flyer starts thus: 'Police officials, colleagues! Is Hitler helping us?' He was accused of distributing 'horror news about the concentration camp Dachau' and 'preparation for treason'.

A score of handwritten reports from recipients of the flyers state that they have no idea where this seditious material came from. The panic is evident: to be caught with these was a death sentence. Once more, he was released for lack of evidence: 'perpetrators not found/searches in vain'. This material comes from that separate Berlin archive, where the file on Rosenbaum was growing.

The years of comfortable flats were over. The family moved to live above the bakery in the Sandstraße. It was here that Inge was horrified to find that the bathroom was separate from the main flat and she had to take a key to use it. *This was the beginning of the 6am visits from the Geheimpolizei* ('secret police'),, she wrote. The outside world was hostile: Jews were pariahs, the streets and school places of persecution. Inge was growing up in a household of three women: a working mother with two daughters who were utterly dependent upon her, financially and emotionally. I note that in Sydenham she eventually replicated a somewhat happier version of this.

Through all these early years little Inge adored her mother, just as I would later adore her. She wrote how she barely recalled anything of her sister or father. Inge was such a passionate child – craving and demanding the love she could not get, unable to be separated from her mother for even one night. The eventual reversal to active dislike of Tilly proved just as absolute and extreme.

By 1934, when Inge was eight, Hitler had taken complete control of Germany and the persecution of the family intensified. The Gestapo did their utmost to catch Arthur in the act: 'Rosenbaum, who was taken into protective custody at the beginning of the National Upheaval, has been continuously monitored and his home and business premises have been repeatedly searched. Proof that he is in contact with foreign communists or emigrants has not yet been produced.' How did Arthur manage to keep his illegal documentation hidden? Inge described how Tilly hid pamphlets under her housedress when the Gestapo surged in early in the morning and how she followed the men from room to room to ensure that they didn't plant seditious material. They never searched her. Blue-eyed Tilly with her red-gold hair must have realised that her Aryan attractiveness was protection, of sorts. But what risks this brave couple took. Gestapo files later state that 'There is nothing disadvantageous, whether political, criminal or espionage-related, known about the Rosenbaum wife'.

Outwardly at least, Tilly managed her double life with great calm. But these searches engendered terror. Big sister Hanne Lore watched her mother conceal whatever the Gestapo were searching for about her person. Perhaps stress did exacerbate the diabetes that killed this gentle child. At that time, artificial insulin existed but was not available to them.

Arthur was frequently taken in for questioning and Tilly was never told where. *So my mother started doing the rounds to find where my father was locked up. She was totally fearless and always found out (a lot of wives were never able to trace their husbands),* wrote Inge. It was a stressful and lonely life for a woman with two children, one of them sick, striving to keep a business going. Tilly had little support. Her brother Willy, unfailingly kind and loyal, was far away in Morocco. Other members of the Lindemann family found it expedient not to know the wife of the Jew. After the war, Tilly in turn chose not to frequent most of the Lindemanns.

In the few photographs of that era Tilly looks haunted and anxious, as well she might. The Aryan Frau Rosenbaum was regularly urged by the Oberhausen Gestapo chief Herr Kolk to divorce her husband and always refused. Inge wrote that *she didn't divorce him because she wanted to be supported (financially).* But the reverse applied. My grandmother was now thirty-two years old, working day and night to hold the family together. With no family support, she must have felt panic and distress, but kept up a brave front. Little Inge noticed that *my mother was not intimidated by anyone.* The fact that she wasn't Jewish probably gave her more freedom than others in her situation.

Arthur had developed his own way of dealing with the authorities. Arrested (again) in November 1934, this time for preparing to commit high treason, his statement reads:

'My customers consisted mainly of former Communists, whom I got to know during my activities in the KPD, or of others who were recommended to me. In Oberhausen I was delivering [bread] to the following people, who previously belonged to the KPD [six names are given]. I am not able to give any information about the political views of the clients above. If I am accused of distributing this or that Communist propaganda during the carrying out of my business, I deny this. I have never delivered Communist pamphlets and have never received any from anyone.'

He goes on to state:

'I do not recall telling clients in the Uhlandviertel in Oberhausen that I had been checked by the police in Mülheimerstraße in Oberhausen, and that if this control had been carried out yesterday, it would have gone badly with me.' In other words, he is accused of admitting to his clients that he had indeed been carrying communist pamphlets the previous day and was lucky not to have been caught with them. The statement ends: 'I have entirely broken with communism. This can be seen from the fact that my elder daughter (aged 11) is a member of the Bund Deutscher Mädel. I am a Jew. My wife and the child were baptised Protestant.'

This mention of Hanne Lore gave me pause. Inge so desperately wanted to join the BDM – could Hanne Lore possibly have been a member? Was a half-Jewish girl permitted to join? But he is lying, of course. Arthur has a method that serves him well. He admits what's incontrovertible, such as his past link with communists, and the names of the people arrested with him. He flatly denies incriminating activities and claims that his days of political activity are over. Then he throws in an Aryan link, to see how that pans out. The Gestapo file reeks of frustration that they had to let such 'an extreme radical' out that same evening because 'there was insufficient evidence that could be used in court'. As Hitler further tightened his hold, such niceties as evidence would disappear.

Eight months later, on 11 July 1935, Arthur was sentenced to three years in prison, again for preparation for high treason. He had had his bread van converted to take passengers and drove the wives of political prisoners back and forth from Lüttringhausen prison in Remscheid, where their husbands were incarcerated, a journey of about an hour. Arthur admitted the offence but denied knowing who the women were. 'On oath, I firmly deny that I made the connections between the individual women myself and then later expanded them.' The Gestapo knew that he organised and ran the network but could not prove it. He was released early; new charges were brought the following year.

Nineteen thirty-six was a particularly bad year. The family were now subject to constant house searches and the confiscation of radios. Ten-year-old Inge wrote how she was told that *every time the police want a new radio, they come to us.* The Gestapo record the confiscation of a radio with built-in loudspeaker, brand 'Mende', M type, found in his apartment at Sandstraße 71: 210 W, apparatus number 13893. Arthur stated that:

'I also have to admit that on some occasions I listened to the Moscow radio station myself with my own set. In one case there was talk of socialist construction in the Soviet Union, on another there was talk of crèche work. I also know that my wife also tuned in to the Moscow channel on several occasions. I do not know what the subject was;

The Duisburg Gestapo file on Arthur for 1936: arrests, reports, telegrams
from Berlin demanding more information. Document courtesy of the
Nordrhein-Westfalen Archive

anyway, I can no longer remember the given topic. This would have been in 1935. I did not listen to other news, particularly not atrocity news. To be completely clear, I wish decisively to deny that I listened to the Moscow station or later made it the subject of special discussions any more times than I have detailed here. I knew that I had committed a criminal offence, so I did not listen to the Moscow station after this time.'

The pattern of partial admission (crèche and wife are good touches) plus straightforward denial was well established. Another arrest followed in July 1936, again on the grounds of preparing for high treason. Was this the year when Inge was forced to take part in a demonstration of wives marching to the prison where their husbands were held? Tilly led the parade and Inge had to march beside her shouting 'Free Arthur Rosenbaum!', a traumatic event she remembered with horror. She would have heard catcalling and booing, maybe worse; people had little sympathy for prisoners of any persuasion and none whatsoever for political prisoners and Jews. Inge was already the subject of abuse and vilification at school. To have school friends point and jeer, to be exposed on the street was utter shame and humiliation. She carried that resentment to the grave; she didn't really get how heroic her mother was. For her, persecution was always personal, never political.

A postcard Tilly sent to her husband in the prison in Düsseldorf (which still exists, at Ulmenstraße 95), dated 9 September 1936, depicts her life. The previous day she had visited him in prison, got home at 5.30 p.m., changed and then completed the bread round, finishing at 9 p.m. The next day she would be up early to

The postcard featuring the Rosenbaum ladies which Tilly sent to Arthur
in prison. Tilly, second from the left, is sitting next to her mother-in-law.
The formidable matron on the far right is Tante Mally

run the bakery. At the end of this exhausting and difficult day, she writes: 'I hope I can get the visiting day on Thursday, it would be better for me and more pleasant now that the days are getting shorter. We only get home in the dark. I am going to the lawyer tomorrow, I will write a letter by then, although there is nothing to be expected from it. Many warm greetings and kisses, your Mathilde.' Many women divorced their Jewish husbands; Tilly, with a business in her name, could have done so. But she was committed to Arthur. He clearly treasured this postcard (it has a photo of his wife, his mother and the five Rosenbaum sisters on the reverse) and kept it.

In 1937, Diepgrond, the Dutch national living in Amsterdam, denounced Arthur and the heat was really on. The Gestapo were convinced that Arthur was working with Rudolf Mintgens, the owner of a bookshop in Hindenburgstraße in Mülheim known for printing what was known as 'hate literature'. Mintgens' premises were searched constantly but nothing was found. Telegrams from Berlin continued to demand corroboration. Multiple reports on Rosenbaum circulated between Berlin, Düsseldorf and Oberhausen, where V. Kolk was head of the local Gestapo branch.

Herr Kolk rose to the challenge. This is the man who organised the searches of the flat, advised Tilly to divorce her husband and would later order her to leave Germany. It was Kolk who, after the family had left, took it upon himself to write to Berlin demanding that their citizenship be removed. Numerous notes and reminders bemoan the fact that Rosenbaum was never caught with incriminating documents and that they could not prove that he had been in contact with foreign communists or emigrants. Berlin constantly seeks corroboration and Oberhausen cannot provide a satisfactory response. The cat and mouse game went on for a long time. The Gestapo needed to capture his whole ring of associates, including those abroad. Being caught with pamphlets was a death sentence for die Weiße Rose (White Rose) students, Sophie and Hans Scholl, who with three other Munich students produced leaflets and graffiti calling for an end to the Nazi regime. Four days after their arrest, the Scholl siblings and their friend Christoph Probst were guillotined. Their sentence came after a show trial, during which none of the defendants were permitted to speak. Arthur, more experienced, always eluded the Gestapo. By any counts, this is a most remarkable achievement.

Nineteen thirty-eight was the worst year of all. Hanne Lore was dying. All Tilly's energy went into ensuring that the child had the confirmation she yearned for and that she would be buried in the main cemetery and not the Jewish one. She died in the Evangelical Hospital at 8 a.m. on 12 April 1938, aged fourteen. Her death certificate lists the causes of death as diabetic coma, otitis media (ear infection) and acute heart failure. This sweet and clever child who understood what was going on, who protected Inge and let her play, would be sadly missed by the entire family. I once asked Tilly why her hands trembled, and she said that it started on the day Hanne Lore died.

On Kristallnacht (9/10 November 1938), the bakery with Tilly's name on it was spared; Inge said that her terrified aunts and their children fled to them. Tilly's five Jewish sisters-in-law had their own troubles. Their mother, Johanna, died that year at the age of eighty, which was perhaps a blessing given all that was to come. Her two surviving sons would die in death camps. Though married to Aryans, four of the five sisters ended in camps; three survived. Only Gerta Silbermintz (the youngest, and the only Rosenbaum to marry a Jew) had succeeded in emigrating to America.

That November, Tilly and Inge moved with a few personal possessions into their last address in Mülheim an der Ruhr, that wretched room at Eppinghofer Straße 134 where the two Stolpersteine now shine bright. Arthur dared not join them at this, his registered abode; he was living underground and working as a manual labourer. It was open season on the Jewish community. On 14 November, Arthur was taken into the euphemistically named '*Schutzhaft-Jude*': Protective Custody – Jew. There is no court case in the files, no specific accusation or formalities; such punctiliousness had fallen away. Innumerable Jews were arrested in these days: not just troublemakers but lawyers, doctors, accountants, teachers. The judiciary, courts, lawyers and their staff all knew what was going on, as did the many people who witnessed the multiple arrests of the Jews and their disappearance in large numbers.

Arthur was transferred to Dachau concentration camp on 16 November 1938; he was prisoner number 30115. Christmas Eve – the most special night of the year for German children – must have been desolate for Tilly and Inge in their miserable room. Earlier that day, Tilly took Arthur's First World War medals and 'Front line status' documents to the Gestapo and applied for him to be released from protective custody because of his combatant status. That took some courage. There's a note of surprise in the Gestapo account of her request. Correspondence between the various Gestapo stations now weighed the danger he evidently represented against the certainty that he would soon be leaving Germany. On 11 January 1939, her application was granted: 'This time there is no objection to his release. I will however instruct Frau Rosenbaum to initiate the emigration process for herself and her husband. On April 10, 1939 I will ask for a report on the emigration status of the Rosenbaums.' It seems likely that the unnamed 'I' was local Gestapo chief V. Kolk.

On 20 January 1939, Arthur was released from Dachau and went underground. Tilly concentrated on the urgent task of getting Inge out of Germany to safety. Armed with Inge's visa to visit Willy in French Morocco, they rushed from one office to another, striving to obtain passports. As Inge wrote, Tilly was *indefatigable and undeterred.*

Before dawn on 22 March, Inge embarked on the first stage of her long and lonely journey through France to Meknes, sunshine and her beloved Uncle Willy. She remembered the car pulling over on a street corner not far from the Eppinghofer Straße and her father looming out of the darkness. One can imagine how startling it would have been to see his pale face suddenly appear, to feel the stubble on his cheek as he kissed her goodbye, to watch him dematerialising into the shadows as though he'd never been there. This fleeting and unexpected moment seemed wholly unreal. Inge would write how strange it was that she felt and remembered so little. It is more likely that she felt everything deeply and shut down, unable to process such terrifying events. For this child to leave the mother she had never been separated from and travel with a succession of strangers into the unknown went beyond her worst fears. That March morning marked the end of her childhood, the end of her Heimat and any concept of security.

Tilly and Arthur had no visas, no money, no exit strategy. Inge remembered being told that they had obtained one ticket to Shanghai but that Arthur would not leave without Tilly. It's possible. The local Gestapo chief followed up on his plan to check for news of the Rosenbaums' 'emigration status' by 10 April. He notes that on 14 April, the official registration office recorded

Arthur Rosenbaum and his wife as registering their intention of leaving for Meknes, French Morocco. They had no way of getting there but by making this declaration, Tilly obtained a passport on 15 April 1939. There is no record of Arthur obtaining one. That same night, they passed secretly over the border into Belgium. They avoided the frontier and border guards by walking through the woods carrying a suitcase between them. Somehow, they reached Brussels. One more destitute couple in a flood of German Jewish refugees, they were supported by an organisation Tilly later described as the 'Hilfskomité der israelitischen Gemeinde Brüssel' (Jewish Help Committee in Brussels).

That September, reluctant Inge was sent back from Morocco to rejoin her parents. It was around this time that her father apparently said he regretted having spent so much time on politics and so little with his family. *Too late*, was Inge's terse comment.

On 12 April 1939, a first official request for removal of citizenship was made. That June, Herr Kolk took it upon himself to write to Düsseldorf setting out all the reasons why Arthur Rosenbaum, his wife and surviving child should be stripped of their citizenship. His surveillance continued even after their departure; in that letter, he noted that the Rosenbaums had left neither debts, liabilities nor assets in Germany. This seems an extraordinary assertion. How many enquiries and visits to family, associates, landlords and suppliers lay behind this one line? Kolk is a man obsessed; he was the one who had urged Tilly to divorce the Jew. I wonder whether he had it in for Tilly because she had refused his advice – or his advances. But perhaps he was just a typical Nazi in his thoroughness and appetite for punishing others.

On 9 August 1939, a letter from the office of der Reichsführer SS, the Chief of German police in Berlin, confirmed to the

Gestapo in Düsseldorf that the official expulsion process of the Jew Arthur Rosenbaum had been initiated. This letter is signed by Jagusch, employee of the Chancellery. Though it came from the highest authority, it was not processed with the usual alacrity. A year later, the Oberhausen Gestapo (no doubt the assiduous Herr Kolk) wrote to Düsseldorf noting that the Rosenbaum names had not as yet been published in the lists; had the request for expulsion not been passed on? Cards in the Berlin archive declare the three Rosenbaums stateless on 2 July 1940. The official declaration that the German citizenships of Rosenbaum husband, wife and surviving 'Mischling 1 Grades' (half-breed grade 1) child were forfeit was published in issue Nr 154 of the Government Gazette on 4 July 1940, over a year after they had left the country. By then, Germany was at war.

It seems scarcely credible that the Belgians, fighting invaders on all fronts, would give priority to expelling male Jewish refugees. But within hours of the invasion on 10 May 1940, Belgian police started rounding up all foreign Jews. Arthur Rosenbaum was arrested on 15 May and transported to south-west France. Before the Jews from Belgium arrived, Saint-Cyprien was a peaceful rural village of a thousand souls in the Pyrénées-Orientales. Conditions in the barracks were appalling. Those interned succeeded in getting a letter to the Red Cross describing the unfiltered water used for drinking and to prepare food, the open latrines, insupportable numbers of flies, mice, rats and other vermin infesting the straw mattresses, an absence of medicine, disinfectant and all articles necessary for hygiene.

The names, dates and places of birth of the men who landed here are recorded in Marcel Bervoets' precisely researched and passionate book, *La liste de Saint-Cyprien*. Bervoets examines the

Belgians' shameful act of expulsion in detail; his own father was one of those who perished. Arthur is one of sixteen Rosenbaums listed. This wretched camp, thrown up on the beach, was one of many ante-chambers to the extermination camps.

Late in 1940, Arthur Rosenbaum was one of 3,870 men (mainly Jews) transported from Saint-Cyprien to Gurs. He wrote to Tilly and Inge in their freezing attic in the Rue Tiberghien in Brussels, asking them to join him. It is most unlikely that Arthur would have written of his own volition; it was standard practice for such letters to be sent, to gather more Jews into the net. As well that Tilly preferred the known deprivations of Brussels to the unknown camp, a decision that saved her and Inge's life. Unable to function outside her language and country, Tilly couldn't find regular work. Overwhelming grief for her child was exacerbated by the terrible insecurity of their situation, the loss of her husband, hunger and cold. It seems likely that she was suffering some sort of collapse. Fourteen-year-old Inge now dug into her own resources, getting herself baptised, going to night school, sewing hooks and eyes for corsets, working to learn French and typing. She was determined to better herself in the sweet factory.

Tilly could not have known that her German citizenship had been withdrawn, because on 16 April 1941 she applied to renew both her and Inge's passports, attaching the birth certificate proving her Aryan origin. She was of course still married to 'the Jew'. The saddest thing in these voluminous files is the hand-written letter, dated 24 April 1941, that Tilly sent to Herr Kolk, whom she knew so well.

'Dear Herr Kolk!

Due to special circumstances, I see myself compelled to divorce my husband, as the Gestapo asked me to do two years ago. My husband has been in an internment camp in southern France (Gurs) for a year and is waiting there to continue his journey to the USA. Since I don't want to end my life with my daughter in a camp and I also don't want to go to America, this should be the reason for divorce. My husband's past life is well known to you, I no longer have the strength to take on anything more. I have already brought my matter to the German Embassy, where I was told that given the remote circumstances it could take several years here in Belgium for the divorce to go through. Since it is very important to me to give my child a secure future, I turn to you, Herr Kolk, with the request that you will assist me in this matter. You know my past life and you also know how I kept everything going while my husband was imprisoned.

'The local authority here has advised me to initiate the affair in Mülheim, my former place of residence. As I am not currently in a position to raise the necessary funds for this matter, I most politely request your kind support. I thank you most sincerely in advance for your valued efforts.

Mathilde Rosenbaum Née Lindemann.

My birth certificate is enclosed.

It is a desperate plea. Tilly does not say that she wants to divorce Arthur, rather that she finds herself 'in special circumstances' and compelled so to do. She doesn't denounce or reject her

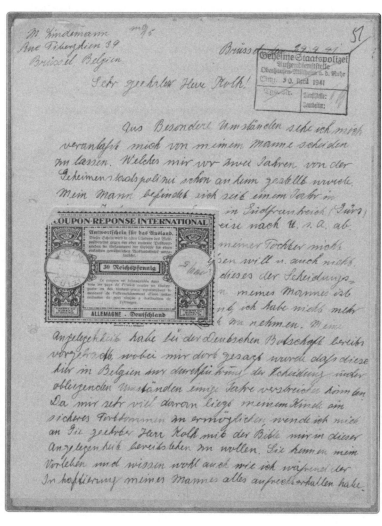

Tilly's letter to Herr Kolk, complete with international response coupon. But no response came. Document courtesy of the Nordrhein-Westfalen Archive

husband; she has not given in to blackmail. The line about not wanting to go to America is pure fantasy. Without papers, Tilly and Inge could not obtain rations or lodging or think of travel; divorce and a possible reacquisition of German citizenship were their only way forward. Letters went back and forth from the German Embassy in Brussels to Düsseldorf as the interminable bureaucracy pondered whether to grant the passport extension request of the '*deutschblütigen Emigrantin*', the 'German-blooded emigrée' – the euphemism for 'not Jewish'. On 3 May 1941, a lengthy letter from Oberhausen to Düsseldorf restated the usual litany of Arthur Rosenbaum's crimes, pointing out that as the Rosenbaums' citizenship had been removed on 4 July 1940, 'there is no need for us to take a position re the passport renewal'.

On 12 May, the Removal of Citizenship documentation for all three Rosenbaums was forwarded to Brussels with the brusque comment that 'an opinion on the passport application is therefore unnecessary'. This too must have gone astray, because Tilly went on striving to regularise her position and obtain papers. On 8 October 1941, the German Embassy in Brussels again asked Mülheim to respond re the passport extension request. This letter notes that Mathilde Rosenbaum had asked for the J in her passport to be removed and stated that she could prove her Aryan ancestry back to the fifteenth century. She intended to divorce, it is noted, her husband being in Gurs camp in France.

Tilly also asked for a certificate to prove that her husband had been expelled from the Reich for 'reasons of enmity to the state', to facilitate the divorce. How resolute she was. I never saw the stubborn defiant side of her, but Lorie did. It wasn't by chance that she would later marry another Jew, another larger-than-life character – this time a man she passionately loved. And it wasn't

by chance that after the war she reclaimed the German nationality that had been stolen from her.

In May 1942, over a year after her letter to Herr Kolk, the
Düsseldorf Gestapo finally responded to Tilly's request for this
certificate, directing 'the applicant to ask the court responsible
for the divorce for the document'. This was of course impossible.
She did not have the funds to apply to a court; besides, no court
in Germany would issue a document of that nature. Why help a
woman who married a Jew?

There is one final thrust from the Oberhausen Gestapo; an
unsigned letter requests the Brussels HQ 'to refrain from review-
ing the applicant after the divorce for the purpose of returning to
the Reich territory in view of the Grade 1 Mischling ('half-breed'
Grade 1) product of the marriage'. The mere existence of the
'half-breed product' was damning; the Rosenbaum wife needed
to be told that, married or divorced, there was no way back. Do I
detect the unsubtle hand of Herr V. Kolk?

This horrible word 'Mischling' was in common use. A huge
chart in Room 4 of the Wannsee villa where the Final Solution
was conceived sets out the Nuremberg laws of 15 September
1935, designed 'for the protection of German blood and honour'.
The chart illustrates the precise grading of Jewish pollution,
reaching back through grandparents and great-grandparents
with numbing clarity; a pure German is represented by a white
circle and a Jew by a black one. Marriage is forbidden and sexual
relationships between the two the crime of 'race defilement'.
A Mischling Grade 1 such as Inge (two Jewish grandparents)
could not marry a pure 'German blooded' individual or indeed
a Mischling Grade 2 (one Jewish grandparent). Inge could
only marry another Grade 1 and her children would also be

Mischlinge. Every German knew his or her grade of Aryanship back through generations.

Did Inge know that her existence as a Mischling meant that her mother could never regain her nationality after a divorce? Perhaps she didn't; perhaps she blocked this out. She certainly felt all the shame of being a Mischling. Such concepts were branded into the flesh, in Inge's case marking her soul for a lifetime. Though her uncles, aunts and cousins were taken to the camps, she later refused to accept that her life had been at risk – more victim-denying. Yet she clearly knew it at the time. Why else, in December 1942, did sixteen-year-old Inge go to all the trouble of getting herself baptised in Brussels?

Though there was no chance of the family returning to Germany, the Gestapo continued to interest itself in the affairs of Arthur Rosenbaum. A handwritten sheet at the back of the file logs the initials and dates of those who consulted it; the last entry is on 7 October 1943 – coincidentally Tilly's forty-fourth birthday. By then, Arthur had been dead for ten months.

From Gurs, Arthur was moved to Les Milles. His name appears on the list of those taken from Les Milles to Drancy. According to the Allied High Commission, on 7 September 1942 Arthur Rosenbaum was transported from Drancy to Konzentrationslager Auschwitz. He arrived there two days later, on 9 September. Four months later, on 15 January 1943, his name appears in the sick book of Block 28 with an entry stating that he was moved to Birkenau. The Allied High Commission state that he can be presumed to have died in the gas chambers on the day he arrived. That is all I know.

It is unnerving and distressing to discover that the trajectory through France that I invented for my fictional grandfather when

writing *The Children's War* fifteen years ago – Les Milles–Gurs–
Drancy–Auschwitz – so nearly matches the real one. Decades
on, the French railways paid compensation to the descendants
of victims of those journeys; Inge followed this story avidly but
declined even to apply. What if the neighbours noticed her name
on the correspondence?

CHAPTER 18

. . . . .

Auschwitz

In the summer of 2020, I visit Auschwitz with my husband, Alex, and my bald facts about Arthur's end become horribly real. Take that anodyne word 'transported'. From Drancy, the north-eastern suburb of Paris, to Auschwitz via Germany is 760 miles as the crow flies, a journey that now takes thirteen hours by car. Jews were transported by cattle truck. En route, trains were stopped for hours and left to wait, mostly in sidings. People crammed into tight spaces with no seats held babies above their heads. They had no privacy or air, no water and no food beyond what they had brought. Religious Jews prayed where they stood. Sometimes at stations or sidings, voices were heard. People pushed banknotes or gold jewellery through the slats in the hope of a glass of water that might or might not be brought. Jews had been encouraged to bring food, warm clothes, their cash, valuables, silver and jewellery, all the better for these items to be looted at their destination.

Auschwitz is perfectly located: an existing army barracks between two rivers, its remote location easily kept secret.

Importantly, it is served by a very good railway network leading to nearby Oświęcim. There was more than one kind of 'camp'. Auschwitz was a work camp; ten minutes down the road is Birkenau, a death camp built on the site of the eponymous village. The Nazis expelled the people of Birkenau and demolished the place, reusing the bricks to build the two barracks that still stand here.

A cattle truck built in 1932 now stands on the railway lines in Birkenau. It was donated by Australian property magnate Frank Loewy, whose father, Hugo, survived incarceration here. Typical of the type used, it is made of thick wooden planks and rides high on its huge wheels. The heavy door is bolted and padlocked from the outside; there isn't the slightest hope of getting out. What would you do if you passed a siding, heard the screams and howls from the inside and smelled the stench of the terrified occupants? Almost nobody tried to help the Jews escape. People shat themselves and died, degraded, in those trucks. They were already in hell.

When Auschwitz opened in 1940, prisoners (mostly Poles at the start) were shaved and photographed in their striped uniforms by a father-son team, in order to identify them if they ran away. But in the short period between arrival and death (average survival time being two to three months), starvation and brutal labour made these men and women unrecognisable. The introduction of a tattoo solved the problem. Everyone who could work received a number, and their name and date and place of birth was recorded with high accuracy. Arthur was given the number 63201. He was forty-nine, lean and pugnacious, fit enough to be chosen to work.

From September to his death in January, Arthur was marched out of the camp daily with a work detail, counted out and counted back; returning work details carried the bodies of those who had died during the day. If anyone absconded, all would be shot. In the morning he received a black liquid called coffee, in the evening watery soup with vegetables and a piece of bread. These rations amounted to 800 calories. The workers used mass latrines, which exposed them to dysentery. Soon they could not wait to go, soiling themselves and their clothes before they could get near. It becomes clear why prisoners became part of the Sonderkommando, transporting dead bodies, cutting off the hair of the dead and extracting their gold teeth, hoping to survive.

The infamous sign ARBEIT MACHT FREI – work makes free – is much smaller than expected. We drive from Krakow and arrive here early on a sunny day in late August, when the orderly grid of neat red-brick buildings, mature trees and mown grass looks innocent. Covid is keeping the usual crowds at bay and the camp is eerily quiet. Lines of poplars that were there in Arthur's day have grown tall and stately. The low cream-painted building with numerous chimneys, reminiscent of a Tudor hall, seems ominous – here, all chimneys hold menace – but it is only the kitchen. The 'base' camp, the Stammlager, containing thirty-two barracks, measures 300 metres by 300: it is small, yet huge in infamy.

Our exceptional Polish guide, Wojciech Smoleń, born in Oświęcim, is a true son of the camp. His parents met in Auschwitz – his father and grandfather were both interned there during the war, but his grandfather did not survive. He leads us in and out of the various barracks. Displays and photographs show the innumerable towns and cities in Europe from where people were transported: so many faces, so many yellow stars, so many children.

We tramp up and down stone steps worn into the shape of waves from the footsteps of four million people who have visited this place since the war. One barracks is crammed with the artefacts and objects people brought here in their optimism – little camping stoves, kettles and teapots. Suitcases and shoes lie piled in unfathomable quantities. A blonde plait placed on a roll of fabric made from human hair triggers me and (like Inge at Yad Vashem) I cannot stop weeping. When the Allies arrived at Birkenau, they found 70,000 kilos of hair waiting to be sent away.

Because of Covid, we are all wearing masks; I can't tell what people are thinking. Outside the barracks, a mobility scooter is parked; children in pink leggings skip around incongruously. Chatty mini vans come here and when they return, the people are completely silent. The drivers play music and by the end of the hour and a half drive back to beautiful fairy-tale Krakow, people have warmed up sufficiently to be able to talk.

Block 10, where medical experimentation took place, is closed because it is one of the places that needs renovation; the authority that runs the camp continues to fund-raise. I am grateful to be spared Dr Josef Mengele, the notorious *Todesengel* (Angel of Death). We walk on to Block 11, the punishment block. Anyone who tried to escape was shot against the 'death wall' here. Anyone outside who helped a prisoner was brought here and tortured; their whole family, including babies, were shot. This is the only place inside Auschwitz where people leave flowers.

In Birkenau we will see little stones placed on memorials, according to the Jewish custom. But there are no memorials or monuments here; Auschwitz is perfectly preserved as it was. Wojciech tells us that of all the hundreds of thousands who came through here, only two hundred escaped. Most ran away when out on work detail – but who, knowing the penalties, would help these emaciated people, with their tattoos? On the contrary, he says, escapees were hunted down by locals seeking a reward. He tells us a particularly gruesome story about one woman who tried to escape and was run over by a train, amputating both her legs. The local 'hyenas' stripped off her clothes and left her naked on the railway tracks to die.

We come at last to Block 28, the sick block, where Arthur was sent that January day in 1943. It occupies one corner of the site under the watchtower beside two layers of barbed wire and concrete-posted fencing. A skull and crossbones sign screams HALT! I note the thick concrete lintel, two steps, some sort of secondary glazing on the window above. Alex and I say a kaddish for him. I walk round to the back of the barracks, where it is very quiet, and tell my grandfather in German that Tilly survived, as did Inge, and that I am one of Inge's two daughters. His line continues. I refrain from mentioning that his wife married a man she truly loved, another Jew. Why disturb his peace of mind? What do you tell the dead who haunt you? I thought for years about this moment and this place, expecting some sort of release. No moment of epiphany comes.

Wojciech has worked out where my grandfather died. In January 1943, he says, Arthur alongside any other sick prisoners in Block 28 would most probably have been transported by truck over to Birkenau to an interim building where the first gassing was done – a pilot scheme for the gas chambers. We get back in the car. A journey of ten minutes brings us to Birkenau's infamous red-brick tower with its huge arch and the railway tracks underneath, which run directly east to west and then stop abruptly. As Auschwitz II Birkenau is a *Vernichtungslager*, a destruction camp, there is nowhere left to go.

In the distance, the twin chimneys of the Buna artificial rubber factory rise up; this is where Primo Levi worked. His memoir of his incarceration, *Se questo è un uomo* (*If This is a Man*), was published in 1947. On the side of the camp to the left of the railway lines as you enter are the two brick barracks. On the other side, isolated pairs of brick chimneys stick up like weird monuments as far as the eye can see. These are all that remain of the hundreds of prefabricated wooden buildings that once stretched for miles. Wooden stables designed to take fifty horses were assembled here between 1943 and 1944 to house the huge influx of people. The chimneys are the remains of a 'patent' heating system. Two long horizontal flues with a fire at one end and a chimney at the other drew heat along the length of these stables, never intended for humans, where prisoners slept huddled on bunk beds. All the heat escaped through the huge gap between the flimsy wooden walls and roof: those lucky enough to get a place near the fires were less likely to freeze to death overnight.

This place is like Gurs camp in the Pyrenees: an endless array of low buildings in a grid on a flat plain – churned mud in the winter, blustery dirt and baking heat in the summer. It must have been bleak indeed on that cold January day in 1943.

We walk for twenty-five minutes across the fields, passing the jumbled remains of the gas chambers and crematoria blown up by the Nazis to destroy the evidence of their crimes. We notice moat-like areas: water so foul that prisoners were forbidden to drink it. Those who did, maddened by summer heat, soon died. The guards were told to boil the water they shaved in because even one cut could infect them fatally. Museum staff pass like aliens on Segways, strangely upright, swerving to avoid the puddles on the grass. Ahead is the triage building where people were sent when they arrived, their names, addresses and dates of birth carefully recorded.

Sonderkommandos removed their spectacles, shoes, clothes and their papers and passports, which would be burned. People left their suitcases in a locker area where the prescient perhaps observed that no ticket was issued – by then it was too late. They went to one office to receive a number, then to another place to be tattooed.

These men and women destined to work were sanitised and deloused with cold or burning hot water, depending on how the SS chose to amuse themselves that day. They stood naked for hours on that cold concrete floor with no towel or soap, not knowing that they were lucky to survive; others on their train had gone straight to their deaths. In the next room they received prison clothes. A large area was devoted to sanitising clothes to be sent back to Germany as rewards for the faithful German people. This process was elaborate and thorough, with hot air for furs and animal skins and big steam vessels for ordinary clothes, which passed from one side of a wall to the other: from the dirty to the clean side. Filthy people queued on one side alongside bundles of clothes – and on the other, clean clothes emerged. Everything is mechanised and well designed; the trolleys still stand on the rails used to shunt them back and forth.

Beyond this building, in a clearing surrounded by trees, is Bunker 2, the 'provisional gas chamber' where the first experimental gassing took place. Arthur was probably among the first people murdered here. I'd like to believe that this stubborn man resisted to the very end, but he was sick, perhaps barely able to stand. Bunker 2, a farmhouse formerly known as the 'white house', was converted by bricking up the windows and chimney and closing the door. The four large gas chambers and crematoria that turned this place into an efficient killing machine would come into operation in the spring and early summer of 1943.

There were five gas chambers eventually: four in Birkenau plus one in Auschwitz.

The building itself is long gone. What remains is a small square patch of foundations, rough stone and bricks with a looping rope to stop people walking on it. We lay little stones here and on the memorial beside the field. A sign in Polish, English and Hebrew reads: 'Bunker 2 was also known as "the white house". Men, women and children were murdered here by gas.' Before the crematoria were built, bodies were burned in the nearby fields and ash carried on the wind to surrounding places. They still dig up bones here. Something always remains, or so you might think.

Wojciech tells us how efficient the crematoria were – that you don't need much coke (which burns at very high temperatures) because the fat in human bodies burns well. Later still, he says that men without women are no good. I take this as some philosophical point – remarking stupidly that women hold up half the sky. That is not what he means. He explains that as men's bodies have less fat, the Nazis found it more efficient to burn the sexes together. Combustion at 1,000 degrees ensures that nothing at all is left, not even ash. In this way and in this place, over a million people vanished – completely – into thin air. Ninety per cent of the murdered were Jews.

The Auschwitz-Birkenau Museum states that 'the second most numerous group, from 70 to 75,000 was Poles, and the third most numerous, about 20,000, the Gypsies [sic – Sinti and Roma]. About 15,000 Soviet POWs and 10 to 15,000 prisoners of other ethnic backgrounds (including Czechs, Byelorussians, Yugoslavians, French, German and Austrians) also died here.'

All that remains of them is their names, saved thanks to the Nazi's bureaucratic bent. The Book of Names is stacked upright

All that remains of Bunker 2, where Arthur was gassed

in Block 27 in Auschwitz; this massive volume fills a room and is the height of a person. Its 8,000 plus pages gather all the names of victims of the Holocaust collected by the Yad Vashem Institute. Each person's name is printed in bold, followed by the date of birth, place of birth, the date and place of murder. One human being occupies between a line and a line and a half. By 2013, Yad Vashem, assisted by partners around the world, had collected over four million names of the six million Jews murdered. They continue to seek the remaining names. Among the multiple pages of Rosenbaums – so many that your eye slides over them – we find Arthur Rosenbaum, Mülheim an der Ruhr, Germany, and his brother Otto.

On the ground floor of Block 27 is a large room where home movies of families are projected on a permanent loop across four walls. We watch Jewish families eat picnics and play on beaches; they sing, laugh and eat in cafes, waving to the camera. Children stand in their best clothes, bold or shy; they ride bicycles, turn cartwheels and ski. Here is the everyday life of the Jews of Europe, ordinary people on family outings.

These are not the bearded Jews from the shtetl who turned up in Germany after the war for the first time, disconcerting many. Holocaust survivors returned to their towns and villages in Eastern Europe to find their homes occupied; their neighbours met them with outbursts of anti-Semitism and violence. In 1946, a horrific pogrom in Kielce in Poland killed forty-two Jews and injured many, in daylight, while police stood by – final proof there was no hope of rebuilding life here. A mass flight from Eastern Europe ensued. Ironically, defeated occupied Germany was seen as the safest place in Europe for survivors hoping to go to Palestine or the USA.

The Jews depicted in Block 27 are assimilated people in modern clothing. They loved life, they loved their children and enjoyed everyday pleasures. That their fellow Europeans, the seemingly civilised Germans, were barbarians capable of creating the hell that is Auschwitz/Birkenau was literally unthinkable. That is why, stepping out of the trains, dazed and exhausted, they did not turn on the guards they so greatly outnumbered.

CHAPTER 19

. . . . .

Russian dolls

Late in 1971, when I was twenty and Inge forty-five, my mother suggested that we go on holiday together at Christmas. And so it came about that she, I and seventy-two-year-old Tilly flew to icy, snowed-in Moscow. The weather was bitter, the city unrelentingly grim from the ride into town past concrete blocks of worker housing to our vast and bleak hotel. The accommodation lived up to every dour cliché, with sinister women in tatty overalls keeping watch on landings, each bathroom having its plug-less soap-less bath. No risk of wallowing in decadent Western froth in those pre-perestroika days. No danger of festive cheer either. The wide streets were empty of cars and we few tourists were moved about en masse in ramshackle coaches.

With her usual generosity, Inge brought a suitcase of tights and blue jeans to give away; she instantly befriended our lovely official guide, who asked whether we might bring dress patterns when we next came. There were no sewing needles to be had in all Moscow, but this lady was an optimist. Inge felt for her deeply. She gave her the contents of her suitcase and even the newly hand-knitted mohair sweater she was wearing – unheard-of luxury – devising the most complex hole-and-corner subterfuges to meet at a street corner and hand over the gifts unobserved. Inge derived enormous pleasure from these manoeuvres, which played to her well-established penchant for intrigue.

We dined on slabs of unknown meats plus the ubiquitous pickled red cabbage. Sometimes a pickled gherkin added a green note. Caviar and vodka appeared erratically. We were hungry, Tilly in particular, but every morning drank plentiful cups of delicious Cuban coffee. Russians, we told ourselves, were used to extremes. So was Inge, who presented the caviar and vodka to our guide. Our itinerary was crammed and Tilly, always intrepid, didn't want to miss a thing. But the conditions were treacherous and the cold bit into the soul. We tottered over the ice rink of Red Square arm in arm to see Lenin's tomb, propping my grandmother between us in her astrakhan coat, fur hat and thick boots. The building was closed: his body was being restored. We had tickets to the Bolshoi but the bus travelled past the building. When Inge complained, we were taken to a concert of Russian patriotic songs. Frustrated and disgusted, she refused to go in, so we sat for hours on the bus waiting for the others. We hopped on and off trains in the grandiloquent marble underground system and wondered self-importantly if we were being followed. We weren't. But the three of us stood together, arms linked in solidarity, three generations of females on thin ice.

Inge persevered in her efforts to enjoy this thin gruel. Her assertive behaviour, bursts of exuberance and generosity-edging-on-fanaticism embarrassed me. She kept a keen lookout for KGB agents and sent a postcard to Lorie 'from Russia with love'.

We shopped in the regulation tourist store using our carefully counted foreign money, contemplating badly made expensive fur hats. She was scathing about the quality yet kept urging me to acquire one. The money we'd exchanged had to be spent on something. She bought Russian dolls – not the amusing political ones, but cheap ones with crazed red cheeks.

GUM department store at number 3 Red Square wasn't the champagne-swilling temple to grand luxe it later became. The magnificent building was empty; one stall on an upper trading row had something to sell. The queue stretched through the whole building and out on to the street. People joined the back with no idea what was on offer. If you went to the front to look, you risked losing any chance of a purchase. Just like the war, said Tilly. There was nothing to buy really, and nowhere to go.

By the end of the week, our guide grew unhappy that her generous new friend had experienced none of the promised treats and excursions. So she wangled us a troika ride, pushing a long queue of people to one side and falsely claiming that we had special priority. Wrapped in a fur blanket, Inge was thrilled. When we got off the troika, she sang 'Lara's Theme' from the film of *Dr Zhivago*, loudly and rather off-key. This histrionic performance astonished people waiting in the queue because the frozen tourists neither smiled nor sang. I was ashamed of her. How false and forced, how very look-at-me. Tilly, as usual, seemed oblivious to these antics. After all, her daughter was known for this sort of thing – wasn't Inge regularly '*en folie douce*' – in sweet madness – as René wrote on the back of that photograph of them dancing. But this wasn't Inge's normal exalted-happy state. She was manic in her determination to make this weird trip into something special, while outwitting the opposition. What opposition? She was no female James Bond and, hard as we looked, there was no knife-shod Rosa Klebb on our trail. Why Moscow? Why was she like this?

Now I know. The break-up with René had happened earlier that year. The great hope of living with the love of her life had receded and her heart was breaking. The previous Christmas, we had all been together in Austria on that festive ski holiday where nobody skied and Inge danced into the new year in René's arms. She must have been in a state of desolate distress. She needed to get away – somewhere – anywhere – ideally to the ends of the earth. Hence Moscow, hence the distraction of seeking more distraction. She had read about how poor ordinary Muscovites were, so filled a suitcase with presents for strangers. She was intent on outwitting those unseen and invisible enemies who were always on her tail. And, because she had paid for the three of us, she wanted her money's worth: every failure of organisation galvanised her further. She needed to sing, to be extravagant, to 'show them' just how great everything really was precisely because she was so unhappy. It was utterly bonkers and also remarkable. Even in despair, a huge life force erupted from her. Grand gestures were her thing: heroic outbursts against the darkness within. I wonder how many of her 'it's-my-day' performance effusions over the years covered terrible distress.

So many things have become clear. Ploughing through those 560 pages of Gestapo files on my grandfather, I found answers to questions that had long puzzled me. Why was Inge so stubborn? How could such a deeply kind person, adored by her friends, be so lacking in empathy at times – unbending, unreasonable, unable to shift direction? Why did she need to dominate and assert herself? And how did she succeed in living a secret life for decades, misleading and misdirecting those who loved her and thought they knew her best?

Inge knew that stubbornness was one of her defining characteristics: *I've started with A so I will continue to Z.* Ironically, she probably inherited this and other obdurate characteristics from the man she blamed for all her misfortunes. Arthur's insistence on remaining an active communist in Nazi Germany and his refusal to leave were extreme. These decisions brought him to a horrible death and nearly destroyed his wife and surviving child. Even in extremis he could never consider another path. He was a tough, gritty, strong-minded man fighting tyranny. Because he was also a rogue and opportunist, he had the strength and wiles to fight on when the entire state apparatus focused on hounding and persecuting the individuals who dared to defy it. A complex and exceptional man, a roustabout with principles, he was a father to be proud of.

Inge never saw it that way. She never acknowledged their shared characteristics; perhaps she didn't recognise any similarities. But it took the sort of guts Arthur possessed to answer back in the street as Inge did when very young, rounding on the bullies who called out 'Jew'. *Half-Jew! See? You're completely wrong!*

Both inside the Nazi state and in her home life, adults' rule was absolute. Hers was a surreal world of harsh unmerited punishments and inexplicable behaviour by people who should have been kind. That permanent state of outrage Inge describes as a young child, that sense of never understanding how the world functions and resentment at not being told things, indicate profound alienation. Feeling all the injustice and unfairness of life, she had no way to express herself. 'I am a little raft paddling on the ocean alone,' she used to say. 'I have to look after myself.' She could not confront parental authority directly, though she bitterly resented it. Her father was always absent, her much-loved mother desperately overworked and emotionally absent, overcome with sorrow as her elder daughter was dying. They barely had time to listen to her, focused as they were so entirely on Hanne Lore. Inge felt this deeply and could not forgive the neglect.

This toxic, tragic mix was heightened by constant danger and puzzles no child could fathom. Inge's parents were subject to intense pressure from a brutal regime; she observed that their reaction was to dissemble while secretly fighting back. To protect her, they concealed their precise acts and motivations. How then to understand and process so many contradictions? Inge never received the education that would have enabled her to weigh ideas and balance them in a measured way. A lifelong autodidact, she tried so hard to learn. But for all her intelligence and all her reading, she could not change. *Once I have decided, that's it*, she wrote in her account of her life, even when she regretted her errors.

Inge never consciously sorrowed for her father and sister's death until she wrote her fragmentary memoir. But this doesn't mean that she didn't care about them. Looking through her account of her life, I found this sentence about Hanne Lore: *I am unable to write of the slow process of her fading away.* Six decades on, she still pushed away emotions too overwhelming to deal with. Going through Tilly's papers on the second anniversary of Inge's death, I chanced upon an airmail letter of 1955 to Tilly in Casablanca from her least favourite sister-in-law, Mally, in Mülheim – the aunt who offered Inge undrinkable ersatz coffee. Almost indecipherable because the ink has bled through the back of the thin sheet, this letter appears to be a reply to a request from Tilly for help with restitution. Written on the back of the envelope in Inge's distinctive handwriting is this message: *I have kept this letter because Mally's writing is identical with my father's.* It must date from after Tilly's death, from a time when she sorted her mother's papers. Who is Inge talking to? Nobody. It is a small, sad message to herself.

Those lasting feelings of powerlessness explain why Inge was conflict averse. She brooked no argument, but she wouldn't kowtow either. I think of her demanding her share of Tom's estate. I think of her deliberately failing to regularise paperwork after the purchase of the square metre she needed to join her two flats. The last year of her life was dominated by an exhausting battle fought against the French telecom giant that sold her a Wi-Fi system and then refused to accept her cancellation of it. Between her natural bolshiness and powerlessness, the internal conflict must have been exhausting. All that emotion had to find an outlet, to the detriment of us all. Her grandstanding makes sense in this context. The triumphalism coexisted with pain and damage to herself as well as others.

Much of her behaviour was formed by the cruel and bizarre circumstances of those first thirteen years in Mülheim an der Ruhr. When the gilets jaunes were demonstrating in Tours in 2018, my mother said how terrifying she found the police lined up beside the Préfecture near her home in full riot gear with shields – 'exactly like the Nazis'. She pushed her empty wheelchair up Rue Jean Jaurès to inspect them, outraged that these young men might use their batons to beat demonstrators. The traumas of early childhood had inoculated her against active involvement in politics; there was no way she was ever going to be a communist – or any kind of 'ist' – just as she was never going to be a Jew. But she followed the news with great anxiety and worried about whatever the far right was up to. Herself extreme, she was always wary of extremes. Always on the side of the poor and oppressed, she worried for the future.

I'm beginning to see an answer to the question I posed about her strange lack of empathy (for Tilly and Lorie in particular) and that unbending unreasonableness. Because Inge thought emotionally and not rationally, she could never progress. She knew very well that her emotions led her to behave in a certain way, but she could not work out the logic. And so she became a creature of contradictions. Unable to change direction, she had to dominate and assert herself, even and particularly when this made no sense. She was simultaneously victim – the abandoned wife and overworked mother, the worker sacrificing herself for our education – and aggressor.

Despite or because of that powerlessness, she insisted on being obeyed by her children and could not stand it when we didn't toe the line. 'You're either with me or against me,' she would proclaim. But we were never the enemy. The real enemy was far too powerful for her to fight. Abandoned on that small raft of hers, she couldn't see all the other people clinging on and bobbing about on the vast horizon. Propelled by overwhelming emotions, she didn't realise what power she held over others; it did not occur to the inner frightened little girl that her own daughters might be hurt. And even if we were, she could not go back and unravel the deceptions of a lifetime.

I have spent an age puzzling over my last question: how did she succeed in living a secret life for decades, misleading and misdirecting those who loved her and thought they knew her best?

Just as emotions clashed yet continued, a barren external life coexisted with a rich hidden one. Inge's gift for misdirection is surely all Arthur. His pattern of explaining himself to the courts was carefully devised. He would admit such facts and contacts as could not be avoided, lie about the rest and leap into an alternative story. Inge did something similar as she reinvented herself in Brussels, in the North of England, in London and finally in France, easily fooling all those nice people who liked her and who wanted to know more about her. She was brilliant at avoiding direct questions, a mistress of obfuscation. The charming English eccentric leaped into all kinds of diversions and random topics whenever the conversation took a dangerous turn. She was protecting herself, but she was gleeful too. I think she deeply enjoyed bending and manipulating people (her daughters included) into accepting the stories she had invented, never quite lying outright.

Perhaps those 'it's-my-day' moments that set my teeth on edge are the clue I misread. Whenever there was an audience present to appreciate her, Inge's dramatic inner life surfaced. In her head, the diva (who claimed to be a mouse) was playing out the grandest parts. She was starring in a cinematic epic of passionate romance and lost love that ran for decades and mattered more than anything else. Not so much Birkenhead as Hollywood. That rich inner life propped up this fragile being. That was why the slightest encouragement brought out Madame la Marquise. Exuberance was willed, a mechanism to cheer herself up, no matter what. She won by being cheerful amazing it's-my-day Inge, suppressing the sad inner child. She refused to be miserable. Into extreme old age, she never once complained or said that she was sad. She never dropped her standards. To the last day of her life, she was bathed, dressed and made up with great care by 8 a.m., hair in a chignon. One can indeed only marvel at such a performance, sustained over a lifetime.

I see too how Inge's marriage to Tom became a story to bolster her myth. In hard times she'd made a pragmatic decision, choosing a man who, like her father, looked as though he'd have his wits about him. Marrying a man you don't love when you're in love with somebody else takes quite a degree of conscious deception. A decade later, when she and Tom divorced, Inge adopted the role of the abandoned but devoted, sorrowing wife. She truly did have deep inner sorrows, just not the ones she declared.

That game-playing, role-playing side of Inge had deep roots. Her father was an expert in doing one thing and saying another, as the court records showed. Her mother played the innocent housewife when the Gestapo stormed in early in the morning. They became chameleons to survive. So did she. She spent her entire life in love with a man she couldn't have and couldn't even talk about. She was totally convincing. I never doubted her for one moment.

Inge's greatest piece of misdirection was telling us over and over again that René was '*l'homme de ma vie*' – the man of my life. This grandiose-seeming statement was indeed true. She had loved him all her life from the age of thirteen until her death nearly eighty years later. She made this pronouncement knowing we would never take her words literally.

She and René corresponded and met secretly over decades. The lifelong habit of secrecy, and of associating secrecy with pleasure, became ingrained. Here was one beautiful thing that nobody could take away. I searched through all her papers and her suitcase with stamps and letters hoping to find old love letters but never found incriminating material. The Gestapo never found anything on Arthur Rosenbaum either. She fooled us, her supposedly clever daughters, for our entire lives.

CHAPTER 20

• • • • •

A German and a Jew

I've learned a lot about myself, and about mothers and daughters. Patterns repeat. The patterns in Inge's life repeated but none of us could see it: she lost her father and so did we. Tilly's second marriage was to a man she loved passionately; Inge had that luck too. Like Tilly, she was a mother adored by her children, a mother raising two girls alone. In each generation, the sisters disconnected. Hanne Lore was lost and so, for a long time, was Lorie.

Inge strove to keep Lorie and me apart but may never have consciously articulated why. She feared our sharp wits and quick ripostes; together we might have dominated or unmasked her. The irony is that for all our faults and transgressions, Lorie and I were Team Inge – her greatest supporters – and we could (and did) support her to the death. We won't be divided now. Sisterhood is fun.

Despite those protestations of love for her two girls, our mother was most alive in her utter passion for René and in the great friendships she formed. Teenage Inge surfaced in that wonderful friendship with Martine in the very last years of her life, brimming with laughter and silliness alongside deep shared interests.

How fortunate we sisters are in inheriting so much complexity and creativity from this complex, troubled woman. She strove to give us the excellent education she so longed for, never suspecting how far it would carry us from her. If she'd understood how negatively we were affected by her, she would have been devastated – but she could not have acted otherwise. It was our refugee mother, not our father, who made us what we are, and we are both grateful.

She would be fascinated to read this book, which is also a monument to her. And she would be appalled. When I asked my son, Jonny, if it was a betrayal for me to write about her, he thought about it. He understood Inge very well and was tolerant of her peccadilloes. Though her highly developed critical arts sometimes infuriated him, he remained very fond of her, and she adored both him and Sophie. His overwhelming image of his grandmother was a woman with her nose in a book who lived to read and existed primarily through literature. She had spent the last decades of her life teaching English, reading challenging books in three languages, pursuing the life of the mind that so delighted and fulfilled her. Therefore, he reasoned, to become a literary figure would be taken as the greatest mark of respect.

I hope he's right. I've worried a good deal whether in writing this I would do justice to my mother or bitterly wound her. I'm still anxious. A relationship this strong does not simply end. Lorie and I will never stop talking and thinking about this unforgettable woman.

As I was finishing this book, I wrote to Inge's closest friends in France and with some trepidation told them about her tragic past. All three were deeply moved and thanked me for confiding in them. Hélène remembered that Inge had once hovered on the brink of telling her something very important, but in the end could not bring herself to speak: 'I just can't do it.' Hortense wrote of Inge's joy in life, her youthful spirit and how her parting words were always the admonition to 'be happy'. They loved her for her independence and freedom of spirit, and they benefited from her wise advice. Martine remarked how lucky she was to have known someone like her, albeit for too short a time. *'Il faut dire les choses,'* she said – one must speak of everything. It was affecting and also sad to see how the revelation of these dark truths only increased their love and compassion.

Did Inge wonder who the father of her children was – or did she know? Calling me Monique in honour of René's niece and speaking French to us strongly suggests that she wanted us to be René's. The more similarities I see between Inge and her father, the more curious I feel about my own inheritance. If Tom isn't my father, am I still me? Inge and Tom were both bookish and lifelong readers; I spend my life reading and writing. I admire Tom's intellectual gifts, not his bad behaviour. But in his early years, René was bookish too. The charming Frenchman who wanted to adopt us seems more attractive than the Englishman who didn't care.

The DNA tests prove that Tom is our father, not René. Lorie's results are conclusive. She and I are full sisters with no connection to Sylvain beyond our delightful chosen cousinship. Having relished the idea of being a mixture of French and German, my first reaction is disappointment. I want René to fill the emotional hole in my heart. But the mildness of my response shows that I don't need a father as much as I thought. Both Tom and René were peripheral in my life.

I've learned something about fathers too. Led by my mother's stories, I projected emotions and wishes that Tom could never fulfil. Maligned, adulterous, dead Tom has borne quite a burden.

I never really knew him; I both denied myself and was denied that opportunity. But he wasn't crucial in the way that Inge was. My mother had towering importance. Losing her – distant and difficult though she was – was devastating. The subsequent shock of discovering that she had lied and lived a double life propelled me to write this memoir.

I've written about Germany, terrorism, about civilians and children suffering in wartime, about absent and difficult fathers, the problems of creativity, about secret lovers and unfaithful wives – at some level it was always about Inge. I felt compelled to write about the past she fled from without seeing the story behind the story. But now I understand how she underpinned my life's work.

Lorie and I lead very different lives. She lives in Birkenhead and has delved deeply into its past. As Reader in Law and History at Liverpool John Moores University, she published a seminal history of poor law, establishing that the poor always had a legal right to relief. Like Inge, she's passionate about the rights of the underdog, but her roots are proudly British. I live in London and am pulled to Europe, its languages and literature.

The DNA results explain a lot. Lorie comes out as 65.4 per cent British and Irish ancestry versus my 24.6 per cent. She's 2.8 per cent French and German to my 21.3 per cent; she's 6.8 per cent 'broadly Northwestern Europe' to my 27 per cent. On the Ashkenazi Jewish front, she has 15.9 per cent to my 21.3 per cent. As I should have guessed, she has a great deal of Viking in her: 8.7 per cent Scandinavian to my 3.4 per cent.

My remaining 2.4 per cent is Eastern European and broadly European – Spanish, Portuguese and Eastern European with just a touch of Western Asian and North African, Iranian, Caucasian and Mesopotamian. Lorie is 0.4 per cent 'broadly European'. I really am the mixed-up foreign one. I had no idea that sisters could inherit so differently through the maternal or paternal side. But this makes sense in terms of our lives, characters, feelings, and choices. Lorie has so much of Tom: his sharp wit, his questioning intelligence. I have a lot of Inge, not least in my obstinacy, as evidenced in this dogged pursuit of her past.

I now believe that Inge probably knew we were Tom's. It seems highly likely that she decided that Lorie was his and punished her accordingly. She may have had her hopes and doubts about me, the favoured French-named child. Either way, she must have told René that we were both his and he believed her. Even inside the perfect marriage to René, Inge kept her secrets; that must have been exhausting. She was so charismatic – so convincing – so certain of everything.

A year after Inge's death, an email arrives from the delightful Angela Grossman at the German Embassy: 'I have now viewed your documents, which are impressively comprehensive. I would now like to invite you to come to the Embassy in order to submit your applications in person.'

Eventually, another email comes from Angela: 'I am very pleased to inform you that the Federal Administration Office has approved your applications for naturalisation.' Here is the home-coming I longed for, that Wiedergutmachung (restoration) of the soul. Born in Birkenhead, on the outside totally English, I have spent my whole life yearning for some lost Heimat. When, aged twelve, I discovered Inge's heritage, something clicked. That moment shaped so many choices. It is weird and, some might feel, perverse that the trajectory of my life, this determined effort to become Jewish and German, so precisely reverses the trajectory of Inge's. But becoming joint British/German and Jewish knits together the problem of who I am, and why. My mother's child and also Tom Charlesworth's: two wholly unsuited people who met by chance in wartime, muddled through a short period of their lives together and found happiness apart.

In 2002, when she was seventy-six, Inge returned to Germany for the very last time. The occasion was the wedding of Lili Zimbehl, the granddaughter of Willy Zimbehl. This was the man who had presented small Inge with chocolates when it wasn't even her birthday, the kind friend who had affectionately called her 'Inge mouse'. The family friendship has continued through generations; Lorie became best friends with Ilka Zimbehl (mother of the bride). Willy's son, Jochen, took Inge on a tour of all the places she knew in Mülheim, starting with Broich where she was born, the part of town with the ancient castle. When they got to the big flat near the Town Hall where the little girls used to roller-skate, she broke down. 'They took my Heimat away,' she said, and cried.

The Zimbehls' magnificent house on the lake was the venue for a huge party that went on for half the night. Lorie and Ilka were having fun waitressing, bartending and laughing with the staff. All through the afternoon and into the warm summer's night, hundreds of friends and relatives of Lili and Michael, her new husband, partied in the house and on the vast lawns sloping down to the lake, decorated with pots of wildflowers and buddleia. A music system had been set up in the emptied swimming pool and everyone danced.

By 2.30 in the morning most people had gone to bed, but not all. The music was still playing. And Inge, glass in hand, was still at the side of the pool, entirely happy, dancing by herself. She didn't notice the enraptured twenty-somethings admiring her. But when the music finally stopped, the young people – every person there a German – stood to applaud her, clapping and cheering.

THANKS AND
ACKNOWLEDGEMENTS

Good friends have kindly read (and reread) this memoir and made excellent comments. Sincere thanks to Karen Brown, Camilla Cavendish, Alyson Corner, Patricia (Tricia) East, Jane Edwardes, Cecily Engle, Julian Evans, Caroline Goldie, Moneer Hobart, Eva Jiricna, Mary Mulholland, Jeremy Rosenblatt, Simone Sandelson and Claudia Zeff for their enthusiasm and help. Tricia contributed invaluable memories and thoughts about Inge. I learned a great deal about relationships (and mothers) through talking to my friend Alyson Corner, clinical psychologist and co-author of the *My Horrid Parent* website. I'm grateful to my agent Annabel Merullo for her support. Julian Evans went above and beyond, championing this book with kindness, enthusiasm and vigour.

Martin Fletcher edited the first draft of *Mother Country* and Sam Boyce the subsequent draft with great skill. I am indebted to them, to Caroline McArthur who brought the book together so beautifully and to Jenni Davis for her line editing and meticulous fact-checking.

The immense Gestapo file on my grandfather, Arthur Rosenbaum, resides in the large Nordrhein-Westfalen Landesarchiv in Duisburg. The Bundesarchiv in Berlin holds further material. Both archives produced and digitised many files with great efficiency and I thank Landesarchiv Nordrhein-Westfalen for permission to publish material as follows: Gestapo photographs on page 246: Landesarchiv NRW – Abteilung Rheinland – Archivsignatur RW 0058 Nr.62454 Bl.32; Duisburg Gestapo file on page 261: Landesarchiv NRW – Abteilung Rheinland – Archivsignatur RW 0058 Nr.62454 Bl.16; Tilly's letter on page 272: Landesarchiv NRW – Abteilung Rheinland – Archivsignatur RW 0058 Nr.62454 Bl.50. Nicky Trainor of LDS and Gage Solaguren of Bayeux achieved wonders retouching and scanning old photographs.

I received invaluable assistance from Annett Fercho in the Mülheim an der Ruhr archive; thanks to the archive's participation in the Stolpersteine project, the Rosenbaums are forever commemorated in the pavement of their town. Frau Fercho has been unfailingly kind in supplying documents and helping me decipher files. Thanks also to Penguin Random House UK for permission to quote from Eva Hoffman's *After Such Knowledge*.

My thanks also to history teacher Frau von Bancels at Broich Gymnasium, who used the Stolpersteine project to give a new generation insight into Germany's dark past. Particular gratitude goes to Broich students David Bakum and Angelina Mehler, who serendipitously chose to research the Rosenbaum family. The archive kindly put me in touch with my first cousin once removed, Hans-Joachim Rosenbaum. He and his delightful wife, Inge, welcomed Alex and me to their home in Menden in Mülheim an der Ruhr most warmly; we all regretted not having got to know each other years earlier. Sadly, Hans died in 2022, aged 92.

Angela Grossman at the German Embassy in London mentored me through my parallel project of becoming a German citizen, making the process as effortless as she could. It was, she said, 'the least they could do'. She has made me feel all the prouder to be German.

In France, Hélène Maurel, the professor whom Inge so cherished, and Toscan Indart, her son, kindly permitted me to describe their part in Inge's last day, as did Inge's great friend Martine Bac-Saule. I thank them and Hortense Thirion for their innumerable kindnesses to my mother. Martine generously gave me so much of her time in Tours after the shock of Inge's death. René Cocard's nephew Sylvain Cocard and his wife, the poet Cynthia Hogue, unveiled a big part of the mystery; I am grateful to the two professors for their enthusiastic collaboration in this project.

My patient family has put up with three and a half years of obsessional behaviour. I thank my sister- and brother-in-law, Viv and Peter Lawrence, for reading the text, their kindness and support. My children, Sophie and Jonny, have provided huge encouragement and love, commenting on the text and on their grandmother with intelligence and sweetness. I very much appreciate Sophie's line edits, a glorious melding of rigour with tact, and Jonny's generosity and clarity as a reader.

I could not have put this puzzle together without the help of my big sister, Dr Lorie Charlesworth, to whom this book is dedicated. She read each draft instantly and remembered much that I didn't. She and I have spent many hours talking over the past and in the process recovered our happiest sisterly selves.

The final thank you must go to my adored husband and best friend, Alex, who for forty years was the most perfect and generous son-in-law to Inge. On this subject, she and I for once agreed. He has travelled back and forth to Tours and Germany, supported this project (indeed all my projects) in every conceivable way, read every iteration and commented with his usual cleverness, discernment and charm. He makes every single moment of my life happy.

THE ROSENBAUM FAMILY

Salomon Rosenbaum (1862–1912)
marries
Johanna Kaufmann (1857–1937)

children:
Arthur (1892–1943)
Otto
Nelly
Mally
Röschen
Toni
Gerta
(+ one died in infancy)

Arthur
marries
Mathilde (Tilly) Lindemann (1899–1982)

children:
Hanne Lore (1923–1938)
Inge (1926–2019)

Inge
marries
1. Tom Charlesworth (1911–1972)
2. René Cocard (1913–1993)

children:
Lorie Charlesworth
Monique Charlesworth